I0762806

PRAISE FOR

FUTURE-PROOFING LEADERSHIP

"This isn't another book about coping with disruption. It's a guide for becoming the kind of leader people trust in disruptive times. One who builds cultures where people feel seen, valued, and capable of doing their best work."

Zach Mercurio, PhD, author of *The Power of Mattering* and *The Invisible Leader*

"As our world at work rapidly changes, we risk losing what makes us strongest: our connections to each other—and ourselves. That's why I love that Dr. Ward centers and celebrates our shared humanity in *Future-Proofing Leadership*. She doesn't just offer a path forward; she dives deep into what makes us who we are and how we can leverage that to shape the future. Whether you're a seasoned leader or just starting out, *Future-Proofing Leadership* is your road map for learning how to thrive through change and stay grounded in what matters most."

Kristen Hadeed, author of *Permission to Screw Up*

"Dr. Rosie Ward has written the definitive guide for leading in an era of nonstop disruption. By exposing the faulty programs that quietly sabotage even the most well-intentioned leaders, she gives us the tools to upgrade how we think, relate, and show up. *Future-Proofing Leadership* belongs in every leadership development library."

Alain Hunkins, bestselling author of *Cracking the Leadership Code: 3 Secrets to Building Strong Leaders*

"*Future-Proofing Leadership* is a timely and essential guide for any leader navigating today's relentless pace of change. Rosie brilliantly normalizes the messiness of being human while offering a practical blueprint for leaders to move beyond self-limiting narratives and thrive in disruption. Her insights into the 'Stuckness Zone™' and the faulty programs that hold us back are both eye-opening and actionable. This book doesn't just prepare leaders for the future—it empowers them to create it with courage, adaptability, and authenticity."

BRIAN GARISH, CHIEF CLIENT OFFICER, MARS VETERINARY HEALTH

"The world won't get less chaotic, but you can get more intentional. In *Future-Proofing Leadership,* Dr. Rosie Ward shows readers how to navigate disruption by mastering the messy inner game first. With candor, compassion, and a little sparkle, she gives leaders the tools to replace fear with courage, control with connection, and burnout with purpose."

MORAG BARRETT, EXECUTIVE LEADERSHIP COACH, GLOBAL KEYNOTE SPEAKER, AND AWARD-WINNING AUTHOR OF *CULTIVATE* AND *YOU, ME, WE*

"As someone who spent a career helping high-performing teams build championship cultures, *Future-Proofing Leadership* is a game-changer. Dr. Rosie Ward reminds us that 'culture is everyone's responsibility'—a message I champion deeply because winning organizations are built person by person, moment by moment, habit by habit, Monday by Monday. A must-read for leaders and beyond!"

PAUL EPSTEIN, FORMER NFL & NBA EXECUTIVE; TWO-TIME BESTSELLING AUTHOR; FOUNDER, WIN MONDAY™

ROSIE WARD, PHD

FUTURE-PROOFING LEADERSHIP

NAVIGATING CHANGE *and* DISRUPTION *to* THRIVE *in* *an* UNCERTAIN WORLD

www.amplifypublishinggroup.com

Future-Proofing Leadership: Navigating Change and Disruption to Thrive in an Uncertain World

For more information, please contact:
Amplify Publishing, an imprint of Amplify Publishing Group
620 Herndon Parkway, Suite 220
Herndon, VA 20170
info@amplifypublishing.com

Library of Congress Control Number: 2025926847

CPSIA Code: PRV0226A

ISBN-13: 979-8-89138-815-4

Printed in the United States

To my amazing son, Peyton: Thank you for inspiring me every day to build a better future for you, your fellow native digitals, and everyone who loves and supports our future leaders.

CONTENTS

Introduction

- Have you experienced challenges when it comes to change on a personal level?
- Have you experienced challenges when it comes to change on a team level?
- Have you experienced challenges when it comes to change on an organizational level?
- Does it sometimes feel like it's harder to navigate change today than it was a few years ago?

If you answered yes to any of these questions, you're in good company. The reality is that change is hard. But have you ever stopped to think why that is the case? I invite you to consider that most efforts to change are mediocre at best or fail completely for one critical reason: They fail to care for the messiness of how humans show up in the face of change. Senior partners at McKinsey & Company describe this phenomenon well in their book *Deliberate Calm*:

> Adaptability, learning, innovation & creativity are most challenging in high-stakes, uncertain situations—exactly when they are most needed . . . The human brain is wired to react to these situations with the exact opposite of learning and creativity.[1]

Organizations are then paying us for a second job that they never intended and never hired us to do: impression management. We spend a lot of time and energy trying to look favorable in the eyes of others (to look good and not bad), which impedes our effectiveness. Not only is it a waste of time and money, but it is also exhausting! The root of impression management started for most of us long ago—in the first ten or so years of our lives. And whether we realize it or not, that ten-year-old version of ourselves is in the driver's seat today much more often than we think or would like to admit, and it is largely what makes change so difficult and impedes our ability to be future-ready.

I grew up the youngest of five girls in a very overachieving family and was constantly trying to carve out my identity beyond the hand-me-downs. I felt so different from my sisters that I was convinced I was adopted. You see, my sisters were into science, musical instruments, and watching reruns of TV shows like *Get Smart* and *Star Trek*. All I wanted to do was watch *The Facts of Life* and *Fame*, dance, and sing and talk into my thumb like I had a microphone in my hand. Plus, my favorite color is sparkle; yes, I assure you it *is* a color! I just knew that there was no way I belonged in this family.

One of my older sisters happily fed into my story about not belonging in our family. One day when I was about five or six years old, she told me that I was adopted and our next-door neighbors were my birth parents. I instantly believed her. After all, they had dark hair and dark eyes and kind of looked like me. Never mind that so did my parents. It was all I needed to hear to validate my story that I didn't belong in my family. I was determined to find where I belonged.

After dinner that evening, I packed my things in a Tinkertoy tub. I grabbed my teddy bear, blankie, and pillow and told my sister I was running away to go live with my *real* family. I started sobbing as I slowly walked down the driveway to go next door. I only got about two-thirds of the way down the driveway before my sister came charging out the front door to get me. (I'm guessing she must've had an "oh crap" moment.) But rather than tell me she was kidding, she said something like, "Rosie, they gave you up. Remember? They don't want you. You might as well just come back inside." Ahh, can't you just feel the sisterly love?

The thing is that while I desperately wanted to have my uniqueness honored, I also wanted to belong—which is probably why I was so willing to go live with my neighbors. I was seeking a place where I felt it was okay to be me and let my sparkle shine. I think this is where my impression management journey began. I thought I had to be more like my sisters and convinced myself that I had to work hard, be super productive, accomplish things, and be the best at everything in order to be accepted and loved. I thought love and belonging were conditional for me, so I had to prove I was worthy and enough.

This story served me well—to a point. I got good grades, earned multiple degrees and certifications, launched a successful business, and more. My friends even had an ongoing joke that I was Wonder Woman. Truth be told, I kind of liked that people thought I was somehow superhuman. On the outside, I may have appeared to be superhuman and successful, but on the inside, I was exhausted by trying to outrun my fear of not being enough and trying instead to be who I thought others wanted me to be!

Despite lots of work on myself, this story can still creep in for me today. After all, I am only human. When the insecure, ten-year-old version of me kicks in and I feel the need to prove my worth and value, I get into hyperindependent, hyperproductive, pain-in-the-ass, get-shit-done mode and take on way more than I can handle. And because I don't want to let people down, I push myself to make it all work at a possible great cost. On more than one occasion, this vicious cycle has led me to illness or injury. At one point, it almost eroded my marriage. I was so busy trying to prove myself and receive the accolades of people around me whose opinions probably don't really matter, while my poor husband got the crappy, leftover version of me. Yikes!

I share this because I know that my experience and story aren't unique. After years of coaching thousands of leaders at all levels across industries and working with hundreds of teams to help them be more effective, I started to see self-limiting stories reveal themselves to everyone. As I looked more closely, patterns started emerging in terms of how and why people get in their own way, preventing them from having the results they desire. While details vary from person to person, I find that everyone has a story they created early in their lives that still runs the show more than they realize, showing up in the form of impression management.

When I launched the *Show Up as a Leader* podcast in the fall of 2020, I wanted to normalize the messiness of being human. I decided to ask every guest to share a self-limiting story they still tell themselves at times and how they move beyond it so they can show up as leaders in their lives. The responses to this question aligned with what we were seeing in our coaching and consulting work, so we decided to examine these patterns more closely to see what we could learn.

And because I'm also a research geek, I went to the data. Recent studies have confirmed what we were experiencing with our clients:

- Sixty to seventy percent of all organizational change efforts fail.[2]
- Seventy-four percent of leaders are not well equipped to lead change.[3]
- Seventy-five percent of companies believe their leadership development is not delivering high value to the company.[4]
- Seventy-six percent of companies say their leadership development model is not up to date or not highly relevant.[4]
- Seventy-three percent of employees are experiencing change fatigue.[4]
- Sixty-four percent of workers are feeling exhaustion and burnout.[5]
- Eighty-five percent of companies aren't caring for and mitigating leader burnout.[4]

When I see these stats, the image of Dana Carvey as the "Church Lady" on the 1990s cast of *Saturday Night Live* immediately pops into my head. Especially his voice saying, "Well, isn't that special?" I don't know about you, but it gets a little tiring and deflating to hear these stats year after year that not only aren't changing for the better but in fact keep going in the wrong direction.

What if it doesn't have to be this way? Imagine a world where people aren't struggling with change. One in which you, your leaders, and your leadership development efforts are thriving, and collectively we're leaning into discomfort and making progress on goals that matter to us. I've learned that it is definitely possible. And it starts with reconciling this vision with our current reality.

I have seen that a key contributing factor is a critical, growing gap between what our disruptive and increasingly complex world continues to demand from us and our innate human biological wiring to self-protect and preserve the status quo. We refer to this gap as the Stuckness Zone. When we are in the Stuckness Zone, it's as though our ten-year-old self is in the driver's seat rather than our hopefully more evolved adult self. Consequently, we get in the way of leading ourselves and others through change, impede our effectiveness, and experience elevated levels of stress and burnout.

The more disruptive our world becomes, the more we find ourselves trapped in the Stuckness Zone. This leads to increased disconnection and defensiveness when what we need is adaptability, creativity, and collaboration. When we react out of stress and fear, we can't adapt to meet the present challenges. We aren't open to learning, we can't think creatively, and ultimately, we can't implement new ways of doing things.

This is the work we do every day at Salveo Partners. We future-proof organizations by strengthening culture and equipping leaders and teams to show up courageously and to better navigate change and disruption. The core of future-proofing organizations is future-proofing leadership, formal and informal. Future-proofing leadership isn't about predicting what's next; it's about being adaptable, human-centered, and willing to embrace change. If we are going to be future-ready leaders, we must recognize what keeps us trapped in the Stuckness Zone and then find a way to move through it and close the gap so we can thrive amid change and disruption, because they are here to stay.

The good news is we have done that by analyzing interview and coaching data spanning 250 leaders across industries (unless otherwise noted, all statistics come from this study). We've identified the seven core faulty programs and their "cousins" that derail progress and effectiveness. These are core patterns of thinking and self-limiting narratives that quietly shape how we lead, work, and live. We've also learned how these faulty programs impede leaders from growing and making progress on the goals that matter to them.

And the really good news is that we've learned what it takes to upgrade our faulty programs and create environments so we can move through change more effectively, turn these trends around, and future-proof leadership within our organizations and ourselves.

What to Expect

This book provides all the context, details, research, and practical application steps to help normalize the messiness of being human and understand why we get in our way. It then gives you a blueprint to start future-proofing your leadership. It's divided into three parts:

- Part 1 sets the context by providing details, research, and examples to help you better understand and normalize our current state, why we have the challenges that we do, and why it is critical that we do things differently to future-proof leadership and have a sustainable future.
- Part 2 unpacks the most common areas in which we get stuck when it comes to change and the faulty programs that trap us in the Stuckness Zone. It includes tangible steps you can take to start the upgrade process and make progress on goals that matter to you.
- Part 3 pulls everything together so you can leverage your new insights to future-proof leadership from two perspectives: within your organization and within yourself.

Along the way I share real stories from leaders who have done the courageous work necessary to upgrade their faulty programs and kick their ten-year-old selves to the back seat so they can take back the driver's seat. Unless specifically noted, their names and any specific identifying information have been altered, but my hope is that you will feel a little less alone and be inspired by their stories and equipped to pave a new path for a more effective and sustainable future. I have learned that when people are in the Stuckness Zone, they can easily find themselves in a place of self-judgment, as if there's something wrong with them. By normalizing the messiness of our shared human experience, I hope to make it less scary to lean into vulnerability and do the inner work that's essential to be future-ready.

In a world with increasing disruption that includes technology and artificial intelligence, the demand for courageous human leadership has never been greater. The world needs everyone to be able to show up as a leader in their lives, regardless of title or role. After all, only humans can truly feel, show care, inspire, foster a sense of purpose and belonging, and build authentic relationships. And that is difficult to do when our brains are running an outdated program. We need to stop the insanity of doing the same things over and over and expecting different outcomes.

Are you ready? Let's do this!

PART 1

UNDERSTANDING AND NORMALIZING OUR NEW REALITY

CHAPTER 1

Why Change Is So Hard

That "change makes us uncomfortable" is now one of the most widely promoted, widely accepted, and under-considered half-truths around . . . it is not change by itself that makes us uncomfortable; it is not even change that involves taking on something very difficult. Rather, it is change that leaves us feeling defenseless before the dangers we "know" to be present that causes us anxiety.

—Robert Kegan and Lisa Lahey, *Immunity to Change*

We know that most change efforts fail and most leaders are ill-equipped to lead change. But why is this? It comes down to two key reasons:

1. We use a mismatched approach for the challenges and changes we're facing.
2. We don't acknowledge our current environment and how it activates deeply ingrained self-protective instincts.

We live, work, and lead in a world where disruption is the norm. The world and our environment are frequently referred to as VUCA—volatile, uncertain, complex, and ambiguous. The acronym has been around for decades, and it gives us a common language in which to normalize our experiences. And while disruption can be helpful—it's how we evolve and grow—it makes us bump against our innate biological wiring to self-protect, leading us to avoid discomfort and cling tightly to what is familiar. (I'll dive into this more in chapter 2.)

The more VUCA our world becomes, the more our self-protective instincts are triggered. This gap between the VUCA demands and our human instincts continues to widen, and we find ourselves trapped in the Stuckness Zone. In fact, the American Psychological Association reports that 87 percent of adults believe there has been a constant stream of crises since 2020 and it's taking a toll on us.[6] So it's not surprising that today's average employee can only absorb half as much change as they could in 2019.[7]

Think about that for a moment. This VUCA-extreme environment we're living, working, and leading in is amplifying the Stuckness Zone, making it harder to adapt when the pace of change is exponential. But again, why?

As a start, it's important to distinguish between the two main types of challenges we face as human beings and their influences on how we show up in the face of change.

- *Technical challenges* are those for which there is a known solution. We can use our existing knowledge and skills (or easily obtain or find the necessary resources) to solve them. As an example, using standard operating procedures and checklists and looking back at what has been done before can be helpful to successfully navigate a technical challenge.
- *Adaptive challenges*, on the other hand, are more complex and have us venturing into uncharted territory. There is no known solution. In fact, relying on our existing knowledge, resources, and experiences won't work. These challenges require experiments, discoveries, and adjustments. We also can't simply will ourselves to the solution. We can only solve these issues by reframing how we think and operate.[8]

Another way to think about this is that technical challenges require *information* to find a resolution, whereas adaptive challenges require *transformation*. Adaptive challenges elicit a sense of loss because they force us to let go of what is familiar to solve them. They bring us face-to-face with our faulty programs and force us to lean into vulnerability so we can move through the Stuckness Zone.

A common request we receive is to conduct communication training for a team or group of leaders so that they can better handle difficult conversations. We have come to realize such requests have a lot behind them. There are usually many underlying cultural issues at play, making it much more than a training solution. But let's set that aside for a moment and say that we are going to provide courageous conversation training for a team within your organization.

Several models are available that provide a structure and framework (including scripts, checklists, and conversation starters) for having a courageous conversation. If the training is done well and includes lots of practice and applications and this is a technical challenge for your team, the information provided will be all they need. They should be able to leverage the tools from the training to effectively navigate difficult conversations.

However, if having to *use* the information to have the conversation elicits anxiety and has your team members wanting to throw up in a garbage can at the thought of having the conversation (or they'll ruminate for days afterward), you are dealing with an adaptive challenge. Until you support your team in transforming and shifting their mindsets to upgrade the faulty programming that makes the courageous conversations feel so cringey, they won't be able to effectively *apply* the information or the technical aspects of the solution.

With adaptive challenges, we are faced with a sense of loss. We must let go of what is familiar and predictable and many times what has allowed us to be successful until this point. Doing so can cause great discomfort. We are essentially forced to let go of part of our identity and change how we see and do things. Consequently, when the familiar personal and organizational equilibrium is disturbed, not only do people push back, but they also seek what is familiar and try to use technical fixes to solve problems that are actually adaptive.[9] This is why we tend to seek quick fixes or magic bullets rather than acknowledge the complexity and uncertainty that accompany adaptive challenges. But it tends to be about as effective as playing a bad game of Whac-A-Mole. Ronald Heifetz put it well: "The single biggest failure of leadership is to treat adaptive challenges like technical problems."[10]

Unfortunately, we do it all the time, reaching for a short-term technical fix rather than face the discomfort required to address the complexities that adaptive challenges inevitably bring. Welcome to being human!

Susan is a senior director who was struggling with leading her team. The organization used Six Sigma and a well-known change management model in many of their processes. But despite following the frameworks, Susan's team struggled with adopting the various organizational changes and kept falling back to its old way of doing things. As more pressure came from executive leadership, she found her team's communication eroding with lots of drama, negativity, blaming, and us-versus-them thinking. She tried bringing in people to lead workshops on change management and effective communication, but they never seemed to work. Her team was deeply entrenched in the Stuckness Zone, and no amount of training was helping; neither were pep talks or directives. Susan didn't realize it at the time, but she was falling into the trap of trying to use a technical fix for a largely adaptive challenge. She was failing to care for the messiness of being human among her team members.

Because Susan's team needed to use transformation to effectively move through adaptive change, we started by normalizing their experiences and providing a common language. We introduced the concept of VUCA and how the nature of work can trigger us to go into self-protection mode. People shared that they felt comforted to know why things seemed harder than they needed to be and to better understand what they were experiencing. When their threat responses were calmed a bit, they were in a better place to listen and do transformation-based work.

The organization had been in a constant state of flux, including significant changes in leadership and organizational structure, acquisitions, and expansion of its product and service lines. Susan's team didn't know where it fit among the changes and had no say in how the changes would impact its work. All the uncertainty activated the team's instinctive human wiring, encouraging team members to act in the exact opposite way than they needed to. And they didn't even realize it.

We facilitated them through a multisession program we frequently use with intact teams. It helps them navigate the transformation process needed to move through adaptive change. We provided tools and a common language for Susan's team members to become more aware of their triggers to self-protect and how often they were showing up guarded rather than as collaborators. We were then able to teach team members skills and techniques to pause, self-reflect, and start upgrading their faulty programs by trying on new stories that served them better. Team members started showing more empathy for one another as they realized their shared humanity was working against them. Once Susan's team members stopped fighting one another and let go of their blame and "rightness," they were able to see the collective purpose and work through the discomfort of the organizational changes rather than avoid it. As they did, they were better able to take in the information provided and engage in dialogue to help make the processes even better. Information alone wasn't working; it was only when the team embarked on doing the transformation work that the team was able to move through the adaptive changes facing it.

Thousands of stories like that of Susan and her team happen every day across organizations. We think if we simply give people information or follow a standardized process, they should be able to easily adopt whatever change we're asking to be made. But we forget that the humanity we all have quietly works against us.

In reality, most of the challenges and changes we face have some technical components, and we would benefit from information to help us increase our knowledge or enhance our skills. But the overwhelming majority of the challenges and changes we need to make to thrive in a VUCA world require that we can embrace adaptive change. Just like Susan's team, we need to be able to let go of comfort, upgrade our faulty inner programming, and find a way to move through the Stuckness Zone.

Closing the Gap to Move Through the Stuckness Zone

Hopefully you're beginning to see that being a future-ready leader requires us to set aside our reactive instincts to apply a quick technical fix and be willing to accept the discomfort of adaptive change. There's no way around it. Dr. Brené Brown has studied leadership for more than twelve years. She asked C-suite leaders from around the world what needed to change for leaders to be successful in a complex, rapidly changing environment. One common answer sums up what is needed to move through the Stuckness Zone and close the gap between the VUCA world demands and our physical biology: "We need braver leaders and more courageous cultures."[11]

That being said, it's important to recognize what leadership actually is. At Salveo Partners, we define leadership as:

> Maximizing our positive impact on the world by becoming our best, fully authentic self and supporting those around us to break past barriers and step into their greatness.

This means we must show up as braver leaders by doing some adaptive change work on ourselves. Then we can show up authentically and move past our limiting faulty programs. In doing so, we can start to create and nurture courageous cultures by supporting others to do the same and learn how to effectively call them to greatness. Sounds simple, right? Yet we know how challenging this can be.

It's also important to recognize that leadership never has been, and never will be, simply about a title or role. We all likely know people who have the power, title, authority, and job description but are in no way leaders. And we all likely know people who do not have the power, title, authority, or job description who do show up as leaders in their lives. In this VUCA-extreme environment, we have an opportunity—and I am so bold as to say a responsibility—to equip *everyone* to show up as leaders. And if you happen to hold a formal leadership position, it's even more important for you because of the influence you wield over the culture and employee experience.

While we were supporting Susan's team members to show up as leaders, we did additional work with Susan herself. She realized that she needed to relearn many of her leadership practices to be effective in this VUCA environment. She had to learn to regulate her own emotions and self-protective instincts and then to show up differently to create a safe space for building a courageous culture with her team. As Susan worked to identify and upgrade her faulty programming, she grew in confidence and clarity. When she moved beyond her fears and frustrations, she was better able to embrace calmness and move from trying to push her team to change to enabling them to do so. That shift was a game changer for Susan, her team, and the organization. Many other teams inquired about what she did and asked for similar support.

Viktor Frankl once said, "When we are no longer able to change a situation, we are challenged to change ourselves."[12] When we show up hijacked by our faulty programs, we are unable to experience true connection and growth; our creativity and innovation become stifled. If people within organizations aren't showing up with authenticity, it increases barriers to the ability to thrive in a VUCA world. Susan and her team experienced this and struggled more than they likely needed to.

We can't change the VUCA nature of our world, so we have no choice but to change ourselves. Showing up as leaders by becoming our best, fully authentic selves isn't for the faint of heart. It requires bravely addressing the Stuckness Zone head-on by doing the work to change ourselves in ways that can be unsettling but are necessary. It starts with exploring and shifting our mindsets.

KEY POINTS

- We live, work, and lead in a VUCA (volatile, uncertain, complex, and ambiguous) world in which disruption is the norm.
- A key contributing factor to our challenges with change is a failure to recognize the critical difference between technical challenges (which require information to solve) and adaptive challenges (which require transformation and some discomfort) and using a mismatched approach.
- The past several years brought us a VUCA-extreme environment full of constant adaptive challenges that exacerbate stress and burnout. Consequently, our capacity to handle change has been cut in half from where it was in 2019.[7] Yet the pace of change continues to increase exponentially.
- The gap between what our VUCA world demands from us and our biological instincts to do the opposite of that in the face of adaptive change is widening and leads us to become trapped in the Stuckness Zone.
- To be future-ready, we must equip ourselves and others with the ability to move through the Stuckness Zone and show up as courageous and authentic leaders, regardless of title or role.

CHAPTER 2

How Mindset Impacts Individual and Organizational Effectiveness

If we continue to believe as we have always believed, we will continue to act as we have always acted. If we continue to act as we have always acted, we will continue to get what we have always gotten.

—attributed to Marilyn Ferguson

Like all species, we are hardwired for survival. The problem is that our brains don't know the difference between an actual physical threat (for example, a wild animal is charging us) and a perceived social threat (for example, someone might judge or reject us).[13] We have the same physiological reaction to both. When we perceive a threat, our brains are triggered to respond automatically in a fight-or-flight manner (often referred to as the "amygdala hijack"), which results in going into self-protection mode and behaving in unproductive ways. These threat triggers are largely activated by our subconscious programming.

In the early years of life (referred to as the imprint period), our brains subconsciously download programming from our lived experiences and through observing our surroundings. This is how we learn the rules of the road; we learn what is right and wrong, when to speak up and when to be quiet, when we'll be accepted versus rejected, and more. This programming serves a critical function. It helps us to survive, stay safe, feel in control, feel loved, and find acceptance. Essentially, our brains are hardwired to maximize rewards and minimize threats.

Herein lies the predicament. Subconscious programming is running the show approximately 95 percent of the time. Even more problematic is that studies have shown that more than 70 percent of the programming we download is fundamentally flawed, negative, and self-sabotaging.[14, 15] Think about that for a moment. We're predominantly operating based on subconscious programming from those first ten or so years of our lives that is essentially head trash. That flawed programming and head trash together put us in a threat-response state that still runs the show way more than we realize or likely want to admit. And the nature of living in a VUCA world increasingly activates the brain's threat response, keeping us from being able to adapt, make meaningful and lasting change, and make progress on goals that matter to us.

The combination of flawed programming and the activation of the brain's threat centers helps to shape what Harvard's Bob Kegan and Lisa Lahey refer to as our psychological immune system.[16] Just like we have a physical immune system that works to protect us from threats of disease and infection, our brains are working subconsciously to protect us from our perceived threats of judgment, rejection, imperfections, lack of being in control, and more. But these immune systems can go astray. For example, people with any sort of autoimmune disorder deal with the body falsely perceiving threats and attacking itself. On the psychological level, our brains spend so much energy trying to keep us safe so that our deepest worries and fears don't see the light of day. Consequently, we end up quietly working against ourselves when we're trying to accept adaptive change and make progress on goals that matter to us.

Our Psychological Immune System at Play

If we're going to upgrade our faulty programs and heal our psychological immune systems, we must first identify and name them. One of the most impactful ways we have found to support leaders in navigating adaptive change and upgrading their faulty programming is the Immunity to Change (ITC) coaching process. I was first introduced to the process in 2014, when the leadership team I was on was asked to collectively go through the process with a coach. Although I had been a certified coach for over ten years at that point, I'm always up for coaching and working on myself, so I was excited to see what this process entailed. It was so transformative that I knew I needed to get certified so I could bring this process to others.

ITC starts with creating a four-column map. In column 1, you identify an adaptive change goal by clarifying behaviors you want and need to change to achieve the outcomes you desire. Then, in column 2, list everything you are doing or aren't doing that undermine your column 1 goal. You'll now be able to see how you're working against yourself.

Next comes column 3, which starts with listing all your worries and fears related to what is at risk if you do the opposite of the behaviors you listed in column 2. You then translate those fears into "competing commitments," which essentially are the brain's subconscious motivations and commitments that work to keep us safe so that our column 3 fears never see the light of day.

The first three columns of the ITC map represent the psychological immune system. The harder we push ourselves on our column 1 goal, the harder our brains simultaneously push back to keep us safe. It's like having one foot on the gas and one foot on the brake at the same time. The key to unlocking this cycle is not to continue pushing harder on the goal, which is the usual approach.

The key lies in column 4 of the map, where we identify our underlying assumptions about how the world works and our perceived self-value that anchor our psychological immune system. Column 4 is where we find our faulty programs and what we use to guide the upgrade process. Here is what my initial ITC map looked like:

Column 1: Improvement Goal	Column 2: Doing and Not Doing	Column 3: Competing Commitments	Column 4: Big Assumptions
To be better at speaking up directly and promptly at work and at home.	Ignore frustrations at home and don't say anything. Make excuses for any poor performance by my team and jump into hypersupport mode (i.e., "train them to success"). Procrastinate having corrective conversations. Get sucked in during corrective conversations. Apologize, fumble over my words, get derailed, and so on. Ruminate for days before and days after when I've spoken up. Then go into hyper-doing mode to try to make up for having the conversation.	**Worries and fears:** I won't be perfect. People won't like me; I won't be loved. I'll be rejected. I'll appear selfish. **I'm committed to:** Being perfect. Having people like me . . . at all costs. Never risking being rejected. Doing whatever it takes to never appear selfish.	If I speak up, I might be subjected to explosive anger. People won't like me; I will be rejected and end up alone. My sole value comes from what I accomplish and being perfect. People can't disagree with me or be upset with me and still love me; these ideas can't coexist.

When I look at my original map, I think how exhausting this was. Although I had done a lot of work on myself, the missing piece was upgrading the programming. There was a part of me stuck in those early years, desperately trying to feel like I was enough and lovable. As long as my faulty programs were running the show, it didn't matter how many books I read or how much training I had. Nothing would help. I had to face the discomfort of the upgrade process. There isn't a fast-forward button!

My upgrade process started with naming which faulty programs I was running and then owning where they came from and how they were showing up in the present. Owning it began by reflecting on early childhood moments that stood out to me and likely formed my faulty programs. In my early years, I was often yelled at when I messed up. Enter the script of needing to be perfect to be loved so I wouldn't get yelled at and so on. I also had moments when I felt that I only received love or validation when I did something extraordinary and "performed." Enter the story of underlining my hyperdoing and overachieving tendencies. Most of the time, I felt like I was compared to my older sisters. I was expected to attend their band and orchestra concerts throughout the year, but no one ever came to my dance competitions, and everyone complained relentlessly the one time per year when they had to attend my dance recital. Then I'd get crap for being upset by their lack of support. Enter more stories about not being lovable or enough and to not be selfish.

Although difficult, this part of the process is important because most of our fears were formed in those early years of our lives as we tried to make sense of our experiences. These fears helped to shape our psychological immune system. Every feeling we experience and every story we tell ourselves today is a programmed belief system from those early years of life that created some sort of meaning, identity, or causality (that is, if I do *this*, then it means *that*). Once we become more aware of which faulty programs we're running and where they came from, we can start to observe when they hijack us—and their associated costs—and when they don't get in our way. Armed with this rich information, we can move into the last phase of the upgrade process, where we challenge our faulty programming. This involves running mini-experiments in which we collect data to poke holes in the validity of our assumptions and faulty programs. With each hole we poke, the old programming starts to upgrade, and we leave our subconscious childhood reactions further behind.

I admit that I still don't like having difficult conversations on any level. But I now enter into them sooner and mostly calm, clear, and curious. And I do so as a courageous adult rather than an insecure, scared ten-year-old deeply worried about rejection. Because of doing the necessary work to upgrade my faulty programs, when they do try to hijack me, I'm able to recognize what's happening and remind myself that I'm not ten years old anymore. I ground myself in my values and other tools that help me to reset and proceed. You see, this isn't a one-and-done event. The upgrade process needs continued nurturing to keep us from reverting to our factory resets. This is why we need to tend to both facets of leadership in a particular order.

The Two Facets of Leadership

Most of us have likely heard of the iceberg analogy: What we see on the surface is only about 10 percent of what is really going on beneath the surface (that we can't see). In other words, only our behaviors are visible to others and sometimes to ourselves. What ultimately guides our behaviors is hidden underneath the surface and is often messy. It includes our thoughts, feelings, mindsets, beliefs, and meaning-making systems. It is also home to our core identities, which include our met and unmet needs, values, dreams, fears, and purposes.[17]

The 90 percent beneath the surface is essentially our inner operating system (IOS). When our IOS is outdated, we impede ourselves when trying to make progress on goals, even when we're highly motivated to do so. Motivation isn't enough when our IOS needs to be upgraded. As you can see from my initial ITC map, when my psychological immune system and faulty programming were in the driver's seat, the foot on the brake in my brain, trying to keep me safe from rejection or appearing selfish, was hindering my ability to make progress on my goal of speaking up timely and directly.

In their book *Mastering Leadership*, Bob Anderson and Bill Adams describe two facets of leadership:

1. *The Inner Game (a.k.a. our Inner Operating System).* This consists of what drives us; our internal beliefs and assumptions that make up our identity and guide our actions; our meaning-making system that we use to make sense of the world; how we analyze and make decisions; and our level of self-awareness and emotional intelligence. This is the 90 percent of the iceberg that is below the surface.
2. *The Outer Game (a.k.a. Leadership Practices).* This consists of our domain knowledge, experience, managerial capability, leadership competencies, and behavior. It is the 10 percent of the iceberg that we can see.

Although the outer game is where we spend most of our time (and it is important), the inner game *runs* the outer game. "Mastery in anything is a well-honed outer game arising on a highly mature inner game."[18] It is reminiscent of the saying that what got you here won't get you there. In many cases, the behaviors and tendencies that stem from our inner programming have helped us and contributed to our current success to some degree. But they keep us from going further and hinder us in a rapidly changing, complex, and disruptive environment. This is why most approaches to development are mediocre or short-lived at best. They don't tend to the messiness needed to upgrade the IOS *first* to be able to support the outer-game work of leveling up skills and capabilities.

Bryan is a physician leader. He had a long history of leadership in the military, where VUCA certainly existed. However, there were such clear processes and practices that disruption was mostly a nonissue for him. Like so many people with a long tenure of leadership, Bryan completed numerous leadership training programs and worked with a handful of leadership coaches over his career. As a result, he seemed to be an ideal candidate for a prominent senior leadership role outside of the military in a complex health care organization. Initially, his drive to get results and provide a sense of order amid chaos appeared to be just what this organization needed. But a few months into the role, Bryan hit a wall when his previous way of successful leadership no longer worked.

Because of the developmental work Bryan had done along his leadership journey, he was highly self-aware and knew he had controlling tendencies. Every assessment he took affirmed this. Despite this, he had convinced himself that his controlling style was necessary, and if people would simply listen to him and do things his way, many of the issues within the health care system would be resolved. He teetered between self-awareness and blame. Bryan couldn't see a path forward other than being an inauthentic version of himself. He didn't need more outer-game tools; he was well equipped for the most part. He needed to tend to the inner game and take a good, hard look at his IOS. This was when the executives of the organization contacted us for help before things went incredibly sideways.

We started with a suite of assessments (some that Bryan had previously completed) to paint a complete picture of his IOS and understand many aspects of the hard wiring of his thinking process that guides his behaviors. We leveraged these insights to guide Bryan in completing his ITC map so we could have a clear adaptive change goal to guide our work and help him to identify what faulty programs were getting in his way. Bryan was highly motivated to get better at holding space for others in conversations. This included listening to understand, staying present, being open and curious, and facilitating people to work through challenges (versus him jumping in and taking over). The problem was that he had one foot constantly on the brake, preventing him from making progress. His faulty programs led him to a deep need to be productive and a "fixer," and he couldn't slow down enough to behave in ways aligned with his goal.

Knowing how to develop others, have feedback conversations, create strategy, provide clear direction, and get results—all outer-game aspects of leadership—weren't helping Bryan in this environment. To some extent, they were making it worse because he overused them to push his need to fix and produce. His behaviors were disabling others from stepping up, taking the initiative, or being accountable. And they frustrated his fellow leadership colleagues. Bryan could see his psychological immune system at play and how he was working against himself, so he set aside some of his pride and ego. As we began the upgrade process, he started to reframe his value proposition and moved from reactive, fear-based leadership practices to more intentional, courageous leadership practices. Once his faulty programs were upgraded, he was much more effective in applying all of his previous outer-game tools and some of the new ones we added to his leadership toolbox.

Rethinking What It Takes to Effectively Lead in a VUCA World

Living, learning, and leading in a VUCA world require a different mindset and approach than what works for us during times of familiarity and certainty. Under times of stress, pressure, and all that comes with VUCA, we are biologically wired to act in ways that protect our core identities at the root of our icebergs. This is where we enter the Stuckness Zone. So we put on masks and spend an enormous amount of energy hiding our flaws and inadequacies, pretending to be something we're not, and overcompensating for feelings and fears of being less than. And sometimes we even dim our own sparkle so we can feel like we belong. Not only is it a waste of our time and energy, but it's also exhausting!

Now, put a group of us together on a team or in an organization, and we wonder why we have the challenges we do. I believe that most people don't wake up in the morning thinking, *I'm going to be a difficult butthead today.* But when we're in the Stuckness Zone, being hijacked by our faulty programs, that's what ends up happening. It's kind of like having a group of ten-year-olds running the show in our lives and in our organizations without realizing it. I don't know about you, but I wouldn't let a ten-year-old make major decisions for our household or our business or even drive our car. Yet we're doing it all the time when this flawed programming is in the driver's seat.

Unfortunately, the more VUCA our world becomes, the more our threat responses and faulty programs are activated, leading us to double down on self-protection and cling tightly to what is familiar because it feels comfortable and safe. Consequently, we see an increase in disconnection and defensiveness when what we need are adaptability, creativity, and collaboration. When we react out of stress and fear, we can't adapt to meet the present challenges. We aren't open to learning, can't think creatively, and ultimately can't implement new ways of doing things.

I see so many people getting frustrated with themselves and others, which isn't helpful. Just because we have this Stuckness Zone predicament doesn't mean we have to stay stuck. What I have found to consistently make a difference with our clients—on both individual and organizational levels—is caring for the inner aspects by identifying the faulty and flawed programs getting in people's way and then supporting them to upgrade that programming. Bryan is a great example of this. All his previous outer-game training was working against him. It was only when he did the messy inner work that he was finally able to get out of his own way and become the leader he was meant to be and that his organization needed. The reality is that we all have some faulty programs leading us to have self-limiting stories and filters that can block our way, whether we realize it or not. We must own them, or they will own us!

KEY POINTS

- Our brains are on autopilot approximately 95 percent of the time. At least 70 percent of our brains' programming that guides our actions was formed in the early years of our lives and is fundamentally flawed, negative, and self-sabotaging.[14, 15]
- This leads to the formation of our psychological immune systems where we have one foot on the gas, trying to make progress on adaptive change goals, while the other foot slams on the brake as our brains try to protect us. So we stay stuck in a vicious cycle of behaviors because motivation isn't enough when our IOS is outdated and needs to be upgraded.
- We are designed as a species to be on high alert for threats, avoid discomfort, and cling tightly to what is familiar. Most of our reactions today are not coming from our adult self. Every feeling we experience and every story we tell ourselves today is from a programmed belief system formed in those early years of life that creates some sort of meaning, identity, or causality (that is, if I do *this*, then it means *that*). It's like having a group of ten-year-olds running the show.
- The very nature of living in a VUCA world regularly activates our brains' threat responses and our faulty programs, leading us to be trapped in the Stuckness Zone: the gap between what our VUCA world demands from us and our biological self-protective instincts.
- The key to reconciling this gap and moving through the Stuckness Zone is identifying and upgrading our faulty programs (The Inner Game of leadership). Then we can start to hone and level up our skills (the Outer Game of leadership). There isn't a shortcut or fast-forward button if we want to have better results.

CHAPTER 3

The Need for Human-Centric Leadership in an AI World

Real leadership is relational at its core. No matter how skilled or strategic a leader is, if they cannot connect with and support the people they manage, their effectiveness will always be limited . . . We cannot lead today with yesterday's skills.

—Jen Marr, *Lifting Up*

The world is at a pivotal moment. Disruptions from global crises, economic instability, and the rapid evolution of technology have exposed vulnerabilities in our societal fabric. It's like those bad 1990s infomercials with the bearded guy who keeps saying, "But wait, there's more!" Hopefully it's becoming clearer why we are having such challenges adapting and thriving in this VUCA-extreme world. Like it or not, we are wired for familiarity and comfort. This means it takes intentionality and courage to break out of our comfort zones and upgrade our self-protective faulty programs.

We've also seen that it's easier said than done. Unfortunately, the traditional models of leadership and development no longer suffice in meeting the largely adaptive challenges we face. We must relearn what is required to effectively lead in this disruptive environment where people are struggling with change, stress, and burnout. This means we need to take a different approach to developing ourselves and others as future-ready leaders and to be a conduit for a space of connection and healing in a world that is hurting. The problem is that most of us were never trained to do this, so we struggle more than we need to.

If we don't take a different approach to developing ourselves and others, we will continue to be trapped in the Stuckness Zone. We have to stop looking for the shortcut, the "easy" button, and mismatched solutions. Instead, we must recognize the complexities of being human and do the messy work to upgrade our IOS and faulty programming. The generational shift happening in the workforce, along with the rise of AI, expedites the need to rethink how we act as leaders of ourselves and others in a world in which our humanness works against us.

For example, along with all the encouraging advancements that AI can bring come human emotions. Many are related to fear and anxiety. Some people fear being irrelevant or having their jobs replaced. Let's say you've always manually entered information; that's what you know. But now the process is going to be automated. Suddenly, you may feel a potential threat and question what value you can bring. You might wonder where—and if—you belong. Or perhaps the increasing use of AI reveals gaps in your ability to effectively interact, communicate, and make complex decisions. And when you add in all the unknowns, your self-protective instincts go into overdrive. The reality is that AI can't form reciprocal relationships. AI isn't worried about its aging parent or sick kid; AI isn't anxious or stressed. But the humans coming into your workplace are and need human support.

On top of everything, there is a deep lacking but incredible need for mattering, which is the feeling of significance to those around us that comes from feeling valued by others and adding value to their lives. In other words, we feel valued when we're fully heard, seen, and understood by others. We experience adding value when we feel needed by and see the unique impact we have on others. Mattering is a core human need, and we all have it. When it comes to organizations, leaders greatly impact people's sense of mattering.

Unfortunately, we're largely on the struggle bus when it comes to people feeling valued and significant. In his book *The Power of Mattering*, Zach Mercurio presents powerful data on why mattering is needed now more than ever:

- Fifty-eight percent of people feel lonely at work,
- Fifty percent of people feel forgotten at work, and
- Thirty percent of people feel invisible at work.[19]

Let that sink in for a moment. It is in our DNA to feel like we matter, yet half of us, at best, feel forgotten at work. So it's not surprising that the 2025 DDI Global Leadership Forecast (which includes responses from 10,796 leaders from 2,014 organizations across the globe) found that in order for leaders to be prepared to lead in a complex world of constant change, they need to learn to lead differently to create more human-centered workplaces. Yes, results are important. But they need to coexist with creating environments where people feel respected, valued, and able to grow. At the same time, we must build adaptable, resilient teams that can thrive amid uncertainty, and not at the expense of the human experience. Otherwise, talent walks out the door.[20]

While human-centric leadership skills have always been important, they are even more critical in this new digital age that frequently hyperfocuses on business growth, results, and technology instead of human care and connection. Make no mistake: Being a future-ready leader requires us to lead with human skills of authenticity, empathy, and adaptivity so we can foster greater connection and collaboration and a sense of mattering. Technology further amplifies the need to level up these human skills.

How AI Amplifies the Need for Human Skills and Connection

A 2025 McKinsey & Company report suggests that the future of work in the age of AI is "VUCA on steroids" and that we can't treat it as just another tool to be implemented. To do so can put more stress on already strained systems, especially if organizations are not purposefully addressing the human aspects.[21] The report goes on to describe how our human brains are wired to prefer simple solutions, especially in the face of complex adaptive challenges. So leaning on AI that is rooted in past solutions when we're dealing with something new and adaptive that requires novel and complex thinking amplifies the Stuckness Zone. It's not an either/or but rather a both/and. We need to learn to leverage technology while growing our human-centric leadership capabilities.

AI is fundamentally changing how leaders work and interact with their teams. As AI tools are leveraged more to expedite some tasks that used to take up a great deal of time, such as analyzing trends or streamlining processes, leaders have more time freed up for meaningful work. At the top of the list is nurturing cultures where employees feel valued and motivated and are able to see how their work contributes to a greater purpose. Leaders also need to help equip their teams to better navigate the growing complexities of work today and in the future. Essentially, as our understanding and use of AI increases, so does the demand for critical human skills. According to a Workday 2025 global survey:

- Eighty-three percent of employees believe that AI will make uniquely human skills even more critical, and
- Eighty-two percent of employees crave more human connection as AI usage grows.[22]

Some key human-centric skills that AI cannot replace include emotional intelligence and empathy, relationship-building, conflict resolution, and ethical decision-making. Yet all of these become more challenging in a VUCA world as our self-protective instincts are consistently activated. When we're run by our faulty programs, most of our critical human-centric skills go out the window. We are especially seeing a growing need to care for the generational collision that increasingly lands people in the Stuckness Zone.

The Generational Collision in the Stuckness Zone

We are having frequent conversations with our clients focusing specifically on navigating the shifts needed to support more Gen Zers (people born between 1996 and 2012) entering the workforce. The collision between Gen Zers and older leaders can be significant and lead to time spent in the Stuckness Zone. Leaders ranging from older millennials to baby boomers frequently double down on their judgments and perceptions about Gen Zers rather than learn new ways of thinking and leading. We hear things like:

- I shouldn't have to recognize them for doing their job.
- They're bringing too much personal baggage into work. I don't [want to, know how to] deal with it.
- They're too demanding and have unrealistic expectations.
- They aren't motivated and don't want to work hard.
- They don't know how to communicate.
- Why should I invest in them? They're not loyal and are just going to leave anyway.
- Why should I have to change? They need to suck it up!
- I only have a few years left before I retire; I'm not changing now. They can just deal with it.

We recently facilitated a full-day leadership retreat with a group of divisional directors for one of our clients. Our focus was on being a future-ready leader and building more human-centric leadership practices and skills. Over the past few years, we have implemented our Thriving Workplace Culture Survey with them multiple times. One data point we always examine is the "deal breakers" that have been identified as critical for younger millennial and Gen Z employees. These are things they are looking for in employers that will lead them to leave if not present. Unfortunately for this client, there has been a steady decline with these generations in terms of how they perceive the deal breakers. It's now at a critical point because they make up over one-third of their population and will grow rapidly in the next few years as more employees retire.

Additionally, the directors were experiencing a much higher turnover rate with these younger-generation employees.

We attempted to help the directors see that their future depended on being able to retain the employees they were judging and dismissing. We shifted the conversation by presenting data on what we know about these generations—especially Gen Zers—to counteract the largely untrue stories they had created in their minds. As long as the directors held on to their stories and judgments as true, they could stay comfortable and avoid needing to change. After all, it's much easier to sit back and blame others than to accept the necessity of learning new ways of doing things. We also invited them to consider their own kids, as many of the directors are parents to Gen Zers. Suddenly, they set aside some of their judgments and frustrations as they saw the humanity and realities of the growing struggles that workplaces will need to care for if they want to have a robust, engaged, and thriving workforce.

Gen Z: The Original "Native Digital" Generation

When millennials entered the workforce, a lot of debate started around generational differences. But given that millennials now represent over one-third of our workforce, and Gen Zers will soon make up another quarter of our workforce, we need to shift the conversation. As we think about generational differences, one of the best ways I've seen to describe things comes from Christopher Lochhead and Eddie Yoon, who describe adopting a framework that puts us into one of two categories: "native analog" or "native digital."[23] Each has a very different relationship with technology and human interaction.

I'm a Gen Xer and fall into the native analog camp. I grew up using a rotary dial telephone with a long-ass cord you had to wind into another room if you wanted any privacy. If I wanted to see my friends, I had to call to see if they were home or ride my bike to their house. We made stupid mistakes that rarely had photographic evidence because we didn't walk around carrying cameras (although those Aqua Net big-hair bangs still have photographic evidence that won't go away). We passed paper notes in class and took typing classes to learn how to use a keyboard. I remember when computers came onto the scene and the thrills of hearing the dial-up internet connect and figuring out email. I was well into my thirties before smartphones and social media came on the scene.

Most millennials are also native analogs, even though they never knew a world before computers, the internet, or cell phones. The majority were in high school or beyond by the time they had a smartphone or entered the world of social media. So they had many years of interacting with people and building relationships in person, not over a screen. Regardless of generation, for native analogs, technology is largely an addition or even a distraction in their lives. However, native digitals grew up with a very different experience as it relates to technology; many formed relationships largely through a screen. Consequently, they can sometimes view real-life situations as an interference or distraction from their digital lives and quickly become uncomfortable when navigating the awkwardness of human interaction.

My son, Peyton, is a native digital who grew up having access to an iPad very early. Who hasn't done this as a parent these days? You want a nice conversation over dinner at a restaurant, so you give your child a device to keep them occupied. While we still don't allow him to have a social media account, he has a very different experience of life than I did at his age. We'll be driving in the car, and I'll say something like, "Look at that amazing sunset," and he barely looks up long enough to snap a photo and then is immediately texting with his friends. Or a couple of years ago, we went to Hawaii for spring break. Initially, he remarked how beautiful it was, but two days into the trip, he was bored and just wanted to play video games with his friends.

Besides digital preferences, there's a critical impact that's happening with the mental health of native digitals, largely due to having access to smartphones in their key formative years. Jonathan Haidt, author of *The Anxious Generation*, refers to this as "phone-based childhood" and argues that the rapid adoption of smartphones and social media, combined with a decline in unsupervised outdoor play, has led to significant mental health issues in this population.[24] In fact, one study found that while Gen Z may be the most tech-savvy generation to date, they are more physically and emotionally unhealthy and lacking in emotional intelligence due to favoring their phone over live and present social interactions.[25] In other words, they tend to be awkward when it comes to human interactions on a normal day and even more so when things are challenging.

So it's not surprising that the work experience for these native digitals is less than ideal. A UKG Global Workforce Study found that the Gen Z experience at work is suffering greatly compared to the employee population as a whole.[26]

- Sixty-one percent aren't satisfied with their overall employee experience.
- Seventy-two percent say their mental health has worsened due to poor interactions with people at work.
- Seventy-one percent say they may quit due to negative interactions with managers, coworkers, or customers.
- Eighty-three percent of frontline Gen Z employees report experiencing burnout.

These are the native digitals who are currently in the workforce. But have you stopped to think about those who will be coming into the workforce in the next few years and beyond? The COVID-19 pandemic did a number on the mental health of our youth. In late 2021, the American Academy of Pediatrics, the Children's Hospital Association, and the American Academy of Child and Adolescent Psychiatry issued a joint urgent warning declaring the mental health crisis among children so dire that it had become a national emergency.[27]

Ben turned ten during the heart of COVID-19. Like so many kids during that time, it was confusing and unsettling that he suddenly couldn't be around his best buds at school. His new social circle by default became families in his neighborhood, but they were not kids he normally hung out with. As they tried to cope with all the VUCA-ness of the world, Ben's parents saw a rapid decline in his mental health over many months. By the summer of 2021, Ben's outbursts escalated to the point that he started saying he shouldn't be alive and was a horrible person. His parents knew they needed to get him into therapy ASAP. The struggle to find a therapist who was accepting new patients, let alone kids, was a whole other issue. Luckily, they found a therapist for him who was seeing patients over Zoom.

Ben's mom shared her heartbreak as she was filling out the therapy paperwork online. She asked Ben to fill out a couple of the forms and was standing behind him as he came to the question: "Do you ever think about killing yourself?" Her heart sank as he checked yes. The next question simply asked, "How often?" He checked the box next to "3–4 times per week." It was all she could do to hold it together until Ben left her home office. Then she crumbled on the floor and sobbed. Her precious son was already running his own faulty program that told him he wasn't enough—to the point he thought he shouldn't be on this earth. She was absolutely shattered.

Thankfully, Ben's parents had the resources to get him the help he needed, and he is now thriving. And in a few short years, he will enter the workforce along with so many other kids who are struggling with their own mental health and emotional well-being. It got me wondering, *What about all the kids who didn't have the resources or support system to get the help they needed?* What we're seeing is that native digitals struggle even more in the face of adaptive challenges and actively seek to avoid the awkwardness that the real world demands of us. Consequently, they are increasingly finding themselves deeply trapped in the Stuckness Zone.

Not only do we need to support this growing group of native digital employees in developing the human skills needed to thrive in a disruptive workplace and world, but we need to equip other generations in showing up differently to create a psychologically safe and inclusive workplace. Organizations will struggle greatly if they continue to enable leaders from other generations to stand in judgment rather than learn how to lead these individuals effectively. Native digitals also bring many wonderful qualities that help them excel in a fast-paced world. They embrace innovation, can adapt quickly, learn new technologies easily, and think creatively when it comes to solving problems. But they are also looking for mentoring and guidance. Native digitals don't know what it's like to be a native analog, and native analogs don't know what it's like to be a native digital. We must seek to understand and support each other—period. Because, regardless of generation, we are at a critical tipping point where we need to level up our human-centric leadership skills and care for the impact that declining emotional well-being is having on our workplaces.

The Collision of Our Declining Emotional Well-Being and the Workplace

It's also important to recognize that Gen Zers and native digitals are not the only ones who are struggling, and it's impacting business outcomes. SHRM published a report on the state of employee mental health in 2024, and the outlook was pretty bleak:[28]

- Forty-four percent of employees reported feeling burned out from their work.
- Workers who were burned out were nearly three times more likely to be actively searching for another job.
- Thirty percent reported often feeling stressed.
- Twenty-two percent reported often feeling anxious.
- Only 40 percent reported feeling fulfilled.
- Workers who felt a strong sense of belonging were 2.5 times less likely to feel burned out, yet only half of employees reported feeling a sense of belonging.

And it goes beyond feeling stressed and anxious. Gallup's 2024 *State of the Global Workplace* report found that one in five employees feels lonely at work.[29] It has become so concerning that the US surgeon general published an advisory report on our loneliness epidemic and how critical social connection is to transforming our well-being.[30] When the government creates a strategic priority to enhance social connection, you know things are concerning. Add on top of this that microstressors (minor daily annoyances that pile up) act like the proverbial straw that breaks the camel's back, pushing us over the edge and impeding our ability to cope with the challenges surrounding us. It's no wonder we are seeing an increase in incivility. Leadership guru John

Maxwell put it well when he wrote, "[T]he propensity to fight and disrespect other people has spread and bled into nearly every aspect of life. It is becoming increasingly difficult for us to work with one another."[31]

It makes sense when you think about it. As a species, we are hardwired for connection, and it is a core human need to feel like we matter. If a significant number of people are feeling anxious and stressed yet are trying to cope while also feeling alone, ignored, or invisible, and you add on the inherent challenges we face with change, no wonder the VUCA-ness of our world so frequently brings out the worst in us. It's hard to play well in the sandbox with others when we're barely hanging on by a thread. So what do we do?

A 2024 *Harvard Business Review* article suggests that we need to actively and deliberately put loneliness on the agenda and equip leaders to more effectively navigate this space. The authors are quick to remind us that loneliness is not solved by in-person work, more team-based work, or blaming people (usually younger employees) for simply being "needy." It takes a more comprehensive approach; this includes reexamining workflows and practices to allow more space for authentic human connections, removing tolerance for behaviors that work against people feeling connected and valued, and upskilling leaders to be courageous human leaders.[32]

Before you tune out and let the narrative of "It's not my job" creep in as you think about how to address the stress and loneliness epidemic, consider this critical fact: Sixty-nine percent of employees believe that their manager has the most significant impact on their mental health, equal to the influence of a spouse or partner. This is higher than their doctor (51 percent) or even their therapist (41 percent).[33] We can no longer brush off messy human emotions and pass people off to their employee assistance program or HR. We have to get uncomfortable to move through the Stuckness Zone to learn what it takes to lead in this environment.

Additionally, having a clear sense of purpose has been found to have a protective effect on our experience of stress and burnout.[34] So having a clear organizational purpose, operationalizing core values, and supporting individual employees in clarifying their purpose and values (and how they align with the organization's) can be beneficial in bucking these trends. In fact, McKinsey & Company reports from their global work with CEOs that "[g]oing forward, the differentiating factor will be human leadership that gives people a sense of purpose and inspires them, and that cares about who they are and what they're thinking and feeling."[35] Don't worry; I'll be diving into this more in chapters 13 and 14. For now, the point is to see that our current and future worlds demand something different from us as leaders. We no longer have any choice except to lean into the work to upgrade our faulty programs, move through the Stuckness Zone, and pave a path for a different—more effective—future-ready way of leading ourselves and others. The rest of the book will do just that.

KEY POINTS

- The future of work in the age of AI is VUCA on steroids and is fundamentally changing how leaders work and interact with their teams. In fact, it has amplified the need for strengthening human-centric leadership skills.
- The generational collision between native analogs and native digitals in the workplace further activates our self-protective instincts, landing us in the Stuckness Zone.
- It is a core human need to feel that we matter. Yet an increasing percentage of people feel ignored, devalued, or invisible at work. On top of that, we have an epidemic of stress, anxiety, burnout, and loneliness across generations, but it especially impacts our native digital colleagues and shapes their faulty programming.
- Organizations will struggle if they continue to enable leaders in other generations to stand in judgment rather than change their methods so they can lead native digitals more effectively and so that everyone experiences a sense of mattering.
- Being future-ready requires that we level up our human-centric leadership skills of authenticity, empathy, and adaptability to foster greater connection, collaboration, and a sense of mattering.

PART 2

THE FAULTY PROGRAMS THAT KEEP US IN THE STUCKNESS ZONE

CHAPTER 4

Our Faulty Programming

Your beliefs become your thoughts, your thoughts become your words, your words become your actions, your actions become your habits, your habits become your values, your values become your destiny.

—attributed to Mahatma Gandhi

So here we are.

We have a perfect storm with a VUCA-extreme world on a collision course with AI and exponential rates of change—all of which on their own bump us up against our biological hard wiring and self-protective instincts. Now, put them together with a growing population of native digitals and a broad-spread mental health and loneliness epidemic, and we have a potential recipe for disaster. That's certainly one way to look at it. But I prefer to look at it as a recipe for a great opportunity to change the course and pave the path for a journey in which we are future-ready and all can thrive despite the VUCA conditions that are thrown at us.

Remember that we all have an opportunity to show up as leaders in our lives. In fact, the most impactful leaders I know do not have it all figured out. And they don't wait for feedback to realize that something might be off. Courageous, future-ready leaders build in regular moments to pause, reflect, and adjust by asking themselves questions like:

- Where am I growing?
- Where am I stuck?
- What impact am I having?

Because the truth is that *you can't change what you're not aware of.* That's why I got so excited when we identified seven core patterns of thinking and self-limiting narratives—our faulty programs—quietly working against us. We also identified three additional programs that we refer to as "cousins" of the seven core programs. Being able to identify and name our faulty programs and how they guide our behaviors has been a game changer in normalizing our messy, shared human experience and paving a clear path forward to move us through the Stuckness Zone.

The good news is that our faulty programs are not our destiny. Once we become aware of them, we can move past our faulty programming via the three-step upgrade process:

1. *Name it.* When your faulty programs try to take over, call them by name. This helps your brain separate you and your identity from the programming that is hijacking you.
2. *Own it.* Reflect on the origin of your faulty programs that lead you to believe the lies they tell you. Take ownership of the head trash they create by using the phrase, "The story I'm telling myself is . . ." This creates space to fact-check limiting beliefs instead of treating them as truths. It is also important to own how you behave when these faulty programs are running the show and the impact you're having on those around you.
3. *Challenge it.* The final step of the upgrade process is about challenging the validity of your faulty programs. First, start replacing the head trash with something that is more empowering and better serves you and others. Second, visualize what life would be like in terms of how you would think, feel, and behave differently if your faulty programs were no longer in the driver's seat. Finally, start running mini-experiments to collect counterevidence that disproves them.

Whether we want to admit it or not, if we don't identify and then do the work to upgrade our faulty programming, we'll keep repeating the same unproductive patterns, no matter how much effort we give. The upgrade process is something we'll have to revisit from time to time. However, each subsequent upgrade takes less time than the original. It's also important to recognize that most people are running multiple faulty programs simultaneously. Each chapter in this section unpacks the faulty programs in detail along with specific ways to upgrade them using the name it, own it, challenge it process. For now, the following summary will give you some highlights for each one.

Our Brain's Seven Faulty Programs	
Faulty Program	**Key Descriptors**
The Counterfeit	Fears vulnerability. Hides authentic self because they do not feel worthy or enough. Feels a need to be something other than who they are. May compare themselves to others and may overcompensate for the ways they feel less than worthy.
The Overachiever	Fears not being enough. Perceived value comes from achievements, being responsible, or how productive they are. Feels like they must prove themselves, so they work harder, take on more than they can handle, and then worry about letting people down.
The Perfectionist	Fears failure at a high level. Views messing up as something that has disastrous and often unrecoverable consequences. They may sometimes think messing up is okay for others but not for themselves; they tend to have unrealistic standards.
The People-Pleaser	Fears rejection. Has a deep need for belonging, being liked, and being loved that they perceive is conditional; believes rocking the boat means being outcast and alone. They tend to go out of their way to avoid difficult situations so as not to upset others; they also might agree to things they really don't want or have the capacity to do to appease others.
The Control Freak	Fears uncertainty. Has a deep need for certainty and being right, so they can't let go of control. They perceive that being in control and ensuring things are done "the right way" can somehow prevent bad things from happening. They can also use control as a path to perfectionism to avoid judgment and failure.
The Mime	Fears disharmony. Self-silences due to feeling that their voices or needs don't matter. They are focused on keeping the peace and maintaining harmony, so they tend to avoid speaking up and having difficult conversations in which harmony might be disrupted or may jump in to stabilize situations where they perceive harmony is at risk.
The Martyr	Fears dependency. They are hyperindependent and self-reliant, shouldering burdens they don't perceive others can handle. They either don't perceive they can rely on others or don't want to be a burden, so they do everything themselves and deprioritize their own needs. Consequently, they tend to struggle with boundaries and frequently become resentful.

As we identified these qualities, I started laughing because I have been hijacked by at least four of these. Heck, I quite possibly have been hijacked by all of them at some point. And when these faulty programs were running the show, I convinced myself it was just me and that there was something wrong with me. It's affirming to know I wasn't alone in my struggles. In fact, every client we work with breathes a sigh of relief and mentions how glad they are not to be the only one. They feel seen and validated in their messy humanness. Hopefully this is affirming for you as well and starts to explain why things perhaps feel harder at times than they need to be.

It is also worth noting that three additional programs emerged from the data that have their own unique characteristics. We refer to these as cousin programs because they are not as prevalent and do not stand alone. Rather, they consistently show up in tandem with one or more of the core faulty programs. I dive into these in more detail in chapter 12. As we unpack all the faulty programs, I'll also share what we've learned about the adaptive change goals that coincide with each program and how we work against ourselves. For now, it's important to have a broad picture of our leadership landscape as it relates to the most common areas where we inadvertently get in our own way. When any combination of faulty programs is in control, at some level, we are trying to outrun our feelings of inadequacy and insecurity. In doing so, we get in the way of becoming a future-ready, courageous leader. In 2017, I attended a Blanchard Leadership Summit where Brené Brown said that it is normal to care what other people think, but when we are defined by it, we lose the capacity to lead. As we unpack each of these, it will become clearer how the head trash of our faulty programs impedes our ability to lead ourselves and others.

How We Work Against Ourselves

Through our analysis of more than five years of leader coaching data (shown in the following table), we uncovered the faulty programs and saw patterns emerge in terms of the adaptive change goals leaders have, challenges they face, and areas they want to improve but can't seem to fully achieve on their own and find themselves in the Stuckness Zone. These insights are important as we look at how we future-proof leadership because motivation isn't enough when we have upgrade work to do. We identified four common categories of adaptive change goals and then specific goals within each category.

Goal Category	Percentage of Leaders with Goal in this Category	Adaptive Change Goal Specifics	Percentage of Leaders with this Adaptive Change Goal
Communication	74%	Feedback	29%
		Speaking Up	23%
		Fostering Accountability	22%
Mindset	49%	Emotional Regulation	24%
		Listening Fully	16%
		Empathy	9%
People Leadership	35%	Delegating	15%
		Relationship-Building	12%
		Developing Others	9%
Decision-Making	35%	Setting Boundaries	22%
		Time Management	13%

Communication-Related Goals

The majority of leaders from our study (74 percent) find themselves in adaptive change territory as it relates to communicating more effectively. We found three key areas where leaders want to improve the effectiveness of their communication:

- *Feedback:* This includes wanting to get better at having growth-feedback conversations and to handle difficult conversations and conflict in a more timely manner.

- *Speaking up:* When it comes to speaking up and letting their voices be heard more in various settings, most of the leaders specifically report wanting to speak up with greater confidence and assertiveness.
- *Fostering accountability:* Leaders with accountability-related goals describe wanting to get better at setting clear goals and expectations with their teams and fostering alignment with those goals and expectations.

Think about it. How often do you hear people complain about the lack of meaningful feedback or accountability? Or how often do you see people holding back and silencing themselves? But what is our typical approach? We send them to a communication class or give them tip sheets on how to have greater accountability with goals and expectations. That likely only helps a bit, if at all. That's because we're defaulting to the "easy button" by providing *information* (that is, providing a technical fix) when what they need is *transformation* (an adaptive change).

As you'll see more clearly in the upcoming chapters, when we have a faulty program that tells us that, on some level, it's not safe to speak up (especially with the Mime, People-Pleaser, and Counterfeit faulty programs) or there's a need to have certainty and precision (especially with the Control Freak and Perfectionist faulty programs), we'll remain in the Stuckness Zone until those programs are upgraded. Bryan from chapter 2 is a great example of this. He wanted to get better at communicating and fostering accountability, yet his Overachiever, Perfectionist, and Martyr programs were working against him, telling him that he couldn't rely on others, he couldn't risk failing, and he needed to fix things and prove himself through productivity. So despite his best intentions, he struggled when it came to applying tools and skills to foster accountability and have effective growth-feedback conversations.

Another way to think about this is that if you or any of your organization's leaders are struggling with or wanting to level up communication skills, there's a high probability you are running one or more programs underlined by self-silence, people-pleasing, vulnerability avoidance, or the need to control things or demand perfection. We can either address what is holding us back head-on or stay on the merry-go-round of struggle. I don't know about you, but those darn merry-go-rounds always made me dizzy—to the point of puking on more than one occasion. So, as we unpack the faulty programs that work against us when it comes to communication-related goals, I'll share examples of how leaders have gotten off the dizzying ride via the upgrade process and become more masterful communicators.

Mindset-Related Goals

Nearly half of the leaders in our study (49 percent) find themselves in adaptive change territory as it relates to how they manage their mindsets. We found three key areas where leaders want to improve related to their mindset:

- *Emotional regulation:* This includes wanting to be better at managing reactivity due to being emotionally hijacked. Specifically, leaders report wanting to be better at pausing, staying curious and open, and responding in a more neutral manner. Others report wanting to exhibit more patience and understanding with others.
- *Listening fully:* Although listening could be a subset of communication, the leaders with goals related to listening specifically describe wanting to be more fully present with others (versus being distracted) and hold space for connection and for people to feel valued and heard—even if they don't agree with them.
- *Empathy:* This includes wanting to be more accepting and better at giving ourselves and others more grace, showing more compassion, and being able to hold space to learn from mistakes.

Many of these skills fall into the realm of emotional intelligence and the human-centric leadership skills mentioned in chapter 3. Yet, as you'll see in the upcoming chapters, if we're running faulty programs—particularly the Control Freak, Overachiever, Perfectionist, or Counterfeit—this is easier said than done because we're likely struggling with judging ourselves and others harshly and avoiding emotional exposure rather than leading with empathy and leaning into the messiness that comes with dealing with human emotions.

In this case, encouraging people to pause before they react or teaching them listening skills isn't going to get us very far when every instinct they have tells them they need to ensure things happen in a particular way or bad things will happen. However, once the upgrade process is complete, those tools and tactics will be much more effective because they'll be in a better place to use them. I'll share examples of how leaders have moved past these self-protective instincts to upgrade their mindsets and be a more emotionally intelligent, growth-focused, mindset-oriented leader.

People-Leadership Goals

Although everyone in our dataset has a formal people-leadership role, over one third (35 percent) find themselves in adaptive change territory as it relates to how they lead others. We found three key areas in which leaders want to improve the people aspect of their leadership:

- *Delegating:* This includes both letting go of tasks we don't need to own and being better at asking for and accepting help from others.
- *Relationship-building:* This includes tending more to the people side of leadership versus tasks and getting things done. Leaders describe this as wanting to take time to connect with others on a personal level, recognize people, and foster greater collaboration.
- *Developing others:* Leaders seeking to improve in this area describe wanting to develop more trust in their team and to support their team's autonomy, learning, and growth. They also want to get better at listening to their team's ideas and soliciting feedback.

Many of these practices might be considered "Management 101," or the basics of what formal leaders are expected to do. It might seem like a no-brainer that we need to connect and build relationships with those on our teams. For some people, completing information-based training on the mechanics of delegating and developing others is helpful. Yet other people (especially those running the Mime, Martyr, Perfectionist, Counterfeit, or Control Freak faulty programs) struggle more than they need to. This is even true for people who have been in formal leadership roles for decades. Think about that! It's not for lack of trying for most people. Rather, the wiring of the subconscious is working against them. Again, I will share stories and examples of how leaders have leveled up their people-leadership skills by upgrading their faulty programs.

Decision-Making Goals

Leaders need to regularly make important decisions. But over one-third (35 percent) in our analysis find themselves in adaptive change territory as it relates to how they make decisions. We found two key areas related to making decisions where leaders want to improve:

- *Setting boundaries:* This includes setting and honoring healthier boundaries between work and home, such as having more downtime, being present with their families when at home, being more diligent in tending to their own well-being and self-care, and having greater work–life harmony.
- *Time management:* Leaders wanting to better manage their time describe things like being better at prioritization, scheduling, and honoring time for key work; being better at follow-through; and being deliberate about working *on* the business more than *in* the business.

This is one area where the overwhelming urge is to take a technical approach by providing information to people rather than acknowledging and addressing the adaptive transformation that is needed. For example, it's easy to see time management goals and jump to providing productivity classes and tips. Or for people who struggle with boundaries, we might provide inspiration and encouragement to help them see why boundaries aren't selfish and are critical to our well-being and effectiveness. Those certainly can be helpful. But if we have a faulty program telling us our needs don't matter or that we need to take on more to prove ourselves and have things be perfect (for example, the Martyr, Overachiever, or Perfectionist), we won't be able to effectively leverage those tools until we reframe and upgrade our mindsets. So if you're struggling with this, hopefully you can breathe a sigh of relief knowing why it's harder for you than for others. I will also be providing examples from other leaders in your shoes to show how you can start your own upgrade process.

As we unpack each of the faulty programs in detail, it will become clearer how each of these present challenges in navigating the change and disruption of a VUCA world and can keep us in the Stuckness Zone. It will become more apparent why we work against ourselves in specific areas even when we're motivated to improve and change. If we want to change behavior, we must identify the faulty programming running the show and do the necessary inner work to upgrade it. If we only focus on behaviors, we are unlikely to have long-term success.

Each time I've presented this data to audiences, I've asked for a show of hands if any of these faulty programs resonate and if they struggle with these same goals. In every instance, everyone raises their hands. So there's no judgment here. If you or your organization's leaders are struggling in any of these areas, it is hopefully becoming clearer as to why. Welcome to being human! Unless we address the areas where most leaders find themselves stuck and support the upgrade process in ourselves and others, we will remain in the Stuckness Zone with its unnecessary struggle.

I want to emphasize that if, at any point, you find that your inner critic and head trash start doing a number on you, or if you're wondering why someone else can take mantras and inspirational tips and be well on their growth and improvement journey but you're on the struggle bus, let me say this loud and clear:

There is absolutely nothing wrong with you!

You are human and simply experiencing the messiness that comes when our biological self-protective wiring is doing its job. Period.

With that, our first step is to recognize which faulty programs we are running and accept this normal part of our humanness. Standing in self-judgment doesn't help. It can only make our upgrade journey more challenging. As Dr. Robert Holden so wisely said, "No amount of self-improvement can make up for any lack of self-acceptance."[36]

So take a deep breath and start the journey. Scan the QR code below to access your Faulty Program Discovery and gain greater insights into which ones may be hijacking you. While it's feasible to be running more than three faulty programs, the discovery will identify your top three. And although you can certainly jump to the chapters that pertain to those top three, I encourage you to read each chapter for two reasons: (1) One or more of the remaining faulty programs may also resonate with you and provide insights into where you may be getting in your own way, and (2) you'll gain greater insights into others who may be running any combination of faulty programs.

CHAPTER 5

The Counterfeit

You have got to stop apologizing for being who you are because someone may not like it. You were not created to water yourself down to fit the molds of others' expectations. Nor were you born into this world to follow everyone else without making your own waves. The powerful thing about you is that no one else is like you or could ever be you. So stand out in that. Be everything that you are, and don't you dare apologize for it.

—Kayil York, *Brave Soul*

	The Counterfeit
Fears	**Behaviors**
Vulnerability	Hides authentic self. Overcompensates. Compares self to others.

The Counterfeit is the most common faulty program keeping us trapped in the Stuckness Zone, showing up in 36 percent of the leaders in our study. If this is one of the faulty programs that is hijacking you, know that you are not alone and are instead in good company with many others.

The Counterfeit program stems from a fundamental fear of being vulnerable, which we experience when we're faced with uncertainty, risk, and emotional exposure. Some leaders describe this as a fear of being perceived as weak or being taken advantage of. Consequently, they feel that they must always show strength, keep their emotions in check, and appear like they always have it together. Others describe this as a fear of letting down their guard and showing their true, imperfect selves. As a result, they withhold parts of themselves in order to fit in. Or they may put on masks and overcompensate, hoping that people won't see their vulnerabilities.

The Counterfeit acts as a silent saboteur, showing up in thoughts like:

- *I can't let my guard down.*
- *I don't want to look weak.*
- *I'm not enough and have to prove myself, my worth, or my value.*
- *My authentic self doesn't belong, so I need to pretend or be something other than who I am.*
- *I'm not as good, talented, experienced, or valued as that person.*

When this programming is present, we tend to hide parts (or all) of our authentic selves because we do not feel worthy or enough. This can lead to feeling a need to be something other than who we are, resulting in unhealthy comparisons to others and overcompensating for the various ways we feel less than worthy. The irony is that we cannot show up as courageous, future-ready leaders in our lives without leaning into vulnerability. But once we understand how this program is typically formed, we can start to upgrade it and help our brains start to realize that we're no longer children who need protection and it's time for our sage adult selves to take the wheel.

Name It and Own It: How the Counterfeit Program Is Formed

Like all our faulty programs, the Counterfeit emerged during those early years as we tried to make sense of our experiences. At some point, our brains created a narrative that there is something wrong with us, leading us to feel like we must hide parts of ourselves or prove our worthiness. This could be from something simple or traumatic that happened in our family, neighborhood, or school, either directly to us or around us. As we made sense of our experiences, our brains drew conclusions or created rules about how the world works and what it takes to be accepted. Sometimes the conclusion we create is one that shows up in the form of "I'll never do *X* again," leading us to hide from vulnerability and authenticity. Other times, we may conclude that we need to prove ourselves and overcompensate for our perceived lack of worthiness, leading us not to show up authentically.

Michael is a highly renowned and skilled surgeon. He has a great track record with his surgical outcomes and patient satisfaction. At the same time, Michael kept taking on more and more work and was reaching burnout. Even his colleagues expressed concern for him. He recognized his own sense of burnout yet couldn't quite seem to do anything differently. As his stress and anxiety grew, he became increasingly reactive; he would either blow up at people or just withdraw completely.

When we started working with Michael to help him uncover his faulty programming, his current behaviors started to become clearer. Michael had several instances growing up that, at the time, seemed minor but profoundly shaped his internal scripts with the idea that there was something wrong with him. He was homeschooled through high school. Around the age of five, he realized that all of his friends could read, but he had not yet learned how to read. Michael was sad and embarrassed. The story he told himself was "I'm dumb and not as smart as my friends," which quickly turned into "I need to figure out how to read fast." Michael developed a self-imposed rule that he could never be seen as weak and needed to prove that he was worthy and as smart as others.

But it doesn't stop there. Around the age of eight, Michael was caught stealing change from a jar at home. Feeling ashamed, he told himself, "I'm a bad person and am not trustworthy." From that moment on, he vowed to never again let people down. That's quite a burden to carry (not to mention unrealistic)! Yet Michael's faulty program formation was far from complete. When he was twelve, a kid in his class called him ugly in front of others, and the kids laughed. Again embarrassed, Michael told himself, "I'm ugly," and then beat himself up, wondering why he hadn't stood up for himself. Consequently, he developed another self-imposed rule that he needed to prove himself in other areas of his life and show this kid he was wrong.

All of these instances started to script Michael's Counterfeit programming full of the need to compare himself to others, thoughts of needing to prove himself, and the idea that he must always prevail. Michael also had the Perfectionist faulty program, which regularly showed up at the same time. This led him to try to have it all together and be perfect. Anytime he was in the operating room with someone he perceived as having more clout or credibility, his faulty programs were triggered, and his narrative of needing to prove himself would kick into high gear. If the operation didn't go as quickly or smoothly as he imagined it should, he'd get frustrated, beat himself up, and start yelling and swearing, thus creating an uncomfortable environment for those around him. Then he wouldn't take the time to debrief residents and fellows afterward so they could benefit from the learning experience. Michael would withdraw so he didn't need to show his weakness to others. And he would push himself harder the next time he was in surgery to overcompensate for any previous perceived less-than-perfect operation.

This Counterfeit–Perfectionist cycle only perpetuated his burnout. Every tip and trick he tried to be kinder and gentler to himself failed miserably. It was only when he did the work to upgrade his faulty programming that Michael was able to show up calmer, more present, and more confident.

I could share hundreds of stories like Michael's. While each has its unique circumstances, the outcome is the same. A series of events—many of which are seemingly mundane—leads to our brains telling us that vulnerability is a threat we need to avoid at all costs by either hiding parts of ourselves or overcompensating in ways to try to prove we're worthy and enough. In either case, it keeps us from showing up as future-ready, courageous leaders and gets in our way of making progress on goals that matter to us.

Now that you've named it, the time has come to own it; get better acquainted with your inner Counterfeit by identifying and understanding how it shows up for you in terms of your thoughts and behaviors and how it was formed as you navigated the early years of your life. Once you own it by understanding where your Counterfeit tendencies came from and how they show up in the present, it becomes easier to challenge them and embrace the upgrade work so you can move from being reactive and hijacked by that faulty program to acting with clarity, intention, and confidence.

Own It: The Counterfeit Expression and Origin Exercise	
Recognize how you express the Counterfeit in terms of what it sounds like and how you behave.	
What inner head trash does the Counterfeit have you say to yourself?	
How do you behave when the Counterfeit is hijacking you?	
Next, identify the Counterfeit's origin. (This is a key part of helping you to see your brain is usually reacting from past experiences and flawed programming rather than actually responding to the present situation.)	
Identify three to five experiences from the first ten to fifteen years of your life that may have led you to conclude that you aren't enough, you can't show vulnerability, or there's something wrong with your authentic self.	

How the Counterfeit Works Against Us

Once we own how the Counterfeit shows up for us, it is easier to see how it subconsciously works against us and keeps us from making progress on goals, even when we're highly motivated. That being said, the Counterfeit is one of the trickier faulty programs; because of the desire to avoid vulnerability, it can make any adaptive change work feel harder than it needs to be. Additionally, it is usually compounded by at least one other faulty program that only exacerbates the sense that we have to be something other than ourselves.

From our analysis, we identified the top four adaptive change goals experienced by leaders running the Counterfeit program. As you can see, the top three are in the category of more effectively communicating; eighty-six percent of people running this faulty program are trying to get better at communication but are on the struggle bus to some degree as they navigate the waters of adaptive change. So if any of these are also challenging for you, realize that you're normal and human. Hopefully, this gives you some relief as to why you may be struggling in these areas.

1. *Growth feedback:* Thirty percent of the leaders who are running the Counterfeit program are quietly working against themselves as they try to get better at having growth-feedback conversations. It makes sense because, by definition, effectively leaning into challenging conversations inherently requires vulnerability, but the Counterfeit has us wanting to avoid vulnerability at all costs. What happens instead is that we may overcompensate and are overly harsh and demanding (especially if we're also running the Overachiever and/or the Perfectionist program). Sometimes we short-circuit any potential discomfort by fixing things ourselves (like Bryan from chapter 2). Or we may postpone or avoid these conversations so we don't have to feel the cringe that vulnerability brings (especially if we're also running the Mime and/or the People-Pleaser program).

2. *Fostering accountability:* Among leaders who are running the Counterfeit program, 28 percent are inadvertently working against themselves when it comes to fostering accountability on their teams; they aren't setting clear goals and expectations and ensuring alignment with them. For some leaders, the Counterfeit leads them to not want to stick their neck out too far, therefore being vulnerable and exposed, by explicitly stating goals and objectives. They somehow feel safer operating in ambiguity.

For other leaders, this program leads them to avoid growth-feedback conversations and struggle with the vulnerability of having conversations related to accountability. This is especially true when they are also running either the People-Pleaser, Mime, or Fraud programs. (The Fraud is a cousin program that we'll dive into a little later.) Susan from chapter 1 struggled greatly with fostering accountability with her team in the adoption of organizational changes due largely to her combination of the Counterfeit, Overachiever, and Mime faulty programs.

3. *Speaking up:* The same percentage of leaders who struggle with fostering accountability also struggle with speaking up assertively and with confidence. It makes sense because, if we are running a faulty program that tells us we're not worthy or enough and are trying to avoid uncertainty, risk, and emotional exposure, of course we're going to be challenged with owning our voices and speaking up confidently—especially if we're also running the Mime and/or People-Pleaser programs. No amount of encouragement from others will help until these programs are upgraded and the thought of being exposed and owning our voices no longer feels like a threat.

4. *Emotional regulation:* Almost one-quarter (24 percent) of leaders running the Counterfeit are trying to get better at, but struggle with, emotional regulation. It's not surprising because staying open and curious, responding in a neutral manner, or being more patient and understanding all put us face-to-face with the uncertainty, risk, and emotional exposure that comes with vulnerability. To avoid or short-circuit vulnerability, leaders tend to withdraw, take on things themselves and become resentful (especially if they're also running the Martyr), or lash out and overstep their bounds (which is exacerbated if they're also running the Control Freak, Overachiever, and/or Perfectionist programs). Michael, from earlier in this chapter, is a great example of this. He wanted to stay neutral and curious,

> especially when things were challenging in the operating room, but his "not enough" narrative from the Counterfeit, combined with feeling like he needed to be perfect and perform, consistently circumvented his best intentions to regulate his emotions.

Again, let me be clear. If you are running the Counterfeit and are struggling with the adaptive change nature of having growth-feedback conversations, fostering accountability, speaking up with confidence, or regulating your emotions to stay calm and curious, you are in good company. I hope this provides some relief for you as to why these skills might have felt harder for you than you wish or harder than it seems like they may be for others.

When I think back to my goals related to getting better at speaking up to have growth-feedback and accountability conversations, I can see how the Counterfeit combined with the Overachiever, People-Pleaser, and Martyr created a perfect storm getting in my way of communicating courageously and effectively. I've also seen leaders running the Control Freak and Perfectionist programs alongside the Counterfeit be extremely challenged in the gray areas of growing and elevating others. It's messy. Period. The key to getting better at any of these goals is not to try harder. The key is to name it (recognizing and coming to terms with which faulty programs are paired with the Counterfeit), own it, and then start the rest of the upgrade process by challenging it.

Challenge It: How to Start the Upgrade Process

Regardless of which program or combination of programs we are running, how we upgrade our faulty programming is similar. However, each faulty program has nuances that need to be considered in its upgrade. Following are the steps I have found work the best for starting to challenge and upgrade the Counterfeit program.

Start Upgrading the Counterfeit	
Name it when it shows up. When you notice the Counterfeit head trash creeping in, pause, name it, and then remind yourself that you're an adult.	Example: • "I'm not listening to your crap today, Counterfeit! I'm not ten years old anymore."
Replace the head trash. Once you name the Counterfeit, practice replacing its head trash with something that is more empowering. The act of intentionally stating alternative truths is an important part of the process. (*Note:* You don't have to necessarily believe it yet; that will come with time.)	Examples: • "I am enough." • "I know my worth and value." • "Most people prefer realness and authenticity." • "Vulnerability is strength." • "I'm not going to compare my behind-the-scenes with someone else's highlight reel."
Create your blueprint. Spend time visualizing what your life would be like if the Counterfeit program was no longer in the control of your life. Use that image to provide hope and energy as you embark on the next phase of the upgrade process.	Consider: • How would you be thinking differently? (For example, what new thoughts would have replaced your head trash?) • How would you feel differently? • How would you behave differently?
Intentionally challenge its validity. Start challenging the validity of the Counterfeit by running mini-experiments. The intent of these experiments is to collect data that pokes holes in the accuracy of the head trash that is holding you back. One of my favorite ways to start increasing your sense of worthiness is starting a self-gratitude practice and then moving toward stepping more into vulnerability.	At the end of each day, reflect on the following: • What went well for me today? • What qualities about myself am I grateful for? • What squiggles, detours, or setbacks am I appreciative of that brought me valuable learning opportunities? • What did I learn about myself? • As you start to embrace who you are authentically, the next step is to practice leaning into vulnerability more and bringing more of your authentic self forward.

I have so many stories about clients who have leaned into the work necessary to upgrade their faulty programming that give me chills. Honestly, it was hard to pick which ones to include in this book. When I think about the Counterfeit program, one of my all-time favorites has to be my dear friend Rachel Druckenmiller. Yes, I'm actually using her real name with permission. Back when I was completing my yearlong ITC certification, I needed a portfolio client for whom I would submit documentation as they went through the full ITC coaching arc. I had known Rachel since 2007, when she reached out to me as her career was just getting started. We grew both a mentoring relationship and a friendship.

Fast-forward to February 2017. Rachel hit burnout at the young age of thirty-two. In late summer, while she was recovering, she still felt stuck. I invited her to be my portfolio client, and she graciously accepted. Rachel was deeply running the Counterfeit, Overachiever, and People-Pleaser faulty programs. In her case, the more her Overachiever and People-Pleaser programs kicked in, the more they exacerbated her Counterfeit program.

When we first started the upgrade process, Rachel set a communication goal related to speaking up with greater confidence. Specifically, she wanted to take more intentional steps to put herself out there, grow her career, and follow in her parents' footsteps as a solo entrepreneur. However, she had an underlying narrative fueled by her faulty programming that was getting in her way. Her limiting assumption was "If I trust in myself and put myself out there, people won't accept me. I won't be 'enough' by just being me. I won't be loved."

Think about that for a moment. Rachel was desperately wanting something bigger for herself, but she was holding herself back (Counterfeit tendencies) and hid behind being productive and accomplishing things (Overachiever tendencies). Once she named her faulty programs, she had to own them by identifying how they were expressed in terms of her head trash and behaviors. At the core was her head trash of not being accepted or enough and needing to prove herself. Consequently, Rachel wasn't writing as much. Nor was she applying to speak at various events, even though she wanted to do both. She also found herself deep in a scarcity mindset, where she would compare herself regularly to others and get "grabby" and competitive with those who were in a similar space as she was. As a result, she wasn't seeking new networking relationships, even though they could help her. Rachel would also regularly second-guess herself and work extra hard to prove herself and justify whatever fee she was charging (she was usually undercharging for her services).

Next, we reflected on the origin of her faulty programming. She often felt rejected and didn't fit in with others at school. This formed Rachel's narrative of not being enough and that there was something wrong with her. She got good grades and received lots of public attention and praise from teachers. This led to some other classmates becoming envious. They would roll their eyes and talk behind her back. All these experiences told Rachel that she needed to hold back and not be "too big" or successful if she wanted people to like her. So her Counterfeit programming took over, and for years, she muted parts of herself out of fear of what would happen if she was authentically herself. Rachel then poured herself into Overachiever tendencies to try to prove her worth and value.

Can you see how she was working against herself and why she hit burnout at such a young age? And while Rachel had a great network of people who believed in and supported her, it didn't matter. No amount of encouragement from others or self-directed pep talks could override her faulty programs enough to make a lasting difference. Rachel leaned into the difficult but transformational upgrade process by challenging her faulty programs. Once we identified what was holding her back, we created a blueprint for her ideal future state that outlined how she'd be thinking, feeling, and behaving differently if she were successful in her goal and if her faulty programs no longer hijacked her.

The final step of the upgrade process was to start poking holes in the stories and assumptions she was holding as true, which were holding her back. We started with a simple and safe experiment in which she asked people who knew her well what they valued about her. Their responses contradicted the Overachiever part of Rachel that told her she needed to achieve and accomplish things to be valued. They spoke about the light, presence, and energy she brought to a room and to others.

Then we started finding opportunities where she could collaborate rather than compete with others and show up authentically while putting in a normal amount of effort versus going overboard to justify herself. Slowly but surely, the old self-limiting head trash and behaviors started to shift, and she began to get out of her own way and take steps toward making her goal a reality.

Rachel's journey since doing the work to upgrade her faulty programming is remarkable, and she is thriving! In 2019, Rachel left her corporate job. Betting on herself, she started her own business focused on living an unmuted life to become a full-time speaker. She started writing more and created a monthly LinkedIn Live show. She started wearing bold, bright colors and letting herself be seen as she authentically is. Another thing that is important to know about Rachel is that she has always loved to sing, but due to her fear of rejection and not being enough, she held that part of herself back. But she slowly started unmuting herself and incorporated singing into her keynotes and her LinkedIn Live sessions.

Then, in 2024, Rachel released her first original song, "Somebody." I cried as I listened to it. Not only is it a beautiful song, but I also know the hard work she did to get to a place of releasing music into the world. She put her upgrade journey into the song, and I heard the anti-Counterfeit and anti-Overachiever words that her nine- and ten-year-old selves needed to hear, as do so many others. So let some of these lyrics sink in for you when your Counterfeit program tries to hijack you.

> Take a breath
> And just be
> You're not on the clock
> And you don't have to impress me
> There is nothing to achieve
> To be somebody
> Let go of all the expectations
> That keep piling up
> The need to be good, to hold it together
> It's all become too much
> Release the need to prove you're worthy
> What if you believed
> You are somebody already?
> You are somebody
> You are somebody
> You matter and you are enough

Rachel has since released more music, has presented a TEDx talk, is about to publish her first book, and more. She's on a mission to help others live unmuted lives and embrace their authentic selves. This is what is possible when we stop either pretending our Counterfeit program doesn't exist or believing its lies and instead work to upgrade our faulty programs. Your goals and journey may be very different from Rachel's, but just think of where you could be a few months from now if you decide to stop letting the Counterfeit be in the driver's seat. You have that power! Every person I have had the privilege of supporting and witnessing who has upgraded and retired the Counterfeit is inspiring. When we stop fighting ourselves and embrace who we are, life is so much better! After all, as they say, you might as well be you, because everyone else is taken.

For more resources related to the Counterfeit, including downloadable exercises to start the upgrade process, scan this QR code.

CHAPTER 6

The Overachiever

Being "crazy busy" is not a badge of honor;
it's a badge of armor and self-protection.

—Dr. Rosie Ward

The Overachiever	
Fears	**Behaviors**
Not being enough	Overworks. Takes on too much. Proves self through accomplishments.

In today's go-go-go culture, the drive to do more and achieve more can feel like the ultimate badge of honor. But what happens when that constant push for success becomes a hidden barrier? Enter the Overachiever; it is the second-most common faulty program keeping us trapped in the Stuckness Zone, showing up in 35 percent of the leaders whose data we analyzed. One of the challenges with this particular faulty program is that achievements and productivity are typically rewarded in workplaces and elsewhere in our lives, so it can seem like a good thing. But the Overachiever is sneaky because it leads to believing that doing more is our only path to success, often at the expense of balance, well-being, and real growth.

This program is rooted in a fear of not being enough and a distorted view of our value and worthiness. When the Overachiever is in control, we feel our worthiness is conditional and attached to our accomplishments and how productive we are—or how much we get done—versus who we are. It can show up in thoughts like:

- *I have to work hard (or harder) to not let people down.*
- *I have to be productive; I don't want people to ever think I'm lazy or not working hard enough.*
- *Getting results is what ultimately matters.*
- *I'm expected to take on more than I can handle or have the bandwidth for.*
- *My value comes from my accomplishments; if I'm not achieving, what value do I have?*

As a result, when the Overachiever is front and center, we tend to take on more than we can handle out of the need to prove our worth. Then we worry about letting people down and end up experiencing greater stress. It frequently shows up in tandem with the Counterfeit as well as with the Perfectionist, People-Pleaser, and Control Freak. Another thing that is fascinating and unique to this program is that it is a consistent travel companion to each of the three cousin programs (the Dropout, the Fraud, and the Protector). It is not uncommon for the fears that show up in the cousin programs—of sounding stupid or incompetent, being an impostor, or holding ourselves responsible for others' experiences and outcomes—to manifest themselves in Overachiever tendencies. It's a way we cope and try to outrun the yuck factor in these related programs. The Overachiever is one of the faulty programs that can easily lead to illness or injury; our bodies have an incredible way of trying to find equilibrium when we're too stubborn to see the signs. It happened to me as well as Rachel Druckenmiller and so many others. This is a stubborn one that still tries to hijack me from time to time.

One of the things I consistently hear from people running this program is how they like being productive and checking things off their to-do lists, and they don't want to be in a position where they no longer care about getting things done. So I want to be clear: The goal of upgrading this particular program is not to overcorrect you into being an apathetic, slothlike worker. When productivity is in your hard wiring, that won't happen. The goal of upgrading this faulty program is to find a happy medium where you can be productive in a sustainable way and recognize that your worthiness and value aren't conditional on how much you get done. When you start to shift toward knowing your worth and value—versus trying to constantly prove your value—you will find greater fulfillment and peace. But first, you must own it by understanding how it is formed and the extent to which it hijacks you in the present day.

Name It and Own It: How the Overachiever Program Is Formed

As with other faulty programs, the Overachiever is formed in the early years of our lives. It usually originates from an overemphasis on achievements, working hard, and being productive. It sometimes stems from a household where results and working hard were expected and we wouldn't dare go against those expectations. Other times, this program is formed from observing others and concluding that achievements and being productive are ultimately what matter and what are valued. Depending on other faulty programs that may be at play, the Overachiever also shows up as a coping mechanism, a way to prove our worthiness because we feel less than in other areas. We believe if we work harder and gain accolades, we'll somehow feel we are enough.

Blake is a senior-level leader whose role continued to expand within his organization. Due to his reputation for getting things done and his vast industry knowledge, Blake was a natural choice for promotion to an executive position. However, each time his role and scope of responsibilities expanded, Blake found himself more stressed and on the verge of burnout. He wanted to be better at setting boundaries and prioritizing how he spent his time. This included saying no more often, spending more time on strategy-related work and things that optimized his strengths and geniuses, spending more time on the people side of things, being more consistent with tending to his well-being, and being fully present outside of work with the people who matter most to him.

Blake felt that if he could get better at those things, he'd have greater clarity, be less stressed, be more effective, and strengthen his relationships. But every time he had tried to refocus his efforts, it only lasted for a short time before he was back to his default settings. For Blake, this showed up as overcommitting, being too in the weeds of day-to-day work, taking on things he could have empowered his team members to do, being in back-to-back meetings all day with no availability for other people, multitasking while in meetings, not creating personal connections with people, and never fully unplugging. He found himself constantly thinking about work and tending to emails while at his kids' sporting events or with his family.

The Overachiever program started for Blake like it does for so many. Some event, or series of events, leads to the conclusion that we need to work hard to either be accepted or avoid consequences. And while having a strong work ethic can be helpful, it can be taken to an extreme where we work against ourselves. Blake grew up in a household where money was tight. On top of that, his dad had a drinking problem and was very hard on the kids. This combination created much stress and anxiety. Blake didn't like the feelings that came with being under financial pressure or the idea that he wasn't meeting expectations. So as a youth, he started to find ways to make money so he wouldn't be overly reliant on his parents. Blake paid his way through college and strove to succeed in athletics to appease his dad, who had been a successful athlete in the past. Not only did this form the narrative for Blake that he had to work hard and prove himself (classic for the Overachiever), but it also led to Control Freak program tendencies. This combination could have been lethal for Blake as it perpetuated the behaviors that were depleting him.

Once Blake named and owned his Overachiever tendency by understanding how he was working against himself and where his faulty program came from, he was better able to catch it and start to challenge it via the upgrade process. Slowly but surely, he began working with his administrative assistant to be more diligent about his calendar. He started testing the waters by unplugging from work one evening a week. That turned into entire weekends, and eventually, he was able to mostly unplug for a full family vacation. Blake began to extract himself from meetings and projects that were opportunities for other leaders on his team to handle. And he started intentionally creating time for relationship-building. Perhaps what stands out to me the most is that you could visibly see the lightness come back to his face and demeanor, the joy coming back to feeling connected to his family, and the enjoyment coming back to his work.

Upgrading the Overachiever is about arriving at a place of sustainable productivity, knowing our worth and value, and acting with greater intention rather than from a reactive place of self-protection while constantly trying to prove ourselves. Now it's your turn to get better acquainted with your inner Overachiever by owning how it shows up in terms of your thoughts and behaviors and how it was formed as you navigated through the early years of your life. Once you have this information, it becomes easier to name it and own it when it shows up. Then you're better positioned to do the work to challenge and upgrade it so you can move from being reactive and hijacked to acting with clarity, intention, and more confidence.

Own It: The Overachiever Expression and Origin Exercise	
Recognize how you express the Overachiever in terms of what it sounds like and how you behave.	
What inner head trash does the Overachiever have you say to yourself?	
How do you behave when the Overachiever is hijacking you?	

Next, identify the Overachiever's origin. (This is a key part of the process that helps you to see that your brain is usually reacting from past experiences and flawed programming rather than actually responding to the present situation.)	
Identify three to five experiences from the first ten to fifteen years of your life that may have led you to conclude that your value comes from your accomplishments and working hard or that being productive is ultimately what matters.	______________ ______________ ______________ ______________ ______________

How the Overachiever Works Against Us

Once we own how the Overachiever shows up for us, it is easier to see how it subconsciously works against us and keeps us from making progress on our goals, even when we're highly motivated. The biggest area where we see leaders get in their own way is when it comes to mindset-related goals; we found that 63 percent of leaders running this faulty program struggle in this area.

From our analysis, we identified the top four specific adaptive change goals of leaders running the Overachiever program. Because workplaces and society typically celebrate Overachiever tendencies, it's not surprising that people running this program find themselves struggling in three of the four adaptive change categories we identified. So if any of these are challenging for you, remember that you're a normal human. Hopefully, this provides some greater insight—and relief—as to why you may have difficulties in these areas.

1. *Emotional regulation:* The biggest area where Overachiever leaders find difficulty is regulating their emotions. In our analysis, 30 percent of the leaders who are running the Overachiever program find themselves challenged when it comes to being less reactive by pausing, staying curious, being more patient and understanding, and responding in a calm and neutral manner. Just taking the time to pause feels counterintuitive because it means slowing down,

which is a no-no for that productivity-focused wiring. The need to be productive often circumvents everything else when we're hijacked by the Overachiever. If we perceive a threat to things getting done or not being done in a particular way (especially if we're also running the Perfectionist and/or the Control Freak programs), it's easy to leap to reactivity and judgments as our frustration gets the best of us.

2. *Growth feedback:* In our analysis, we found 24 percent of the leaders who are running the Overachiever program are quietly working against themselves as they try to get better at having growth-feedback conversations. For many running the Overachiever program, this leads to jumping in to take care of things themselves (fueling their need for getting things done) rather than enabling and developing others (especially if they are also running the Perfectionist, Control Freak, or Martyr programs). Blake didn't specifically have this as a goal. However, because his calendar was so packed and he was in a deficit with investing in relationships, the quality and quantity of growth-feedback conversations were lacking and part of the equation that kept him from effectively elevating his team.

3. *Fostering accountability:* The same percentage of leaders running the Overachiever program struggle with fostering accountability as those who struggle with growth feedback. It makes sense as these two skills tend to go hand in hand. If you think about what we know about the Overachiever, you can see how this is challenging. If we are overly attached to filling our to-do lists and proving how hard we work, the thoughts of setting clear expectations and elevating someone else to do some of those tasks can be perceived as threats. Besides, why would we take the time to align goals for other people's success when we're too focused on getting our own stuff done and making sure we're proving our worth and value?

4. *Setting boundaries:* It is also not surprising that the Overachiever program makes it challenging to set and maintain healthy boundaries. In fact, the same percentage of leaders also struggle with this as they do with fostering accountability and having growth-feedback conversations. When we attach our worth to how much we get done, it becomes hard to say no to things or to not overpack our schedules with tasks and busyness. All the encouragement about the importance of self-care and well-being goes in one ear and out the other when the Overachiever is in charge. Logically, we know we're supposed to put on our own oxygen masks first, but every ounce of our being is drawn to getting more things done—even if we're depleted. Blake had boundary-related goals of being more deliberate on where he spent his time, including being more present with his family, actively caring for his well-being, and spending time more on strategy and the people side of leadership than on tasks and putting out daily fires. But until he upgraded his Overachiever program, he wasn't able to make meaningful or lasting progress.

As I mentioned previously, if you are running the Overachiever and struggling with the adaptive change nature of regulating your emotions to pause and stay calm and curious, having growth-feedback conversations, fostering accountability, or setting and honoring boundaries, you are in good company. I hope you feel a little less alone and can calm your head trash a bit as you perhaps have wondered why these skills felt harder for you than you wish or harder than they seem to be for others. Remember that the key to getting better at any of these goals is not to try harder. The key is recognizing and coming to terms with which faulty programs are paired with the Overachiever. Then you can start the upgrade process.

Challenge It: How to Start the Upgrade Process

The blueprint for starting the upgrade process for the Overachiever is similar to the steps for other faulty programs. However, the key to upgrading this particular program is helping your brain to see your value for *who you are* rather than what you do or how much you accomplish. Following are the steps that I have found work best for starting to challenge and upgrade the Overachiever program.

Start Upgrading the Overachiever	
Name it when it shows up. When you notice the Overachiever head trash creeping in, pause, name it, and then remind yourself that you're an adult.	Example: • "I'm not listening to your crap today, Overachiever! I'm not ten years old anymore and don't have to prove how productive I am."
Replace the head trash. Once you name the Overachiever, practice replacing its head trash with something that is more empowering. The act of intentionally stating alternative truths is an important part of the process. (*Note:* You don't have to necessarily believe it yet; that will come with time.)	Examples: • "I am more than my accomplishments." • "My worth and value are not dependent on how much I get done." • "I am enough as is. I don't have to prove my worthiness." • "People value me more for who I am, not what I do." • "Do I really have the capacity and interest to take on this task? What's the cost of taking this on?"
Create your blueprint. Spend time visualizing what your life would be like if the Overachiever program was no longer running your life. Use it to provide hope and energy as you embark on the next phase of the upgrade process.	Consider: • How would you think differently? (For example, what new thoughts would have replaced your head trash?) • How would you feel differently? • How would you behave differently?
Intentionally challenge its validity. Start challenging the validity of the Overachiever by running mini-experiments. The intent of these experiments is to collect data that pokes holes in the accuracy of the head trash that is holding you back. One of my favorite ways to help your brain start to detach your sense of worthiness from your accomplishments and how productive you are is by gathering objective feedback from others who know you well via short interviews.	Ask people who know you well the following questions: • What do you value about me? • What is it like for you to observe or be around me when I'm overly focused on getting things done or proving how productive I am? With the first question, it's a bit of a warm and fuzzy conversation. The intent is to note all the ways people value you or see you adding value that have nothing to do with your accomplishments. You're going into the second question prepared for a little sting. The point is to hopefully cause a moment of trepidation the next time your instinct to overload your calendar, multitask, or take over work kicks in so you can pause and consider the potential costs. What you will find is that you slowly start to reframe your value proposition and find that maybe you don't have to be working so hard to prove your worthiness.

Matthew's strong work ethic was instilled in him at a young age as part of family expectations. His grandfather, whom he deeply loved and admired, had a profound influence on him. Matthew spent a lot of time on his grandfather's farm learning the value of hard work and chores. His grandfather also had very high expectations for Matthew and would get on his case if he wasn't working hard enough. As often happens while growing up, there were several instances when Matthew goofed off or tested boundaries that landed him in trouble. This also helped to form his inner narrative of needing to work harder, be more responsible, and not let people down. All these experiences helped shape his Overachiever and Perfectionist tendencies as he got older.

Like many people with the Overachiever program, this work ethic served Matthew well in many ways. He worked hard in school and was a reliable employee once he entered the workforce. Consequently, Matthew was on a fast track for promotions and quickly moved into management positions. He was one of the younger people among his leadership peers within the company, so Matthew was in constant overdrive trying to prove himself and how hard he worked. He tried to never disappoint people. As usual, the Overachiever's behaviors were rewarded and celebrated by executive leaders, which further fueled his tendency to take on too much and impose ridiculous standards on those around him—even at home with his wife. In Matthew's mind, he was doing his job by providing for his family, and working hard was key to earning other people's respect and for him to respect himself.

As Matthew wanted to grow in his leadership skills, he realized that he needed to approach things differently. His improvement goal was related to emotional regulation and fostering accountability with his team. Specifically, he wanted to be better at creating space for others to do things in a way that worked for them and then giving them more grace, especially when he perceived they weren't working as hard as he thought they should or weren't doing things a certain way. But despite being highly motivated to be an effective leader and succeed in this goal, Matthew was quietly working against himself thanks to his faulty programs. He had unrealistically high expectations for his team and was upset when they fell short of meeting them. He constantly pushed people to do better—even if they didn't want it for themselves—and became nitpicky and overly critical. He was constantly on the go and working. As could be expected, this behavior spilled over into his home life, where Matthew would get on his wife's case for not taking the initiative to do things around the house. Of course, he rarely gave her a chance because he would jump to take care of things.

Once Matthew named his faulty program and owned it by understanding where it came from and how it was working against him, he was ready to challenge it by creating the blueprint and starting the upgrade process. Matthew began by interviewing people at work and at home about what they valued about him as well as what the costs were when he was overly focused on working hard and proving himself. This part was critical because Matthew had a difficult time seeing why working hard wasn't a good thing and felt he wouldn't respect himself if he didn't work hard. I assured him that the goal wasn't to squash his work ethic but to help him find a more balanced and sustainable place than what he currently had. Unsurprisingly, many people mentioned that they appreciated how hard he worked. However, what they valued him even more for was who he was as a person, how he showed up for them, and his caring nature. While they appreciated his work ethic, people expressed how it undermined their confidence and ability, frustrated them, and was deflating when he became demanding, wanted things done the way he would do them, or simply took over and did things himself.

This feedback hit Matthew hard. He had trouble reconciling seeing working hard as a good thing with the impact he was having on others. He deeply wanted to be respected but was, in some cases, having the opposite effect on his team members. Additionally, Matthew and his wife were trying to start a family, and he realized that if he didn't take this feedback to heart, he'd be perpetuating this system for his child. Slowly but surely, Matthew started letting his wife do chores her way. As he did, their relationship strengthened, and he felt more connected to her. He leveraged tools we gave him for fostering clarity and alignment with expectations and having growth-feedback conversations to elevate his team versus criticizing or "saving" them by doing the tasks himself. In doing so, his team started stepping up more, and Matthew began to see that perhaps his value as a leader was more about elevating others than showing how much he could get done.

About a year later, Matthew and his wife welcomed their first child. He expressed tremendous gratitude for going through the upgrade process as it allowed him to lean on others and take a paternity leave, which he never would have done when the Overachiever was in charge. Matthew's shift in focus with his team also helped the company. With people being more empowered to step up, their location grew in revenue and became one of the top-performing divisions, leading to Matthew's promotion to a larger leadership role.

Of course, this isn't a one-and-done story. With the larger role, Matthew's Overachiever tendencies were reactivated as he began feeling the need to prove himself again. Luckily, he had the tools necessary to perform some minor upgrade work and not become completely hijacked. This will be his ongoing journey as he is deeply wired for productivity.

As someone who is regularly tending to this faulty program myself, I can tell you that like Matthew, leaning on the tools from my initial upgrade are incredibly helpful for the ongoing tune-ups I need when my humanity gets the best of me. While I've mostly retired my other faulty programs (notice I say *mostly*), the Overachiever is my kryptonite because I'm wired for getting stuff done. At the same time, I've become keenly aware of the costs and have created systems around me to help keep the Overachiever at bay. For example, I live by my calendar and put everything in it. Being more deliberate to schedule personal time, prep, and follow-up time, working on the business time, and more has forced me to be more realistic about my bandwidth. And despite this, I can still sometimes schedule over the blocked time. So I have bright-pink sticky notes on my computer that say, "Do I really have the capacity?" and "What's the cost of taking this on?" Before I am tempted to overschedule my calendar, they help me pause and proceed with intentionality rather than reactivity. Yet I can still ignore them if I'm not cognizant to leverage them as my reminders and decision-making filters. So I've also started adopting the philosophy that if something isn't a *hell yes* for me, it's a *no* and means I either need to find a way to get it to a *hell yes* or decline.

The point is that we sometimes have to keep reconnecting to our tools and find new ones to keep our faulty programs at bay as the seasons of life change. Remember, this isn't a onetime thing; it's an ongoing journey. But once we do the initial work to upgrade the Overachiever and fundamentally reframe our value propositions, it becomes much easier to reset. At that point, it's more about reminders, slight modifications, and brief resets than needing to do a full makeover. And the resets happen without rumination, shame, or guilt. That's the beauty of doing the initial hard work. For my fellow Overachievers, I hope this is helpful.

For more resources related to the Overachiever, including downloadable exercises to start the upgrade process, scan this QR code.

CHAPTER 7

The Perfectionist

There is a huge difference between aspiring to be our best selves and claiming to be perfect. One is a journey of fulfillment. The other is a lie we tell ourselves and others.

—Simon Sinek, foreword, *Permission to Screw Up*

The Perfectionist	
Fears	**Behaviors**
Failure and judgment	Sets unrealistic goals. Hides mistakes. Self-critical.

How many times do you hear people boast or joke about their perfectionist tendencies? The reality is that our society tends to flippantly praise perfectionism, overlooking its pitfalls. In *The Gifts of Imperfection*, Brené Brown says this about perfection:

> Perfectionism is a belief system that if we are perfect we can somehow avoid or minimize painful feelings of shame, judgment and blame. It's a myth and an unattainable goal.[37]

Enter another sneaky faulty program that keeps us trapped in the Stuckness Zone—the Perfectionist. This program shows up in 30 percent of leaders studied in our analysis and is fundamentally different from having a healthy drive for excellence. Whereas a healthy drive for excellence is rooted in an intrinsic value for quality, perfectionism is externally focused on what other people think. It is all about avoiding judgment, blame, and our feelings of not being enough. Although the Perfectionist might initially seem like a strength, it erodes confidence, hinders decision-making, and prevents us from showing up authentically. This deeply ingrained mindset pushes us to chase unattainable standards, creating stress and burnout while stifling innovation and connection.

The Perfectionist is rooted in a deep fear of messing up or failing and consequently being judged or rejected. When the Perfectionist is in the driver's seat, we view the consequences of the failure as being disastrous and unrecoverable. Most leaders report a very binary, either/or relationship with failing. They perceive that they can't mess up or fail—or be less than perfect—and still be liked, respected, or effective. The Perfectionist can show up in thoughts like:

- *I can't mess up or let people down and still be liked or respected.*
- *Failure is not an option.*
- *It's okay for others to mess up or be imperfect, but not me.*
- *If I let my imperfections show, people will judge me negatively or reject me.*
- *Mistakes and failures are unrecoverable and not worth it.*

As a result, when this programming is present, we tend to have incredibly high standards with unrealistic expectations for ourselves that sometimes even bleed toward others. It frequently appears in tandem with the Counterfeit, Overachiever, Control Freak, People-Pleaser, and Martyr programs. Behaviorally, this program typically leads to us working extra hard to prove ourselves, overcompensate for all the ways we feel we may not belong or are inadequate, take on unnecessary things out of our need to have them turn out a certain way that we believe will be just right, or focus on trying to be who we think others want us to be. It can sometimes lead to holding ourselves back (Mime tendencies) because we do not want to speak up until we have an idea fully processed and perfect. In this case, the thought of putting a draft idea on the table is too risky.

What's ironic is that the Perfectionist program can inadvertently lead to a self-fulfilling prophecy where we miss deadlines or delay progress because of our constant need to have things be "just right" (a.k.a. perfect). I've seen this show up in everything from delays in physicians completing patient charts on time (due to the need to go above and beyond with the information provided), leaders taking excess time to respond to emails (due to needing to craft a perfect response), or people getting behind on projects (due to wanting their parts to exceed standards). And when others become upset because of the delays, it reinforces the head trash that tells us that our mistakes cause others to think less of us.

Quite simply, the Perfectionist is exhausting not just for us but for those around us. However, when you upgrade this faulty program and start to embrace your imperfections as part of being human and then build more of a growth mindset, you—and everyone around you—will breathe much easier. The journey starts with owning where the Perfectionist came from and what activates it. Once you know this, you can be aware of and intentionally reframe this unsustainable mindset.

Name It and Own It: How the Perfectionist Program Is Formed

Almost everyone has likely experienced situations in which they were scolded in one way or another for breaking the rules, doing something wrong, or messing up another way. But when and how normal occurrences start to go astray and form the Perfectionist depend on their frequency and severity. Most people I see with this faulty program had multiple instances of being scolded when they made mistakes that eventually formed a narrative of being a bad person or unworthy. They've come to believe that if they can avoid messing up in the future, they will be good or worthy.

This also shows up quite frequently with the Overachiever when people came from a household where good grades and excelling were expected. They either received praise only for perfect scores and being the best, or they were pushed to work harder when they were less than perfect. For me, this was a triple whammy. I equated scolding as me not being lovable or enough unless I was perfect, and it showed up hand in hand with the Counterfeit, Overachiever, and People-Pleaser.

Chad is now the CEO of a well-established, successful manufacturing organization. But it took time and deliberate work on himself to upgrade his IOS to get to this point. He has a long tenure with the company and worked his way to the top. Part of what contributed to Chad's success is his relentless drive for success and to win. This made him a successful salesperson and the eventual leader of one of the company's largest locations. He knew how to get things done and win, and he pushed those around him to succeed.

Chad was eventually promoted to a regional leadership position. That is when the cracks in his default wiring started to show. We learned via 360-degree feedback that, while people greatly respected him and his drive for results, Chad's hyperfocus on results contributed to a lack in broadening his relationships and hindered his ability to be a fully effective steward of the company's culture, purpose, and values.

Although he didn't know it at the time, Chad was running a powerful combination of the Perfectionist, Counterfeit, and Martyr faulty programs. His primary fear was failing, to the point that he had a powerful underlying assumption that winning is what ultimately matters and he had to do things to ensure a win. This consistently worked against his emotional regulation goal. Chad wanted to elevate his effectiveness by getting better at pausing, having more patience, and taking time to gather more info before reacting and making premature decisions. But because of his drive to win and avoid failing at all costs, he would get irritated with people he assumed didn't have his same sense of urgency and push them hard for results. Chad sometimes sent people harsh emails implying that they weren't pulling their weight. He would copy their leader and the leader above that level. And rather than being curious about people, he had a "Suck it up, buttercup" mentality and made quick judgments and assumptions about others. Not surprisingly, Chad also had a bad habit of making decisions without having all the facts.

Once he recognized and named his Perfectionist program, it was time to start owning it. As we started to unpack the origin of Chad's faulty programming, his challenges that were working against his adaptive change goal became clear. Chad had some significant instances growing up of being punished for making mistakes that fueled his narrative of avoiding mistakes and needing to be responsible. On top of that, his parents divorced. Not only were there challenges with a nasty custody battle, but they eventually moved to another state. He felt like an outcast in school. Now living with his dad and stepmom, Chad was on his own a lot. His stepmom didn't make his lunches like she did for her biological kids, and his dad traveled frequently for work. He felt alone and decided that he had to take care of himself (enter the Martyr) and not let his guard down (leading to the formation of the Counterfeit).

At this point, Chad's mom was in another state, and his stepmom mostly ignored him. Vulnerability was a no-no, especially for men. The only real connection Chad had with his dad was over athletics; it was the only thing they communicated about. Unfortunately, the only accolades Chad received from his dad—or anyone—were related to athletics. He desperately wanted to make his dad proud and pushed himself to excel and win. His Perfectionist program began to take shape as he learned that his value was attached to winning. This desire continued to fuel him as an adult and was the reason why he found himself standing in judgment and irritation whenever he perceived someone wasn't working hard enough or they failed in some way (for example, they lost a sale, had a safety incident, and so on). Additionally, Chad realized he was repeating patterns. Not only was he really hard on his son, Alex, about athletics, but he was only really connecting with Alex around athletics and nothing more.

These valuable insights into the origins of his faulty programs and how they showed up in the present day helped us to plan and begin his upgrade journey. We started to challenge his Perfectionist program with some simple interviews in which he asked people what they valued about him, what they experienced when he failed, and what the costs were when he was overly focused on winning. Chad started to realize that the things he considered failures others simply saw as part of learning and growing. And they didn't hold them against him. At the same time, he learned that the costs of his overly focusing on winning and avoiding failure were great, especially when it came to his son, Alex. Chad described the stinging and appreciation of Alex's feedback. Alex shared that he felt like Chad's support and love were conditional and tied to his sports performance. If he didn't win, he dreaded the car ride home, knowing that Chad would get on his case. Ouch! That wasn't the kind of relationship Chad wanted with his son. But he didn't know how else to relate to him.

In order to challenge and upgrade Chad's Perfectionist program, he had to work on it alongside the upgrade to his Counterfeit program as they were deeply intertwined. He couldn't lean into vulnerability enough to admit or accept mistakes. So we began reframing how he viewed vulnerability and equipped him with courage-building skills. This was a game changer for Chad. He started testing the vulnerability waters by sharing with his team what he was learning about himself and modeling vulnerability. He started asking more questions, practiced pausing more, used missteps as learning discussions rather than blame and judgment, and shifted to trusting and growing his team rather than doing things himself to ensure perfection. His actions strengthened the psychological safety within his entire division, and their results got even better. Perhaps even more profound was how Chad reframed his relationship with Alex and built a closeness that he never thought possible. He still hates to lose, but he now has a more sustainable relationship with failing and focuses more on a healthy striving for excellence.

Now it's your turn to get better acquainted with your inner Perfectionist by owning how it shows up for you in terms of your thoughts and behaviors and how it was formed as you navigated the early years of your life. Once you know where your Perfectionist tendencies came from and how they show up in the present, it becomes easier to name it, own it, and then do the work to challenge and upgrade it so you can move from hiding from your humanity to embracing it.

Own It: The Perfectionist Expression and Origin Exercise	
Recognize how you express the Perfectionist in terms of what it sounds like and how you behave.	
What inner head trash does the Perfectionist have you say to yourself?	
How do you behave when the Perfectionist is hijacking you?	
Next, identify the Perfectionist's origin. (This is a key part of the process to help you see that your brain is usually reacting from past experiences and flawed programming rather than actually responding to the present situation.)	
Identify three to five experiences from the first ten to fifteen years of your life that may have led you to conclude that your worthiness, safety, or belonging are dependent on you being perfect or not messing up or letting people down in any way.	

How the Perfectionist Works Against Us

Once we name and own how the Perfectionist shows up for us, it is easier to see how it subconsciously works against us, keeping us from making progress on goals even when we're highly motivated. In fact, we found that two-thirds of leaders running this faulty program are trying to improve some aspect of communication, with another 58 percent having mindset-related goals. Yet they find themselves in the challenging waters of adaptive change and struggling more than they'd like.

From our analysis, we identified the top four specific adaptive change goals leaders running the Perfectionist program desire. This program most frequently puts us on the dysfunctional merry-go-round in three of the four adaptive change categories we identified. So if any of these are also challenging for you, remember that you're a perfectly imperfect human, and hopefully, this provides some sense of calm and relief as to why you may be struggling in these areas.

1. *Emotional regulation:* The biggest area in which Perfectionist leaders find themselves challenged is regulating their emotions. Specifically, our analysis found that 29 percent of the leaders running the Perfectionist program find difficulties with being less reactive by pausing, staying curious, being patient and understanding, and responding in a calm and neutral manner. It makes sense. When every ounce of our being feels that things must be perfect and go a certain way, any variance is a threat and risks facing judgment. Trying to stay calm can be extremely difficult.

   Chad is a great example of how the Perfectionist works against this goal. In particular, the aspect of emotional regulation that is most challenging with this faulty program is being patient and understanding because, by definition, we're usually in a place of needing to be understanding when something is less than perfect. This is especially the case if we're also running the Overachiever and/or the Control Freak programs.

2. *Growth feedback:* One-quarter of leaders running the Perfectionist program are quietly working against themselves as they try to get better at having growth-feedback conversations. For many people running this faulty program, it can mean jumping in to take care of things themselves to ensure they are done perfectly rather than enabling and developing others (especially if they are also running the Overachiever, Control Freak, or Martyr programs). It can also go the other way, in which we completely avoid these conversations (especially if we're also running the People-Pleaser) due to the messiness that accompanies growth-feedback conversations.

3. *Setting boundaries:* Many leaders (23 percent in our analysis) struggle to set and maintain healthy boundaries when they're running the Perfectionist. It makes sense because the head trash of this faulty program has us believe that anything less than perfect is too risky. Whether we take on things to try to ensure they turn out a certain way, spend excessive amounts of time on tasks, or are working hard to try to prove ourselves and avoid negative judgments, we're going to find ourselves challenged when it comes to boundaries. After all, it's hard to know what is and isn't yours to own when your primary focus is running from a fear of failure.

4. *Fostering accountability:* Although you may think that fostering accountability would be a no-brainer for leaders running the Perfectionist program, it's quite the opposite for 22 percent of them whose data we analyzed. While this faulty program leads to having unnecessarily high standards, leaders tend to struggle with equipping others to grow and develop so they can achieve excellence. Think about it for a moment. If you have an underlying fear that things won't be done perfectly, are you really going to take the time to foster clarity and alignment around goals and expectations with others? Probably not, because deep down, you don't trust that they will be successful and won't let you down. This is what happened in Chad's case. He didn't believe others had his sense of urgency or worked hard enough. Chad would shame them with emails to their boss or get upset with them rather than clarify goals and set them on a clear path for success. This created a vicious cycle when they couldn't measure up to his expectations, so he'd skip any alignment conversations and just push them harder.

If you are running the Perfectionist faulty program and struggling with the adaptive change nature of regulating your emotions to stay curious and be more patient and understanding, having growth-feedback conversations, setting and honoring boundaries, or fostering accountability, you are in good company. Hopefully you can have a greater understanding as to why these skills may feel harder for you than you'd like and can recognize the key differences between perfection and a healthy striving for excellence. When you can, you'll be in a good place to start the upgrade process.

Challenge It: How to Start the Upgrade Process

The blueprint for starting the upgrade process for the Perfectionist is anchored in reframing your relationship with failing. It is about recognizing failure as a part of being human, that your worth is not conditional on being superhuman, and that you choose to embrace your imperfections rather than hide or overcompensate for them. I have found the following steps work the best for starting to upgrade the Perfectionist program.

Start Upgrading the Perfectionist	
Name it when it shows up. When you notice the Perfectionist head trash creeping in, pause, name it, and then remind yourself that you're an adult.	Example: • "I'm not listening to your crap today, Perfectionist! Perfection is a myth."
Replace the head trash. Once you name the Perfectionist, practice replacing its head trash with something that is more empowering. The act of intentionally stating alternative truths is an important part of the process. (*Note:* You don't have to necessarily believe it yet; that will come in time.)	Examples: • "Messing up or failing at something doesn't mean I'm a failure." • "Failing is a normal part of the learning journey." • "My imperfections are part of what makes me unique." • "No mistake is unrecoverable." • "No one expects me to be perfect."
Create your blueprint. Spend time visualizing what your life would be like if the Perfectionist program was no longer in control of your life. Use it to provide hope and energy as you embark on the next phase of the upgrade process.	Consider: • How would you think differently? (For example, what new thoughts would have replaced your head trash?) • How would you feel differently? • How would you behave differently?

Intentionally challenge its validity. Start challenging the validity of the Perfectionist by running mini-experiments. The intent of these experiments is to collect data that pokes holes in the accuracy of the head trash that is holding you back. One of my favorite ways to start reframing your relationship with failing is gathering objective feedback from people who know you well about what they experience when you've messed up, failed, or let them down.	Ask people who know you well one or more of the following questions: • What do you experience when I've failed or messed up? • When *XYZ* happened and I messed things up, what is it that allowed our relationship to still be okay? • What is it like for you to be around me when I'm overly focused on things being perfect? With the first two questions, you're picking people you have a good relationship with but feel you've somehow let down. The third question is one where you're going into it prepared for a little sting. The point is to hopefully cause a moment of trepidation the next time your perfectionistic instincts kick in so you can pause and consider the potential costs. You will slowly start to reframe your relationship with failing and typically discover that others aren't holding failures at the same level as you are, and they aren't holding mistakes against you.

For most people, the Perfectionist seems to be one of the quicker faulty programs to upgrade. It takes putting in the reps to embrace mistakes and imperfections. This can be leaning on whatever alternative narratives and truths we find to be most helpful in replacing the head trash when we are less than perfect. Once we lessen our fear of failing and let go of unattainable Perfectionist goals, it becomes easier to lean into the messy work to upgrade our other faulty programs. Just like Chad experienced, the biggest thing I see is people lightening up as they start to embrace their imperfections rather than hide from them. It reminds me of Kintsugi, the art of Japanese pottery focused on finding beauty in imperfections. It's frequently referred to as the "art of precious scars" because instead of trying to hide the flaws of the broken pottery, artists put the pieces back together with gold, silver, or platinum and accentuate the cracks and flaws. There's something energizing and relieving when we can see the value and beauty in our flaws and scars. It reminds me of a line in a Kelly Clarkson song from the movie *UglyDolls*: "I'm broken and it's beautiful!"

Thankfully, the Perfectionist is one faulty program that I have been the most successful at upgrading and have for the most part retired through ongoing deliberate practices. Whenever I mess up on something,

I intentionally say aloud, "I'm embracing my humanity today" to remind myself not to let it hijack me. The other practice that has been a game changer for our entire team is our F-Up Friday share. Every Friday we have an end-of-week huddle where we reflect on the week and share our peaks and our valleys. We frame the valley as F-Up Friday, and everyone shares their biggest missteps, challenges, or obstacles—their F-Ups—and what they learned from them. As the leader, I always go first for this part and last for the peak of the week share. This weekly practice has normalized messing up for everyone. In fact, some of our best process improvements and ideas have come from these F-Up Friday shares. I've heard other people do the same but refer to it as Fail Forward Fridays. Pick whatever phrasing works for you; whatever you choose, having a deliberate practice to normalize imperfections can be hugely valuable.

So when your Perfectionist tries to resurface, remember that most people want realness and authenticity over polish and perfection any day of the week!

For more resources related to the Perfectionist, including downloadable exercises to start the upgrade process, scan this QR code.

CHAPTER 8

The People-Pleaser

Be who you are and say what you feel, because those who mind don't matter and those who matter don't mind.

—attributed to Dr. Seuss

The People-Pleaser	
Fears	**Behaviors**
Rejection	Avoids conflict. Overcommits. Puts others' needs first.

As human beings, we are hardwired for connection; we are a social species. But sometimes that need for connection and belonging goes astray and becomes a liability that impedes what we're trying to create and traps us in the Stuckness Zone. Say hello to the People-Pleaser and join more than one-quarter of other leaders in our analysis who are also running this faulty program. The dark truth about this program is that while many lightheartedly joke about having people-pleasing tendencies, it quietly brews deep resentment and leads to an eroding of well-being, confidence, and effectiveness.

The People-Pleaser is rooted in a deep need for belonging and the fear of being rejected on some level that includes a fear of letting people down, not being liked, or not being loved. When the People-Pleaser is running the show, we go out of our way to avoid these risks and ultimately operate under the fear of being an outcast and alone. It can show up in thoughts like:

- *I can't let people down and still be liked, respected, or loved.*
- *I can't upset people and have the relationship be recoverable.*
- *I'm an outsider on this team or in this group, and I don't belong.*
- *Any pushback or disagreement confirms that I don't belong.*
- *My value comes from keeping other people happy.*

The People-Pleaser can present itself as agreeing to things that we really don't want or have the capacity to do out of a desire to appease others, avoiding difficult situations and conversations to not upset others, or withholding our needs and opinions to not inadvertently go against a person or group.

When the People-Pleaser is in the driver's seat, we feel our acceptance, love, and sense of belonging are fragile and conditional. Consequently, we do anything to not rock the boat and risk being alone. We fear that if we disappoint or upset people, we will automatically be rejected, which will affirm our beliefs that we don't belong. So we can twist ourselves into pretzels trying to appease everyone else's needs before our own at the cost of our well-being, effectiveness, and confidence.

Imagine that the following diagram is a dinner plate. The inner circle is your core; this includes your purpose, values, what you care about, and your interests. The outer circle is the circumference and where the "OPs"—other people—live. That is, this area is comprised of other people's expectations (OPE), opinions (OPO), and attitudes (OPA).

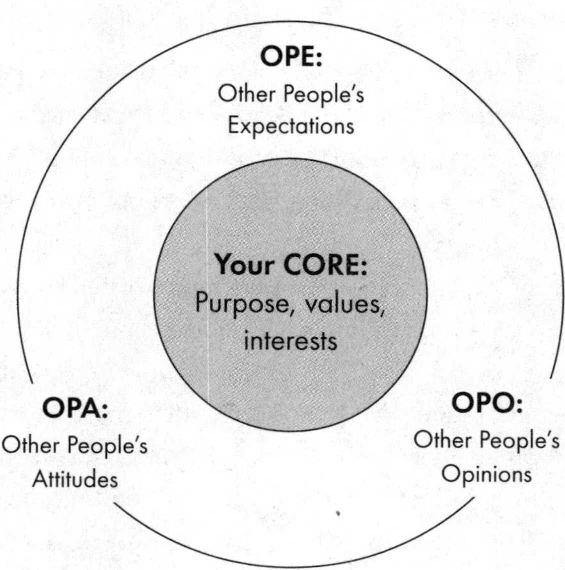

When the People-Pleaser program is in control, we live more on the circumference. As soon as we try to meet the expectations or opinions of one group, we find we're not meeting those of another. We can feel like a pinball bouncing from one OP to another, desperately seeking approval and acceptance. But instead, we frequently end up bruised, resentful, and tired. It would be like loading up a dinner plate and trying to balance it using only one or two fingers on one part of the circumference. Chances are the plate would quickly topple over, and you'd have quite the mess to clean up. And you'd still be hungry. However, if we put our fingers under the center of the plate, we could load it up with delicious food and still have a good chance of keeping it stable. Why? Because when we operate from our core and are clear about who we are, we are more stable and grounded. It is easier to say no to the OPs when they're not aligned with our core without feeling resentment and worry. The journey of upgrading the People-Pleaser includes naming and owning it to understand where it came from and what activates it so that you can move away from the OPs on the circumference and stand confidently in the core of who you are and act based on whose opinion actually matters: you.

Name It and Own It: How the People-Pleaser Program Is Formed

It is a basic human need to feel like we belong and matter. For people running the People-Pleaser, something in their early years threatened or violated that need, telling them that they didn't belong. The rejection left a deep wound that now prevents them from sticking their necks out in any way when they aren't certain of belonging.

Shelly had several seemingly common, minor instances growing up that formed her deep fear of people not liking her and her desire to avoid rejection at all costs. When she was five years old, her family moved, and she had to leave her favorite babysitter (with whom she spent more time than with her mother). This was Shelly's first experience of losing a relationship, and it's a hard thing to process when you're that young. Of course, she didn't understand why they had to move or why her parents were taking her away from someone she loved. In looking back, Shelly believes this experience started shaping her sense that relationships are temporary and at risk of being lost.

Fast-forward to middle school. Shelly didn't consider herself to be overly attractive, and she carried a little extra weight. As is so common with this age group, there was a person who could be a best friend one day and a frenemy the next. This girl told Shelly in front of their neighborhood group that she couldn't play flag football with them because the belt wasn't big enough for her. Even though Shelly didn't think that was true, she was humiliated and went home. But even more devastating for her was that no one stood up for her or went after her. This instance started to craft her head trash stories of not belonging, not being enough, and deeply fearing rejection. Over time, this narrative grew to the point of not initiating social activities with her friends as an adult because she was unable to handle people who said they were busy. She also had a bit of paranoia concerning her social circles as she assumed people were talking about her.

As president of a key division for her company, Shelly's People-Pleaser program led her on many occasions to overshare with people to try to get them to like her. But instead, it started to erode people's trust and confidence in her. Because of her sense of not being enough and fearing rejection,

Shelly leaned heavily on her other faulty programs, the Overachiever and the Control Freak. As we learned is common with these programs, Shelly channeled her hurt into wanting to prove herself by constantly taking on more and heavily controlling situations. Of course, that hard work contributed to her success and ultimately her promotion to president. But it was getting in her way of elevating and growing her team and having the level of professionalism and discretion needed in her role.

Shelly wanted to be a more effective communicator in many ways, including having better guardrails around what she shared and being more reciprocal with others in relationships by speaking up and initiating things. She also wanted to strengthen her ability to stay curious and present and be open to other ways of doing things. It is easy to see how Shelly's combination of faulty programs was quietly working against her. Because her head trash was pretty gnarly, her upgrade process started with some self-gratitude work and learning to talk to herself like she would talk to someone she loves. She also started an active practice of reminding herself that not everything is about her and that she's not the center of everyone's universe. We helped Shelly to identify her core bubble, the people who know her well and have her back. When her head trash tried to take over, she would remind herself who was in her bubble and started letting go of the OPs on the circumference. This helped her establish better boundaries of what information she did and didn't share with people, and it strengthened trust with others. She also started catching herself when her paranoid head trash started to take over; Shelly learned to redirect her energy elsewhere. As this part of her brain calmed, she started taking more initiative in her relationships, thus creating a space for her to do the additional upgrade work needed for her other faulty programs.

Now it's your turn to get better acquainted with your inner People-Pleaser by owning how it shows up for you in terms of your thoughts and behaviors and how it was formed as you navigated through the early years of your life. Once you know where your People-Pleaser tendencies came from and how they show up in the present day, it becomes easier to name it, own it, and then work to challenge and upgrade it so you can move from being stuck on the circumference and hijacked by what you presume other people think to being clear and confident and acting from your core.

Own It: The People-Pleaser Expression and Origin Exercise	
Recognize how you express the People-Pleaser in terms of what it sounds like and how you behave.	
What inner head trash does the People-Pleaser have you say to yourself?	
How do you behave when the People-Pleaser is hijacking you?	
Next, identify the People-Pleaser's origin. (This is a key part of the process to help you see your brain is usually reacting from past experiences and flawed programming rather than actually responding to the present situation.)	
Identify three to five experiences from the first ten to fifteen years of your life that may have led you to conclude that you don't belong, can't let people down, or need to avoid any possible rejection.	

How the People-Pleaser Works Against Us

Once we have a greater sense of how the People-Pleaser shows up for us, it is easier to see how it subconsciously works against us and keeps us from making progress on goals, even when we're highly motivated. In our analysis, an overwhelming 93 percent of leaders running the People-Pleaser are actively trying but struggling to get better at some aspect of communication.

This faulty program tends to fall into one of two camps of coping. The first way the People-Pleaser program copes is by holding back and being more passive to hopefully avoid the risk of rejection. This shows up in tandem with the Counterfeit, Perfectionist, or Mime programs. The second way this program copes is by overcompensating and trying to prove our way to acceptance, like Shelly did. This occurs when the Overachiever or Control Freak programs kick in to try to save us from feeling the pain of rejection by being hyperfocused on doing things. From our analysis, we identified the top four adaptive change goals of leaders running the People-Pleaser program.

1. *Growth feedback:* It's probably not surprising that the biggest area where People-Pleaser leaders find themselves challenged involves growth-feedback conversations. Our dataset showed that 38 percent of leaders would probably rather have a root canal than risk a conversation where they might upset someone. Yet they know it's important and want to get better at it. Think about it. If we're running a program that tells us anyone being upset with us automatically means that they don't like us or that the relationship won't be recoverable, of course we're going to avoid the potential discomfort that inherently accompanies those conversations. No amount of training, tool kits, or practice conversations will help until the upgrade is complete and we no longer believe that giving challenging feedback is always detrimental. Instead, we will avoid, postpone, or fumble through these conversations, inhibiting others' growth due to our discomfort with the process.

2. *Fostering accountability:* Because setting clear expectations and fostering accountability to those expectations inherently risks upsetting someone, it's easy to see why we found that 35 percent of leaders running the People-Pleaser program want to get better in this area but struggle to do so. For leaders who fall into the overcompensation camp and are also running the Overachiever or Control Freak programs, this can lead to jumping in and taking care of things themselves rather than elevating others. This is exactly what happened to Shelly, and her stress and anxiety were amplified as a result. Other leaders will fall into the passive and avoidant behaviors, saying

things like, "I trust and empower my team." They will assume that checking in on progress and firm goals will be insulting to team members, or that the team will perceive them as micromanagers.

3. *Emotional regulation:* At first glance of our data, I was surprised to see that 22 percent of leaders with the People-Pleaser program want to get better at pausing, being curious, responding in a more neutral manner, and being more patient and understanding. But as I thought about it a little more, it started to make sense. If we're deeply concerned about being accepted, we're likely on high alert for signs that we don't belong. That state makes it harder to regulate our emotions. This was certainly the case with Shelly. When this faulty program activates the head trash that tells us our belonging is fragile, we are likely to reject others before they can reject us.

4. *Speaking up:* For leaders who are afraid to upset the apple cart, so to speak, it's not surprising that our study found that 20 percent of leaders running the People-Pleaser program struggle with speaking up with confidence and conviction. But they want to get better at it. After all, it's hard to simply will yourself to speak more in meetings or let yourself be seen and heard when you're afraid that putting yourself out there will automatically mean rejection.

If you are running the People-Pleaser and struggling with the adaptive change nature of having growth-feedback conversations, fostering accountability, speaking up with more confidence, or regulating your emotions to stay curious, patient, and understanding, you're not alone. These things will feel harder for you than you'd like as long as this faulty program tells you it's too risky for your acceptance and belonging. But once you know and realize how much time and energy you're spending on the circumference, you can start to challenge and upgrade this faulty program and move to operating more from your core.

Challenge It: How to Start the Upgrade Process

The blueprint for starting the upgrade process for the People-Pleaser is anchored on getting clear about your core, knowing who you are authentically, and then learning to act on behalf of your core. As you do, you will learn to essentially put on a Teflon coating to not absorb all the never-ending, competing ideas from the OPs on the circumference. Instead, you will be clear about whose opinions actually matter, because we're not for everyone, and that's okay. I have found that the following steps work the best for upgrading the People-Pleaser program:

Upgrading the People-Pleaser	
Name it when it shows up. When you notice the People-Pleaser head trash creeping in, pause, name it, and then remind yourself that you're an adult.	Example: • "I'm not listening to your crap today, People-Pleaser! I'm not ten years old anymore and don't have to prove that I belong."
Replace the head trash. Once you name the People-Pleaser, practice replacing its head trash with something that is more empowering. The act of intentionally stating alternative truths is an important part of the process. (*Note:* You don't have to necessarily believe it yet; that will come with time.)	Examples: • "I don't need everyone to like me." • "I know who I am at my core and am clear on whose opinions matter." • "Upsetting or letting someone down doesn't mean the relationship is unrecoverable." • "I can recover from rejection." • "Someone pushing back on my idea or feedback does not mean they're rejecting me."
Create your blueprint. Spend time visualizing what your life would be like if the People-Pleaser program was no longer driving your life. Use it to provide hope and energy as you embark on the next phase of the upgrade process.	Consider: • How would you think differently? (For example, what new thoughts would have replaced your head trash?) • How would you feel differently? • How would you behave differently?

Intentionally challenge its validity. Start challenging the validity of the People-Pleaser by running mini-experiments. The intent of these experiments is to collect data that pokes holes in the accuracy of the head trash that is holding you back. One of my favorite ways to start reframing your fragile sense of acceptance and belonging is by gathering objective feedback from people who know you well on what they experience when you're in people-pleasing mode. Then do the work to clarify who you are at your core and incrementally start making decisions from there versus the circumference.	Ask people who know you well the following question: • What is it like for you to be around me when I'm in People-Pleasing mode and avoiding speaking up, overcommitting, and so on? Some might say they want you to speak up more and that they appreciate your input. But be prepared for a little sting as some will likely share concern, frustration, or annoyance. The point is to hopefully cause a moment of trepidation the next time your People-Pleasing instincts kick in so you can pause and consider the potential costs. Then do the work to get really clear about who you are at your core. Slowly but surely practice speaking up, setting boundaries, and acting on behalf of your core and notice how much calmer, more confident, and more grounded you start to feel.

Kristen, a leader in a large health system, was promoted to a key leadership role overseeing a critical program that was seen as a growth engine for the organization. However, she had a great deal of self-doubt and was experiencing incredible stress to the point of exhibiting early signs of burnout. Kristen's primary goal was to speak up with greater confidence, which included asking for help when she needed it, setting healthy boundaries, and speaking up when she wasn't okay or was feeling overwhelmed. She felt that getting better at these behaviors would allow her to step more confidently into her role as a leader and know her worth and value. But her People-Pleaser program was actively working against her.

Kristen's biggest fears were that people wouldn't like her, she wouldn't be included, it was impossible to be effective at both work and home, and she would ultimately upset and fail someone. These fears formed her head trash that told her being an effective leader required being perfect and having people like her. It also told her that she couldn't be in disagreement with people and still be liked. Kristen assumed that she couldn't challenge authority and be heard, respected, and valued because she believed her opinions didn't matter. She also assumed that if she wasn't included in something (a meeting, email, project, and so on), it meant that people didn't value her. Basically, everywhere Kristen turned, she was fearful of letting people down and being rejected. No wonder she was exhausted!

As we started to look at where her People-Pleaser program was formed, it became clear that Kristen's ten-year-old self was very much in the driver's seat. When she was ten years old, they moved to a new state, leaving behind the only friends she knew. Coming into a new school was hard because all the friend groups were already well established. Kristen was made fun of for being the new person and for wearing glasses. This started to form her head trash that she didn't belong and needed to work harder so people would like her.

Kristen recalled that for the next several years, her parents argued quite a bit. She concluded that disagreements are bad and meant that a relationship is strained or isn't going to work. One of those consistent arguments was her mom wanting some help around the house, but her dad refusing because he worked all day and was tired. This started to form Kristen's narrative about not speaking up to power because it would be shut down.

The other instance that stood out was her dad not showing up for her special events in high school because he was working. She internalized this to mean that she wasn't enough. If she were, her dad would be present like the other kids' parents.

Kristen coped with her feelings of not-enoughness, not belonging, and not wanting to upset people by overcompensating with the Overachiever program. She believed that how she gained approval and added value was by working hard and her accomplishments. So she would say yes to everything and end up overloaded with work. For Kristen, this resulted in taking phone calls or answering emails while she was with her kids and never unplugging, not even on vacation. When her leaders would ask her if she was okay, Kristen would say that she was fine even though she wasn't. If she offered an opinion and it wasn't initially accepted or there was discussion and debate, she would immediately back down rather than engage or stand up for herself.

Understanding the origin of her faulty programs and how they were working against her was key to taking ownership of them. Then it was time for the upgrade process by actively challenging them. Kristen started by naming it when her People-Pleaser program showed up and trying on some alternative narratives to replace her head trash, which kept her stuck. She did the work to get clear about who she is at her core by identifying her purpose and core values and using them as an anchor for guiding her behaviors and decisions. Then Kristen created her blueprint to have a clear picture of what her life could be like if her faulty programs were no longer in control and used that inspiration to provide some momentum to move into intentionally challenging its validity.

Kristen began interviewing people to find out what they experience when she's in a people-pleasing mode, which is often the case. The most impactful feedback she received was from her husband. He told her that she becomes stressed, anxious, unapproachable, and hard to be around. He said he would rather that she was present than always doing stuff. This hit Kristen hard as she realized the toll it was taking on her husband and kids. The people who meant the most to her were getting the crappy, leftover version of herself. But this feedback helped her start the gradual pausing process. Before she would take on more, she started pausing and reminding herself of the costs, thus creating a space for her to be more intentional about what she did and didn't say yes to.

We had Kristen complete some self-gratitude practices to become kinder and gentler to herself. As her head trash started to shift, she was able to start clarifying and strengthening her core. When she wasn't involved in things, she would practice pausing, leaning into curiosity, and asking herself, "Do I have the capacity to be involved in the first place?" Then she slowly started setting more boundaries with the people on the circumference. This included proactively looking for opportunities to grow others and realizing that other people taking on more responsibilities didn't diminish her value. As her confidence grew, Kristen started slowly speaking up more and well before she was frustrated, overwhelmed, or at her breaking point. As her faulty programs loosened their grip on her, there was a noticeable physical change in her as well. Her face lightened, she was calmer, and joy at work and at home came back into her life.

Most leaders who are hijacked by the People-Pleaser program experience excess stress due to the emotional rumination they constantly carry. It's challenging to regulate our emotions or effectively communicate when that's brewing underneath the surface. What we consistently find is that, similar to Kristen, a sense of calm, confidence, and lightness emerges as this faulty program gets kicked to the back seat. So when your People-Pleaser program takes over and you're doubting yourself, lean on your core and be more like Teflon for all the other people living on the circumference. Remember that we're not for everybody, and that's okay.

For more resources related to the People-Pleaser, including downloadable exercises to start the upgrade process, scan this QR code.

CHAPTER 9

The Control Freak

Incredible change happens in your life when you decide to take control of what you do have power over instead of craving control over what you don't.

—Steve Maraboli, *Life, the Truth, and Being Free*

The Control Freak	
Fears	**Behaviors**
Uncertainty	Takes over situations. Asserts their "rightness." Tries to have things go their way.

The U in VUCA stands for uncertainty and is part of one's reality. But what happens when people fear uncertainty at a heightened level? The Control Freak takes over, and they struggle navigating the disruption and complexity a VUCA world inherently brings. In fact, our study found that 23 percent of leaders find themselves trapped in the Stuckness Zone due to this faulty program. The Control Freak stems from a deep need for certainty and being right. It can show up in thoughts like:

- *It's my responsibility to make sure things happen the "right way" [the way they should].*
- *If I'm not in control, bad things will happen, or this will fail.*
- *I'm the only one who knows how to do this the right way.*
- *My way is the best, right, or most effective approach.*
- *I need to know or be able to predict what happens next.*

In general, most leaders with this faulty program describe a strong sense that being in control and ensuring things are done "the right way" can somehow prevent bad things from happening. As a result, they end up controlling everything from schedules to work products to conversations. But they also typically have a lot of frustration and stress as well. The journey of upgrading the Control Freak requires working to accept what we can and can't control so we can put our focus and energy on the people and things that matter. That journey starts with naming and owning where the Control Freak comes from and what activates it so that you can shift from shouldering burdens that aren't really yours to own to creating space for others to learn and grow.

Name It and Own It: How the Control Freak Program Is Formed

Most people running the Control Freak program experienced one or more events in the early years of their lives when something went astray or something required a great deal of structure and regimen. For some people, they may have had a health issue or a family member with a health issue that required great restrictions and regimen to manage. Consequently, control became a critical part of safety and survival. For others, this faulty program is formed as a result of something unpleasant happening in which they determined if they could control things, they'd never have to experience anything similar again. Having a controlling parent or family member can sometimes activate this program as our brains tell us that we're never going to be controlled again. Rather, we do the controlling instead.

Therese has a large leadership role in a prominent university. She desperately wanted to get better at setting and honoring boundaries and prioritizing her self-care, but she always seemed to struggle in this area. As we started to unpack her faulty programming, it became clear how and why she kept inadvertently working against herself. When Therese was six years old, her oldest brother hid under her bed to scare her. When he jumped out, she screamed. Therese's mother got mad and spanked her for making too much noise. When her brother confessed to what he did, her mom said that she probably deserved the spanking for something else she had done. Therese recalled wondering why she deserved to be punished for something that was out of her control. This began forming her inner narrative that not being in control can lead to punishment or bad things happening. Her Control Freak program further solidified a few years later.

At age eleven, Therese got sick. After four days of being miserable, she called her mom at work, crying. Therese's mom was irritated that she had to come home from work and take her to the doctor because she assumed it was just the flu. The next thing Therese remembers is waking up in the ICU from a hyperglycemic coma and learning she had type 1 diabetes. She didn't understand what that meant, but the doctors told her she would have to monitor her blood sugar and take insulin shots for the rest of her life. Therese's mom helped her for about three weeks but then told her that she needed to figure out how to manage this on her own. As a result, Therese concluded that she couldn't rely on other people and must be self-sufficient (Martyr faulty program tendencies) and in control or she could die. She realized that she was holding the need to be in control at a life-or-death level for everything in her life.

Therese experienced several other instances in which her mom dismissed her needs or accomplishments, activating her desire to work harder and prove to herself and her mom that she was "enough." Enter both the Overachiever and People-Pleaser programs, which made boundaries extra challenging. She perceived that if she were to tell people no, she wouldn't be the go-to person anymore. Instead, she would be irrelevant and rejected and would lose her identity. For Therese, controlling things and taking on projects to make sure they were done correctly were necessities. She rarely pushed back on requests, canceled vacations to take last-minute meetings, took calls from work on evenings and weekends, and sidelined her exercise time for meetings. Therese was also letting herself get pulled into things at work that weren't hers to own, thus further challenging her ability to set boundaries and actively practice self-care. She ended up stressed and resentful and couldn't see a way out of her self-made misery.

This is the irony of faulty programs as they quietly work against us. For Therese, you'd think that self-care would be a no-brainer as part of controlling her diabetes. But her need for control didn't stop at monitoring it and giving herself daily shots and instead seeped into every area of her life, leaving no time for any other form of self-care. Once she owned it and understood the vicious cycle, Therese was ready to challenge it and begin the upgrade process. For her, that meant slowly but surely extrapolating herself from projects and meetings she didn't need to own, elevating her team to take on more, and pushing back on requests that came during off-work hours or while she had scheduled time off. When things didn't completely fall apart, her Control Freak program let go a little more until eventually, she found freedom and peace from not trying to control everything or do everything herself, letting go of trying to prove herself to others, and getting clear about who she was at her core rather than being overly concerned about other people's opinions and expectations.

Now it's your turn to become better acquainted with your inner Control Freak by owning how it shows up for you in your thoughts and behaviors and how it was formed as you navigated through the early years of your life. Once you know where your Control Freak tendencies came from and how they show up in the present day, it becomes easier to name it, own it, and start challenging and upgrading it so you can move away from the stress and pressure that come with shouldering the burden of trying to control situations and people and instead move toward supporting and elevating others and creating a space for them to take ownership of their outcomes. By doing so, you'll be able to take greater ownership of your reactions and responses and the impact they have on others.

Own It: The Control Freak Expression and Origin Exercise	
Recognize how you express the Control Freak in terms of what it sounds like and how you behave.	
What inner head trash does the Control Freak have you say to yourself?	
How do you behave when the Control Freak is hijacking you?	
Next, identify the Control Freak's origin. (This is a key part of the process to help you see your brain is usually reacting from past experiences and flawed programming rather than actually responding to the present situation.)	
Identify three to five experiences from the first ten to fifteen years of your life that may have led you to conclude that you can or need to be in control of situations, ensure things happen the "right way," or somehow hold yourself responsible for preventing bad things from happening.	

How the Control Freak Works Against Us

Once we own how the Control Freak shows up for us, it is easier to see how it subconsciously works against us and keeps us from making progress on goals even when we're highly motivated. Leaders running this faulty program frequently get a bad rep as intentionally being difficult, picky, intolerant, judgmental, or micromanaging. But once we understand that it's usually our brains simply trying to protect us from the dreaded fear of uncertainty and things going astray, it's easier to see why they behave the way they do. From our analysis, we identified the top four adaptive change goals leaders have who are running the Control Freak program. It's also worth noting that, unlike any other faulty program, an overwhelming 72 percent of leaders running the Control Freak program have mindset-related improvement goals. It makes sense because an incredible amount of self-regulation is required when our brains have an overactive sense of needing to control people and situations around us.

1. *Emotional regulation:* It's probably not surprising that the biggest area where Control Freak leaders find themselves challenged is with their mindsets that allow them to pause, be curious, practice patience and understanding, and respond in a more neutral manner. In our study, 35 percent of leaders running this faulty program want to improve regulating their emotions but frequently get sucked into the reactionary trap. It makes sense when you think about it. If you're running a script that deeply feels it's your responsibility to ensure things happen a certain way or you need to control situations and people, then when things don't go the way you want, your instinct will likely be to judge rather than be curious and jump to take over or fix things rather than pause and seek to understand if there is a way to help others. No amount of emotional intelligence training and tips will help until the upgrade is complete and you no longer believe that you are responsible for all outcomes around you. Therese is a great example of this. She experienced challenges with staying curious, pausing, and extending grace to others—and herself—when her Control Freak program took over.

2. *Listening fully:* Another mindset area Control Freak leaders want to improve but struggle with is listening fully; twenty-four percent of leaders running this faulty program actively want to get better at being fully present rather than distracted when with others, holding space for connection and for people to feel valued and heard—even if they don't agree with them—and listening to understand versus listening to reply. Think about it. If you assume you have the right answers or the right way of doing things and someone is speaking or acting to the contrary, it's going to be challenging to hold space for that person to feel heard and to stay present. Every instinct within

you wants to assert that the individual is wrong and to course correct and get things back on the "right" path.

3. *Growth feedback:* It might seem it would be easy for leaders who are running the Control Freak program to have growth-feedback conversations. After all, they're not usually worried about upsetting other people. However, 22 percent of leaders running this faulty program in our research are challenged with growth feedback and want to improve. Where they typically get stuck is having the conversations clearly—or at all—because they end up taking over and do not create opportunities for others, or they presume it's easier or more effective if they just do things or fix them to be "right" according to their definition. This becomes a double whammy if they're also running the Overachiever or the Perfectionist program. Think about it this way. Why would you take the time to give others meaningful feedback to help them grow and get better at things when you feel valued (and calmed) by being the fixer and ensuring results happen in a specific way? And some leaders take it a step further by fearing that growing and elevating others will mean they will no longer be the go-to person, thus threatening where and how they perceive they add value.

4. *Setting boundaries:* For leaders who feel they are responsible for ensuring things go a certain way and are trying to eliminate uncertainty in their world, it's not surprising that just over 20 percent of leaders running the Control Freak struggle with setting and honoring healthy boundaries. After all, if we jump in to fix, take over, or own things that aren't necessarily ours to own, it's going to be hard to back off, say no, and create space for others to step up so we aren't overscheduled. This is also one area where leaders tend to struggle at home as well, taking over projects and chores because they don't feel others in their household can do it right, and then they are overloaded with to-do lists.

If you are running the Control Freak program and find your emotions getting the best of you, have a hard time staying present and curious in conversations, struggle with having growth-feedback conversations, or feel that your boundaries could use some help, you are in good company. These things will likely feel harder for you than you'd like as long as you're shouldering that self-imposed burden of ensuring things happen in a particular way and trying to create a level of certainty that just doesn't exist in a VUCA world. However, similar to other faulty programs, once you start the upgrade process, you will likely experience less anxiety and frustration as you slowly let go of trying to control things that you simply cannot.

Challenge It: How to Start the Upgrade Process

Because the Control Freak is rooted in such a deep fear of uncertainty and the need to have things done in a particular way, the key to challenging and upgrading this faulty program is to go right to the yuck factor. You must help your brain see how much this perhaps well-intended need to control is actually costing you and your relationships. With this realization, you can begin to reduce your controlling tendencies and instincts to push your way as the so-called right way. Following are the steps that I have found work the best for upgrading the Control Freak program.

Alan is a frontline manager for one of our clients who had some complaints about his abrasive communication style and blowing up at people. He wanted to get better at communicating in a more positive or neutral way in which he would stay present, open and curious, and engaged even during frustrating situations. However, he didn't know how to do that. Whenever Alan got frustrated, he would visibly show it and become defensive. His words would be harsh and overly direct to the point of offending others. Additionally, if he didn't feel like he had control of things, he would simply check out and not give any extra effort. Alan's need to be in control was deeply intertwined with his fear of failing. He was running a powerful combination of the Control Freak and Perfectionist programs.

Upgrading the Control Freak	
Name it when it shows up. When you notice the Control Freak head trash creeping in, pause, name it, and then remind yourself that you're an adult.	Example: • "I'm not listening to your crap today, Control Freak! I'm not ten years old anymore and don't have to try to control everything."
Replace the head trash. Once you name the Control Freak, practice replacing its head trash with something more empowering. The act of intentionally stating alternative truths is an important part of the process. (*Note:* You don't have to necessarily believe it yet; that will come with time.)	Examples: • "The only thing I really can or should try to control is myself—my actions, reactions, and behaviors." • "I am not responsible for other people's behaviors or outcomes." • "There is more than one 'right way' to do things. Who says my way is necessarily the best or only way?" • "Uncertainty is part of life. It's pointless to try to make things be different." • "What if my way really isn't the best or only way? Maybe I can learn from others or at least create an opportunity for them to learn and grow."
Create your blueprint. Spend time visualizing what your life would be like if the Control Freak program was no longer in the driver's seat. Use it to provide hope and energy as you embark on the next phase of the upgrade process.	Consider: • How would you think differently? (That is, what new thoughts would have replaced your head trash?) • How would you feel differently? • How would you behave differently?
Intentionally challenge its validity. Start challenging the validity of the Control Freak by running mini-experiments. The intent of these experiments is to collect data that pokes holes in the accuracy of the head trash that is holding you back. One of my favorite ways to start circumventing your deeply entrenched need to be in control and direct outcomes is by gathering objective feedback from people who know you well about what they experience when you're hyperfocused on controlling things and asserting your "rightness" in situations. Then, slowly but surely, start taking steps to let go of control and create clarity and space for others to step up and contribute in a way that adds value and works for them.	Ask people who know you well the following question: • What is it like for you to be around me when I'm trying to control things, asserting my "rightness," or trying to have things go my way? Be prepared for a little sting, as some will likely share frustration, annoyance, or the sentiments that they feel less confident or that they're letting you down. The point is to hopefully cause a moment of trepidation the next time your Control Freak instincts kick in so you can pause and consider the potential costs. Then you can start to slowly find opportunities to let go of control. This could be letting others take a task and not jumping into critique or takeover. It could mean staying present and curious in a conversation rather than jumping in with your thoughts and opinions. Whatever it is, each time you do this and the world doesn't end, you upgrade a little more until you start to see the beauty and relief of not overextending where and when you try to be in control.

Because looking in the mirror can be really unsettling, it took a while for Alan to embrace the work of the upgrade process. Not only is he a very private and low-trusting person, but he also found himself standing more in the blame game of his boss and others than looking at how he was working against himself. He didn't want to go through the process of identifying the origin of his faulty programs. So we came to an agreement: He didn't have to share details with me as long as he could own how the program was formed and recognize that his reactions today were often coming from his ten-year-old self rather than his sixty-year-old self. That worked and allowed us to transition into challenging his faulty programming.

Alan started the upgrade process by recognizing and naming his Control Freak program when it showed up and trying on some alternative narratives than the head trash that kept him stuck. He created a blueprint to have a clear picture of what life could be like if his faulty programs were no longer in control. Alan used that inspiration to provide some momentum to move into intentionally challenging its validity.

Alan began interviewing people at work and home to find out what they experience when he's attached to trying to control things and assert his "rightness" with others. He received some helpful but stinging feedback. People at work told him that they avoid him when he's in that mode, and his wife conveyed that she also withdraws but worries about him and his health when he gets worked up about things that weren't done his way. This is not the type of environment Alan wanted to create at work or at home. So he started finding small opportunities to course correct. When he would have one of his normal negative reactions, interrupt others, or shut down, he would own it and apologize to people. Then he started catching himself more in real time. When he would notice his instinct to assert his way of doing things, Alan practiced pausing and asked himself, "Is my need to be right more important than the quality of this relationship or outcome?" Over time, he started actively seeking others' perspectives and actively leaned into curiosity rather than judgments.

Numerous times during our work together, Alan mentioned wanting to quit the process and quit the company. But his wife told him not to and that she could see positive changes in him. His journey was rough, and he fought it nearly every step of the way. But what stands out to me the most in watching Alan's transformation is how he went from being closed off, angry, and blameful to being more open, humble, and lighthearted.

I recently saw Alan at a leadership workshop we were doing for this same client. It had been nearly three years since we completed our coaching and upgrade work together. He shared how he was still leaning on the tools he learned in our work together to not get hijacked by his Control Freak program. This allowed him to let go of owning some significant struggles his kids and grandkids were currently experiencing. Instead, he was supporting them within boundaries and not taking over. Alan was still just as light as when we wrapped up our work together. He had tears in his eyes when he told me, "You don't understand how much you changed my life. You saved my marriage and me." I told him that I appreciated his kind words. But then I reminded him that he's the one who did the work to upgrade his faulty programs and that he changed his life by leaning into the framework I provided.

Most leaders who are hijacked by the Control Freak program experience excess frustration due to the judgments and/or worry they constantly carry. It's difficult to regulate our emotions or stay present in conversations—especially when we don't agree with the other person—when every ounce of our being believes we know what's best and we are holding ourselves responsible for ensuring those outcomes come to fruition. What we consistently find is that, similar to Therese and Alan, a sense of calm, lightness, and newfound energy emerges as this faulty program is slowly surrendered. So when your Control Freak program takes over and you find yourself judging the behaviors and performances of others, or you feel like your way is best, remember that you are only responsible for yourself at the end of the day. You can influence others and create spaces for them to learn and grow, but remember that people are about as predictable and controllable as the weather.

For more resources related to the Control Freak, including downloadable exercises to start the upgrade process, scan this QR code.

CHAPTER 10

The Mime

Every conflict we face in life is rich with positive and negative potential. It can be a source of inspiration, enlightenment, learning, transformation, and growth—or rage, fear, shame, entrapment, and resistance. The choice is not up to our opponents, but to us, and our willingness to face and work through them.

—Kenneth Cloke and Joan Goldsmith, *Resolving Conflicts at Work*

The Mime	
Fears	**Behaviors**
Disharmony	Tries to keep the peace. Avoids speaking up. Attempts to stabilize situations where harmony is at risk.

If they're honest, most people probably don't enjoy conflict. But what happens when any amount of discord feels unsettling or threatening to the point that what we're left with is artificial harmony? This is exactly what happens when the Mime takes control. Our study analysis found that this faulty program shows up in 20 percent of leaders, keeping them trapped in the Stuckness Zone. On the surface, this program can look very similar to the People-Pleaser, but it stems from a different fear.

Whereas the People-Pleaser fears not being liked or respected and is trying to ultimately avoid rejection, the Mime fears disharmony and is trying to keep the peace. There's something fundamentally unsettling about discord running the show. This can be discord among us and others or having any discord around us. It can show up in thoughts like:

- *Any conflict is bad.*
- *Relationships can't recover if there is conflict.*
- *It's my job or role to be a peacekeeper.*
- *I can't handle conflict and must stabilize situations where it may be present.*
- *Conflict is too uncomfortable for me to handle.*

Issues with conflict can present as avoiding speaking up or having difficult conversations in which harmony may be disrupted. People running the Mime may also get in the middle of potential conflict situations to try to instill peace or take it upon themselves to stabilize situations where they fear harmony might be disrupted. The journey of upgrading the Mime is one of shifting our relationships with debate and discord in order to understand the difference between healthy and unhealthy conflict without needing to intervene or save others when they're experiencing conflict. As with the other faulty programs, it starts with naming and owning how the Mime was formed and what activates it in the present.

Name It and Own It: How the Mime Program Is Formed

Many leaders running the Mime program had one or more experiences growing up in which conflict was—or appeared to be—detrimental. Many people describe parents arguing or having a family member who was emotionally unstable. They attempted to create an environment where they determined not rocking the boat and keeping the peace were safer.

Rhonda's volatile childhood shaped her Mime program. When she was seven years old, her dad had a psychiatric break, requiring him to undergo inpatient treatment and the loss of his job. As a result, they lost their house. Ashamed, Rhonda didn't feel she could tell people and felt instead that she had to keep her family's secret. She determined that her role was to be the good girl and take care of things herself so as not to add to her family's stress. By the time she was eight, her parents had declared bankruptcy, and they had to move. Her parents separated when she was twelve and later divorced. These instances further fueled Rhonda's need to work hard to not get into trouble, get good grades, and stay off the radar to not add to the family's challenges.

In reflecting on things in the present, Rhonda realized how much she avoided conflict and would not speak up if it felt unsafe or she didn't know how it would be received. She also realized how her childhood coping skills were still evident as she would overextend her role as a stabilizer in an attempt to keep the peace around her at all costs, even above her own needs. Additionally, Rhonda had strong Overachiever and Martyr tendencies, leading her to feel the need to prove herself and earn her keep due to the financial and emotional insecurities left over from childhood.

Ultimately, Rhonda believed that her value came from protecting others and creating harmony and that she had to earn her keep and accomplish things to have value. This led to her taking on things to shield others from what she perceived would be painful or a burden for them. She did not take time for self-care, jumped in to keep the peace, and got involved in situations where she probably didn't need to. For example, when Rhonda was copied on an email thread and saw that things were going sideways, she would jump in and redirect the project rather than let others work it out. The irony is that, like in so many workplaces, Rhonda's ability to take on an incredible amount of work and maintain a seemingly peaceful team accelerated her advancement to the company's executive team. This reinforced her Mime, Overachiever, and Martyr tendencies and was quickly leading to her burnout.

Once she owned her faulty program's origin and how much her childhood self was actually in control in the present, Rhonda was ready to challenge it and begin the upgrade process. It became clear that her faulty programs were more easily activated with people she perceived as volatile (like her dad) or in positions of authority who she didn't believe appreciated the value she brought to a project. This was a key insight that allowed her to focus her efforts in those areas. She started testing the waters at executive team meetings by pushing back, thus risking the potential of causing disharmony, and also not jumping into trying to create harmony when others were debating. There had been a history of friction with one of her colleagues in particular. Rhonda stopped shying away from it and leaned into several clarifying and growth-feedback conversations with him rather than avoiding it to maintain the peace. With each conversation she had with that colleague, misunderstandings were cleared up, and they found a place of more effective collaboration. Rhonda also started working to be more diligent about her calendar and elevating other leaders on her team to take on more responsibility. As she incrementally kicked her ten-year-old self and faulty programming to the back seat, Rhonda's confidence grew. She found herself showing up more calm, clear, and energized.

Now it's your turn to get better acquainted with your inner Mime by owning how it shows up for you in your thoughts and behaviors and how it was formed as you navigated through the early years of your life. Once you know where your Mime tendencies came from and how they show up in the present, it becomes easier to name it, own it, and then challenge it so you can move from being reactive and hijacked by it to acting with clarity, intention, and greater confidence.

Own It: The Mime Expression and Origin Exercise	
Recognize how you express the Mime in terms of what it sounds like and how you behave.	
What inner head trash does the Mime have you say to yourself?	
How do you behave when the Mime is hijacking you?	

Next, identify the Mime's origin. (This is a key part of the process needed to help you see your brain is usually reacting from past experiences and flawed programming rather than actually responding to the present situation.)	
Identify three to five experiences from the first ten to fifteen years of your life that may have led you to conclude that conflict is bad, you need to avoid it and/or be the peacekeeper, or your safety requires that you stabilize situations where conflict is present.	______ ______ ______ ______ ______

How the Mime Works Against Us

Once we own how the Mime shows up for us, it is easier to see how it subconsciously works against us, keeping us from making progress on goals even when we're highly motivated. The Mime frequently emerges in tandem with the People-Pleaser. It can also emerge with the Perfectionist, the Counterfeit, and the Martyr.

What is fascinating is that our analysis found 100 percent of leaders running the Mime program struggle with some aspect of communication, yet they want to improve their ability to communicate effectively. Additionally, nearly 55 percent of leaders running this program also struggle with at least one area of people leadership, especially when it comes to delegating. It makes complete sense because all of these present a potential risk that conflict could emerge. This is exactly what Rhonda experienced when her Mime program was in control. She struggled with pushing back with certain people and delegating out of the fear of it creating disharmony.

Herein lies the predicament. At face value, it may look like leaders are effective because their teams appear to work harmoniously. But significant dysfunction is often brewing beneath the surface. Artificial harmony can lead to dangerous silence and inhibit psychologically safe, high-performing teams. This matters profoundly because we need teams in which people feel safe to express ideas, concerns, and opinions without fear of negative consequences such as ridicule, rejection, or punishment.

Psychologically safe teams are not all unicorns and rainbows; it's quite the opposite. Candor is encouraged, expected, and critical to performance.

In fact, Project Aristotle (Google's five-year research study on team effectiveness) revealed that psychological safety is the single biggest attribute of the highest-performing teams.[38] And leaders set the tone for the team's psychological safety. So, if a leader is running the Mime program, there's a good chance that the team will fall into the trap of artificial harmony and ultimately impede performance.

In our analysis, we found that each of the top four adaptive change goals that leaders running the Mime program have also impedes psychological safety and team performance.

1. *Growth feedback:* Forty-one percent of the leaders running the Mime program actively want to get better at having growth-feedback conversations but are quietly working against themselves. It makes sense because in any conversation with the possibility of difficult feedback, there is a potential risk for upsetting someone and creating discord or conflict. When leaders are also running the Counterfeit or People-Pleaser programs, they tend to avoid having growth-feedback conversations so they don't have to deal with someone becoming upset with them or with the situation. It feels too risky.

   When they are also running the Overachiever, Control Freak, or Martyr faulty programs, leaders may also avoid these conversations, but in this case, it's due more to feeling like there's no point to them and they need to take care of things themselves. If there's no avoiding them, leaders may structure one-sided conversations that shut down any potential for dialogue. Then it is likely the other person will leave feeling neither heard nor valued. After all, it's hard to have conflict if we don't create a space where someone could potentially push back with us in the first place.

2. *Speaking up:* The next most common aspect of communication where the Mime finds leaders in the Stuckness Zone is speaking up with confidence and clarity. Our analysis found that 36 percent of leaders want to be better at speaking up in meetings, sharing

their ideas, and contributing to conversations. Instead, they hold themselves back because their head trash tells them not to rock the boat. In these instances, the Mime tells them they risk upsetting the group or derailing an agenda if they speak up. For these leaders, withholding their contributions feels safer, even if they have ideas that could add value to a conversation or process. If these leaders are directly asked for their input, they often say they have nothing to add. Until they do the upgrade work and no longer automatically associate speaking up and sharing ideas or concerns with causing conflict, the Mime will keep them in silence. This was the case with Rhonda. She had no issue speaking up with certain people or in certain situations. But with people who tended to be more volatile, her ten-year-old self was automatically activated. She would then feel the need to avoid causing instability or try to find ways to create harmony to stabilize situations she perceived would get volatile.

3. *Delegating:* A key aspect of leading is being able to delegate effectively and responsibly. However, 29 percent of the leaders in our study running the Mime program struggle when it comes to delegation. Leaders describe fearing that people will be upset if they ask them to do things or that they'll add to their stress and burden. The latter is especially the case when leaders are running the Protector, one of the cousin faulty programs. In Rhonda's case, she wanted to call others to greatness by stretching themselves and solving their own challenges. But her desire to keep the peace and prove herself led to taking on more herself rather than effectively delegating tasks to her team. And when her Protector kicked in, she convinced herself that she was more capable of shouldering the stress than the other leaders within her span of care.

4. *Fostering accountability:* Nearly one-quarter (24 percent) of leaders running the Mime program want to get better at setting and aligning with clear goals and expectations and fostering greater accountability

to meet those objectives. But fear of the disharmony that could be created by having accountability-related conversations gets in their way. They will avoid them altogether, take on work themselves, or be too vague to be helpful. Then they frequently become frustrated or resentful but will rarely say anything because they're too focused on maintaining harmony. All the while, their well-being and effectiveness are quietly eroded.

If the Mime is hijacking you and you find yourself struggling with the adaptive change nature of having growth-feedback conversations, speaking up with greater confidence, delegating, or fostering accountability, you are in good company. Remember that 100 percent of leaders running the Mime program struggle with improving some aspect of communication. To many, speaking up and having potentially challenging conversations feels unsettling due to the risk of disturbing the harmonious equilibrium of the current state (whether it's real or merely artificial harmony). Something in our brains tells us that we can't handle disharmony, so we shouldn't risk it. But once you realize how much keeping the peace actually costs you, it's easier to start challenging the Mime via the upgrade process and gain true psychological safety and team effectiveness rather than false harmony and potentially dangerous silence.

Challenge It: How to Start the Upgrade Process

When I think about the leaders who have effectively upgraded their Mime programs, something that Jim Bishop shared on my *Show Up as a Leader* podcast always comes to mind. Like all my guests, I asked Jim to share a self-limiting story that he still tells himself and how he moves beyond it so he can show up as a leader in his life. Without naming the Mime, Jim talked about his overwhelming sense of needing to keep the peace for everyone outside of himself and how that historically got in his way. Through his upgrade journey, he eventually shifted to focusing on finding and maintaining the peace within himself, which was a game changer.

What Jim described is a hallmark of what other leaders experience when they kick the Mime to the back seat. They shift from fearing disharmony around them to actively nurturing harmony within themselves, allowing them to move forward in their lives with greater calm and clarity. And now it's your turn to find that inner peace. I have found the following steps to work the best in upgrading the Mime program.

Upgrading the Mime	
Name it when it shows up. When you notice the Mime head trash creeping in, pause, name it, and then remind yourself that you're an adult.	Example: • "I'm not listening to your crap today, Mime! I'm not ten years old anymore, and it's not my job to protect people from conflict, assume all conflict is detrimental, or stabilize situations."
Replace the head trash. Once you name the Mime, practice replacing its head trash with something that is more empowering. The act of intentionally stating alternative truths is an important part of the process. (*Note:* You don't have to necessarily believe it yet; that will come with time.)	Examples: • "Healthy conflict is much better than false harmony." • "Not all conflict is bad; it doesn't have to ruin relationships." • "Conflict can be a helpful way to strengthen relationships and processes." • "It's not my job to keep the peace and save others from their own conflicts."
Create your blueprint. Spend time visualizing what your life would be like if the Mime program was no longer controlling your life. Use it to provide hope and energy as you embark on the next phase of the upgrade process.	Consider: • How would you think differently? (For example, what new thoughts would have replaced your head trash?) • How would you feel differently? • How would you behave differently?
Intentionally challenge its validity. Start challenging the validity of the Mime by running mini-experiments. The intent of these experiments is to collect data that pokes holes in the accuracy of the head trash that is holding you back. One of my favorite ways to start reframing your relationship with conflict is by reflecting on and gathering objective feedback from people who know you well about what they experience when you've been in conflict or are overly focused on keeping the peace. Then slowly but surely start taking steps to let go of your peacekeeper role, inviting others to stretch themselves and work through things, and find greater peace within yourself.	Reflect on experiences you've had with conflict or that you've observed with others where the relationship wasn't ruined or it helped strengthen a relationship or process. Then ask people who know you well the following question: • What is it like for you to be around me when I'm trying to avoid conflict or keep the peace? Be prepared for a little sting as some will likely share frustration, annoyance, or concerns for your own well-being. The point is to hopefully cause a moment of trepidation the next time your Mime instincts kick in so you can pause and consider the potential costs. Then you can start to slowly find opportunities to let go of your self-imposed peacekeeping responsibilities. This could be by leaning into challenging conversations, letting others work through their own conflicts and issues, or not taking ownership of other people's emotional responses. Over time, you will likely find greater inner peace when you stop trying to create false harmony around you.

Brett had a long tenure at his organization and was promoted into a regional leadership position. He had a reputation for getting results while also having a harmonious team, so the executives were hoping he could help bring about some much-needed positive change to a region that had been struggling with morale and accountability. Because of this, Brett's goal was to get better at having intentional and timely feedback conversations because he regularly found himself struggling more than he wanted to in that area.

As a result of the Mime programming, Brett was running the limiting narrative that nothing positive comes from conflict or confrontation and that it ruins relationships. This was compounded by one of the cousin programs, the Protector, which told him that it is his responsibility to protect others from hurt and pain. Additionally, Brett was also running the Martyr, which led his head trash to tell him that he needed to be the responsible one and not depend on other people. This powerful combination stopped him every time he was faced with having growth-feedback conversations and fostering accountability with his team. Instead, he would inadvertently focus on trying to protect them from discomfort and take on more tasks himself to assert how responsible he was. Coming into a team where there had been a lot of conflict increasingly activated his faulty programming.

Brett's upgrade journey started with naming and owning how his faulty programs were formed and realizing how much of his ten-year-old self was in the driver's seat in the present day. When Brett was seven years old, his parents divorced. His mom quickly remarried. Unfortunately, his stepdad was abusive to his mom, to his brother, and to Brett. For over two years, they all endured abuse. Brett took it upon himself to be his mom's protector. He also became determined that he would never be the cause of hurting people. His older brother got into drugs and eventually died from an overdose. This fueled Brett's deep need to be the responsible one in the family, to not be like his brother. He needed to be the upstanding one who could hold things together and care for his mom. As he later reflected on these experiences, it became clear to him how he came to take on the role of the responsible one and try to protect others from feeling bad, feeling discomfort, or having any level of emotional pain. Brett said he didn't even like seeing any type of discomfort or conflict on television.

Armed with this rich information, Brett was ready to start to challenge his faulty programs. He created his blueprint to have a clear picture of what life could be like if his faulty programs were no longer in control. He used that inspiration to provide the momentum he needed to move into intentionally challenging its validity.

Because Brett lived in artificial harmony and didn't have any experiences he could recall in which conflict didn't ruin relationships, we had to dive right into having him face his fears in real time. In his new role, he inherited performance issues he was directed to address. So we gave him tools to structure growth-feedback conversations in an effective way and to lean on the mantra, "Clear is kind. Unclear is unkind." This helped him reframe that he was being kind by being clear and direct, even if the message might be hard to hear. The first conversation he had was tough, but the other person appreciated the open conversation and direction Brett gave for improvement. Each subsequent conversation he had yielded a similar result. The real test came when there was conflict between two leaders. Instead of trying to keep the peace, he pulled them into a conference room and instructed them to talk things out. Here he was encouraging conflict to be in the open rather than trying to avoid it or protect people from it.

With each conversation Brett forced himself to have, he incrementally upgraded his Mime program and started kicking it to the back seat. He regularly reminds himself that being clear with people about setting expectations, addressing when things aren't working as they need to, or clearing the air when there are grievances makes relationships and teams stronger. Brett shifted his head trash from believing that having harmony is what made him a good leader to creating a space of strong psychological safety where people are regularly speaking up and working through tough situations rather than avoiding them.

Most leaders who are hijacked by the Mime program experience excess anxiety and worry that frequently lead to resentment due to avoiding conflict or taking over to stabilize situations and create false harmony. Thinking we must keep the peace for other people while our inner peace is in turmoil is quite a boulder to bear on our shoulders. That's why I love the shift that Jim Bishop shared on the power of moving from externally trying to keep the peace to finding internal peace and not owning others' experiences or trying to save them from discomfort. Just like Rhonda and Brett experienced, when leaders start setting aside this faulty program, we consistently find that they are calmer and more energized as they see people around them stepping up, stretch themselves, and let go of their need to shield them from discomfort. We frequently hear that they feel their relationships are stronger due to being authentic rather than just harmonious. So when your Mime program takes over and you find yourself hyperfocusing on trying to keep the peace and maintain harmony, remember that clear is kind, growth doesn't happen within our comfort zones, and the best kind of peace to strive for is inner peace.

For more resources related to the Mime, including downloadable exercises to start the upgrade process, scan this QR code.

CHAPTER 11

The Martyr

If you want to go fast, go alone. If you want to go far, go together.

—African proverb

The Martyr	
Fears	**Behaviors**
Dependency	Shoulders burdens alone. Deprioritizes their needs. Struggles with boundaries.

At some point, many of us have likely thought we needed to do things ourselves. But what happens when that thought becomes a constant and turns into a fear of being dependent on others? Enter the Martyr faulty program that keeps us trapped in the Stuckness Zone, showing up in 19 percent of the leaders in our analysis. Many leaders running this program describe not perceiving that they can rely on others, while others describe not wanting to appear selfish or be a burden. Consequently, they end up doing most things themselves. The Martyr can show up in thoughts like:

- *I have to be self-reliant; I can't count on others.*
- *I don't want to be a burden to others.*

- *I need to take care of things myself.*
- *My needs don't matter or don't count.*
- *I can't appear selfish.*

When the Martyr is in the driver's seat, we tend to become hyperindependent and self-reliant. We typically end up doing most things ourselves rather than asking for or accepting help. Deep down, leaders running this faulty program like feeling needed and want to be valued and acknowledged for serving and sacrificing themselves for others. At the same time, however, they deprioritize their own needs, assuming they don't matter.

For some leaders, the Martyr leads to head trash that conveys they can't rely on others or that others can't handle things as well as they can. For others, the head trash tells them to avoid appearing selfish or to not be a burden to others. Some leaders running this program also describe feeling compelled to be constantly available and responsive to others (and, therefore, deprioritize their own needs). In all cases, this faulty program leads to struggles on some level with boundaries and frequently leads to resentment. The journey of upgrading the Martyr includes learning to recognize the importance of mutuality in relationships and the value of leveraging the power of many over the burden of one. It begins with naming and owning how this program was formed and what activates it in the present day.

Name It and Own It: How the Martyr Program Is Formed

One of the common threads that contributes to the formation of the Martyr is frequently experiencing times growing up when we were left to fend for ourselves in one way or another. This creates the head trash of needing to be self-sufficient or being unable to rely on others. For other leaders, this program emerges as a result of experiences in which focus needed to be on other people or other things, leading to the conclusion that their needs don't matter. Sometimes leaders describe observing dynamics with parents or other siblings where they saw people they care about being told not to be selfish or a burden. Some say that when others tried to set boundaries or advocate for themselves, they were ignored. By observing others in this situation, they concluded that it would be the same for them as well.

Christine is a highly regarded and successful leader. She had a pivotal turning point in her personal and leadership journey. Christine had an overly humble, self-deprecating quality that led her to constantly apologize for herself even when she didn't need to. She worked exceedingly long hours, bent over backward to please people in an effort to help the organization, and worked through vacations. After several major stressful life events, these behaviors became even more pronounced to a fault. Her overly humble, self-deprecating tendencies went too far where people perceived her as not having confidence and doubted her abilities.

Luckily, Christine embraced the opportunity to take advantage of this juncture in her leadership journey to engage in work to develop herself. We examined where she was getting in her own way and the underlying faulty programs that shaped her behaviors. When Christine was six years old, her mom gave birth to twins—a baby girl and a baby boy. The baby boy (we'll call him Max) died two days after he was born. Christine accompanied her mom on countless errands as she made arrangements for Max's funeral and trips to the hospital to visit her newborn sister (we'll call her Angie), who was still in the nursery. Christine watched as her mom literally slept under Angie's crib each night to tend to her in case she stopped breathing. This was hard for Christine to process at such a young age. She decided to become her mom's helper. She thought if she could free up her mom to tend to Angie, she could help ensure that her sister would live.

Fast-forward a few years. Christine's older brother was diagnosed with juvenile diabetes. Christine watched him have several low blood sugar episodes and was determined to help. She even stuffed her cheerleading uniform with candies just in case he needed them during high school basketball games. She put an incredible burden on herself. She felt that the world rested on her shoulders and that she needed to be a good girl and do the right things or the world would fall apart. And where her family was concerned, her young brain literally was running a life-or-death script.

Christine was running a very strong Martyr program. She found her value in helping others and putting others first. The problem was that this narrative didn't evolve as she became an adult. She continued to operate with an underlying assumption that her only value came from being helpful and anything not in service to others meant she was selfish and not enough. In her mind, this meant that she couldn't advocate for her needs and be of service to others; they couldn't coexist. So she apologized anytime she felt she might be perceived as advocating for herself, which allowed others to interpret her actions as being weak. Christine was becoming increasingly stressed and burned out.

In Christine's case, advocating for herself was a trigger for feeling guilty. For example, whenever she tried to take a vacation, people put appointments on her calendar, even though it was blocked. This sparked guilt and a fear of disappointing people, so she'd cancel or work during her vacation. Then she would feel trapped, resentful, overworked, frustrated, and weak. As a result, she was unable to show up effectively under times of stress.

When Christine hit a pivotal point in her leadership journey, her organization invited her to do the transformative work needed to step back into her greatness as a leader. While some leaders might hide their heads when receiving difficult feedback, Christine did not. At first, she repeatedly apologized for herself, but then she decided to lean into the discomfort, do the work to name and own her faulty programming and head trash, and then challenge it via the upgrade journey.

Christine desperately wanted to have healthier boundaries and to speak up for herself with greater clarity and confidence. She started to challenge the assumptions she held that told her she couldn't recover if she let people down and couldn't be in service to others and tend to her needs. Christine eventually stopped apologizing for herself at every turn. She owned her mistakes and began to embrace gratitude for the opportunity to upgrade her faulty programming. In time, she reported feeling calmer and more poised. She told us, "My gut reaction to self-protect and shut down is gone; leaning into the discomfort of my old assumptions actually makes me stronger."

As Christine kicked her Martyr programming to the back seat, she started to reenter her greatness at work and at home. And as her confidence grew, she knew she was ready for the next step and took on the new role of chief nursing officer for two hospitals in the Midwest. Christine describes the value of doing the work to upgrade her faulty programming:

> It was my great fortune to have the type of fearless environment where thinking through why feelings and behaviors appear under times of stress and then being able to do the messy upgrade work allowed me to gain the clarity I needed to show up again as the leader I knew I was. Working with Rosie was a gift I will never be able to repay but will pay it forward!

Thousands of leaders who have done the messy upgrade work to move beyond their faulty programming describe it as a gift. But it's not for the timid. I've experienced a handful of leaders who cannot let themselves lean into this process. Unfortunately, they stay stuck. I always remind our clients that we don't have some sort of special magic wand. People must be willing to accept the discomfort, embrace the process, and do the work. No matter how nice it would be, there is no shortcut. But when they do the work, they find the gift in the upgrade journey, just like Christine.

Now it's your turn to embrace this potential gift. Be brave and get better acquainted with your inner Martyr by naming and owning how it shows up for you in your thoughts and behaviors and how it was formed as you navigated the early years of your life. Once you know where your Martyr tendencies came from and how they show up in the present day, it becomes easier to name it, own it, and then challenge and upgrade it so you can move from being the lone wolf to embracing the value of advocating for your needs and accepting support from others.

Own It: The Martyr Expression and Origin Exercise	
Recognize how you express the Martyr in terms of what it sounds like and how you behave.	
What inner head trash does the Martyr have you say to yourself?	
How do you behave when the Martyr is hijacking you?	
Next, identify the Martyr's origin. (This is a key part of the process to help you see your brain is usually reacting from past experiences and flawed programming rather than actually responding to the present situation.)	
Identify three to five experiences from the first ten to fifteen years of your life that may have led you to conclude that your needs don't matter, it is selfish to advocate for yourself, you can't rely on other people, or that you need to be self-sufficient.	

How the Martyr Works Against Us

Because the Martyr creates head trash that tells us, to some degree, that our needs don't matter, it can be hard to believe that we deserve to focus on ourselves or to accept support in the upgrade process. This Martyr program can lead to significant self-judgment in which we convince ourselves that we should be able to figure this out on our own, which makes adaptive change work feel harder than it needs to be. Additionally, it is usually compounded by one or more other faulty programs that amplify the sense that we need to go it alone or suck it up and figure it out.

Our analysis found that nearly half of the leaders running the Martyr program want to get better at some aspect related to decision-making and/or want to get better at their leadership skills. But this faulty program continues to quietly work against them. So if you also are struggling in either of these areas, know that you're human and give yourself some extra grace as you start to understand why you've struggled more in these areas than other people. From our analysis, we identified the top four specific adaptive change goals leaders have who are running the Martyr program.

1. *Setting boundaries:* The biggest area in which Martyr leaders feel themselves challenged is with setting and honoring healthy boundaries. Specifically, our analysis showed that 35 percent of the leaders running the Martyr program want to get better but find difficulties in constructing healthier boundaries between work and home, having more downtime, being present with their families when at home, and being more diligent in tending to their own well-being and self-care. It makes complete sense because the head trash of this faulty program tells us that our needs ultimately don't matter. Trying to advocate for ourselves by having boundaries and tending to our own well-being directly contradicts the messages entrenched in the Martyr program. And when we're also running the Overachiever or Control Freak program, the need to do things ourselves becomes even stronger. When we're also running the People-Pleaser, Mime, or Counterfeit program, the thought of pushing back on the other people in the circumference of our lives feels way too risky. Consequently, we find ourselves constantly struggling when it comes to having healthy and sustainable boundaries. Christine is a great example of struggling with boundaries due to all the falsehoods her Martyr was regularly telling her and feeling compelled to be constantly available and in service of others. This led to the depletion of her well-being and happiness.

2. *Speaking up:* Given that the Martyr leads to making us believe that our needs don't matter or that advocating for ourselves could be perceived as selfish, it's not surprising that our research indicated that 28 percent of leaders running this faulty program struggle with speaking up with confidence. Even though we may want to have our

voices heard and to advocate for our thoughts and ideas, this program's head trash tells us that no one will listen or that we'll be seen as selfish or ego-driven. So we keep our thoughts to ourselves while a deep longing or resentment brews inside us. This is especially the case if we're also running the People-Pleaser, Mime, or Counterfeit programs. To a lesser extent, this can also show up if we're running the Overachiever, Perfectionist, or Control Freak programs. With these, we simply keep our heads down and take on whatever tasks are given to us out of a need to prove ourselves or have things go a certain way. In these instances, we can end up being so heads down and task/productivity focused that we forget that our needs and voices matter. It's all about getting things done at that point.

3. *Growth feedback:* According to our analysis, nearly one-quarter of leaders (24 percent) struggle with having growth-feedback conversations when they're running the Martyr. It makes sense because the head trash of this faulty program has us believe that our needs don't matter. If we're trying to elevate someone else and give feedback based on our experiences or perception of things, this faulty program can easily activate thoughts of coming across as selfish or that people won't respect and listen to us. Consequently, similarly to leaders who struggle with speaking up with confidence and clarity, we tend to avoid or fumble through those conversations because it likely feels easier to do things ourselves than go through the discomfort of trying to grow and elevate others.

4. *Emotional regulation:* The same number of leaders who struggle but want to get better at growth-feedback conversations also want to improve their ability to regulate their emotions. But instead, they end up hijacked by reactivity. Think about it. If we're constantly doing things ourselves because we think others won't help us or do it as well as we will, we can't rely on others, or our needs don't matter, we will constantly suppress frustration, resentment, and feelings that come

> when we're overloaded. In that state, it is difficult to regulate our emotions so that we can stay calm and curious, be patient and understanding, and respond to others in a more neutral way. It's like the lid on a pot of boiling water just waiting to pop off at any moment. We can only ignore our own needs for so long before something must give.

When I'm facilitating workshops, I regularly ask people running the Martyr program if they struggle with establishing boundaries and managing their calendar by either taking on too much or getting sucked into putting out more reactive fires than being able to be proactive and tend to strategic work. Then I'll say something like, "Let me guess. You tend to do everything yourself and like feeling needed but frequently are resentful, stressed out, and on overload." Nearly every time, their jaws drop and they ask me if I'm psychic or something. I usually laugh and simply tell them that this is what the Martyr does to people. Every prioritization and productivity class in the world won't help until they do the upgrade work and realize that speaking up, setting boundaries, and relying on others aren't a death sentence.

Let me reassure you that if you are running the Martyr and struggling with the adaptive change nature of setting and honoring boundaries, speaking up confidently, advocating for yourself, having growth-feedback conversations, or regulating your emotions to stay curious and give yourself and others grace, you are not alone. Hopefully, it's starting to make sense why these skills may feel harder for you than you'd like. As you begin the upgrade process, you will find that you move from hyper-self-sufficiency, frustration, and resentment to collaboration, connection, and greater harmony in your life.

Challenge It: How to Start the Upgrade Process

If you're going to recognize and value that your needs matter and advocate for yourself, it's critical that you are clear about who you are and what matters to you. Similar to the People-Pleaser, the blueprint for starting the upgrade process for the Martyr is anchored on getting clear about your core and knowing who you authentically are, then learning to act on behalf of your core and shift how you interact with people on the circumference. I have found that the following steps work the best for upgrading the Martyr program.

Upgrading the Martyr	
Name it when it shows up. When you notice the Martyr's self-limiting narratives creeping in, pause, name them, and then remind yourself that you're an adult.	Example: • "I'm not listening to your crap today, Martyr! I'm not ten years old anymore. My needs matter, too, and I don't have to do everything myself."
Replace the head trash. Once you name the Martyr, practice replacing its head trash with something that is more empowering. The act of intentionally stating alternative truths is an important part of the process. (*Note:* You don't have to necessarily believe it yet; that will come in time.)	Examples: • "My needs matter just as much as those of other people." • "I don't have to do everything myself." • "Most people want to contribute and help. I need to give them a chance." • "It's not selfish to advocate for what I need. It's an act of love." • "There's nothing wrong, weak, or incompetent about letting others help." • "I can add more value by including others in the process than by doing everything myself." • "I'm robbing others of an opportunity to grow or contribute when I do everything myself."
Create your blueprint. Spend time visualizing what your life would be like if the Martyr program was no longer in control. Use it to provide hope and energy as you embark on the next phase of the upgrade process.	Consider: • How would you think differently? (For example, what new thoughts would have replaced your head trash?) • How would you feel differently? • How would you behave differently?
Intentionally challenge its validity. Start challenging the validity of the Martyr by running mini-experiments. The intent of these experiments is to collect data that pokes holes in the accuracy of the head trash that is holding you back. One of my favorite ways to start reframing your need to do things yourself and deprioritize your needs is by gathering objective feedback from people who know you well about what they experience when you've been hyperfocused on doing everything yourself or deprioritizing your needs. Then slowly but surely start taking steps to advocate for your own needs, set boundaries, and let others step up and contribute.	Ask people who know you well the following question: • What is it like for you to be around me when I'm deprioritizing my needs and trying to do everything myself? Be prepared for a little sting, as some will likely share frustration, annoyance, or concerns for your well-being. The point is to hopefully cause a moment of trepidation the next time your Martyr instincts kick in so you can pause and consider the potential costs. Then do the work to gain clarity about who you are at your core. Use that as your guide to start finding opportunities to test the waters with boundaries by advocating for yourself and your needs and letting go of your self-imposed assumptions that you must do everything yourself. Remember that boundaries are healthy and an act of love, not selfishness. Most people want to help and contribute, so let them. And the next time you're feeling stress and resentment, see what need you're not conveying or advocating for and take a small action.

Not unlike many leaders running the Martyr program, Rebecca wanted to get better at having boundaries and more harmony between her work and personal lives. She wanted to be more fully present with her family, not answer calls and emails during her off-hours. And she wanted to delegate more and advocate for herself with her peers and leaders. As the newest member of the executive team with a company experiencing a rapid growth period, she had a heightened sense of needing to prove herself. But she had a fear of being seen as whiny or weak if she advocated for herself, and she worried that she wouldn't add value and that people would think she wasn't doing a good job. Rebecca was running a powerful combination of the Martyr, Counterfeit, Perfectionist, and Fraud faulty programs.

Her faulty programs quietly worked against her goal of setting better boundaries. When people from work called her, she would always answer, even if she was already on the phone with her husband or kids. While she was with her family, she found herself distracted and constantly thinking about work. Even worse, when they were having family movie time, she'd tend to work emails at the same time. Rebecca was constantly multitasking, so she was never really present with anyone. Her calendar was her enemy most of the time because she never declined invites or said no. And she never scheduled time for prep, follow-up, or other work. Rebecca would be in back-to-back meetings all day, never took time to delegate and elevate other leaders within her span of care, and jumped in to do things rather than give others the chance to contribute. This pattern started to deplete her, but she couldn't get off the dysfunctional merry-go-round no matter how hard she tried.

When we started to examine the origin of her faulty programs, Rebecca's patterns became clearer to her. Her family had moved several times during her childhood due to her dad's job. While this is a normal occurrence, it's hard when kids must leave their friends and what is familiar to them. With each move, Rebecca worried about fitting in and concluded that her needs didn't matter. After all, if they did, her parents wouldn't move so often. At least that's what her child's mind believed.

She recalled two additional instances that likely helped to form her

Martyr programming. When Rebecca was five years old, her younger brother was born. No longer being the baby of the family, she needed to find different ways to get praise and attention, so she decided to become her mom's helper. Fast-forward to age nine, when her mom went back to work after being a stay-at-home parent. Rebecca took it on herself to step up, help out, and be more responsible and self-sufficient because her mom wouldn't have as much time to give her.

As she recalled these normal but impactful experiences, Rebecca realized how much her ten-year-old self was in the driver's seat in the present. She was constantly trying to earn her keep and make her leaders and peers proud while being ruled by her head trash that told her that her needs didn't matter. Naming and owning her faulty programming were eye-opening experiences for her. Rebecca practiced recognizing and naming the head trash when it showed up, including trying some alternative narratives from the head trash that was keeping her stuck. She got clear on her purpose and values so she had a firm grasp on who she was at her core. Rebecca then used that to create her blueprint and develop a clear picture of what her life could be like if her faulty programs were no longer in control. She used that inspiration for momentum to move into intentionally challenging its validity.

Rebecca started by interviewing people at work and at home to find out what they experience when she's in a mode of needing to be constantly and immediately responsive and take on everything. Her executive team colleagues said that when she is quick to respond, she can miss answering some of the questions. They reminded her that being first to respond doesn't always mean she's giving them the best answers. It can also set unrealistic expectations for others around her, putting extra pressure on them to feel like they have to have the same level of responsiveness, especially during nights, weekends, or early mornings. They said that it sets a tone for imbalance when they're all trying to have greater work–life harmony and expressed concern that she would reach burnout. Rebecca's husband said that while he understood, it was frustrating when she took a call in the middle of one of their conversations. He admitted that her work was taking more and more time away from her family and they felt like a bit of an afterthought. Ouch!

The feedback she got really hit her, especially the cost that her family was paying for her behavior. Rebecca realized that she had too much on her plate and needed to find a way to shift her trajectory.

Once she had some momentum and confidence from the interview feedback, Rebecca was ready to further challenge the Martyr by testing the waters with setting boundaries. She started with unplugging from work emails and phone calls for one evening. That progressed to weekends. Eventually, she found herself mostly unplugging to enjoy a family vacation (this is about better, not perfection). Rebecca also worked with her executive admin to reconfigure her calendar and schedule time for work beyond meetings, thus giving her a clearer picture of her actual capacity. She began delegating some of her work to the leaders within her area of responsibility rather than trying to do everything herself. Additionally, she made a rule and practice for herself that when she was copied on emails, she would pause and give others a chance to respond and handle them rather than being the first to jump in. Most of the time, things were handled just fine. She found that she became more effective at growing and elevating other leaders and more confidently stepping into her executive role while also strengthening her relationships at home. It was a win-win. Rebecca found her stress and anxiety lessened a bit, and her overall fulfillment grew.

Now, because the upgrade process is not a one-and-done, Rebecca has needed to continue to lean on her tools to help keep her ten-year-old self in the back seat. While the initial upgrade is the hardest, leaning on those lessons, tools, and systems helps with mini-resets along the way as the VUCA world tries to reactivate our faulty programming. Since her initial upgrade work, Rebecca's organization has had more growth. Her role expanded again, and the pace of change in recent months has been exponential. On top of that, she hit a pivotal decision point. Not unlike Ben in chapter 3 (and not unlike what is happening with countless native digitals), Rebecca's sixteen-year-old son experienced a mental health crisis. She found herself torn because there was a huge, high-profile meeting that she was to be coleading at the same time her son needed her more than ever. She initially didn't know what to do.

For most people, this would seem like a no-brainer. But when you have a combination of the Martyr and Overachiever trying to take over, it's not an easy decision. Rebecca said that if this happened a year ago, she probably would've gone to the meeting, felt guilty, and simply been checking in on her son because her fears of advocating for herself and sounding whiny or disappointing her CEO were too great. But because Rebecca was clear on who she is at her core and what matters to her, making the decision to prioritize her family was easy. She courageously called her CEO and executive colleagues and informed them of what was happening and told them she would be skipping the meeting to care for her son. Of course, they were completely supportive. Rebecca had tears in her eyes when she told me how thankful she is for the work she did the previous year and the tools she continues to lean on so she could have her priorities straight. And her son is out of crisis mode and getting the ongoing help he needs.

When we've been running the Martyr, the instinct to take care of things ourselves or deprioritize our needs may never fully go away, even after a successful upgrade journey. However, it will lessen. Like Rebecca, it will be easier to lean on our core to make decisions when we're faced with difficult situations. When leaders kick this faulty program to the back seat, they find peace and renewed energy as they embrace asking for and accepting help, leveraging it as a skill rather than viewing it as a weakness.

One of the things that immediately comes to mind when I think of sidelining the Martyr is an incredible conversation I had on my podcast with Mark McFatridge. He is the founder of Quade, which facilitates meaningful connections and peer groups for CEOs. During our conversation, he talked about how critical it is that we shift from the "go it alone" mentality to having a robust network he refers to as the three A's: Allies, Advisors, and Advocates.

- *Allies* are people who are like-situated and similar to you in terms of position, role, and so on. These are your peers, the people you share your dreams with, and will be your circle of support to cheer you on (for example, friends, colleagues, support groups, or employee resource groups).

- *Advisors* are more like mentors. They are typically people who have been where you want to go. They take it to the next level from simply being an ally. Not only will they listen to your dreams, but they will also challenge you and help you grow and get to the next level.
- *Advocates* are those who have taken a liking to you and see something in you that you may not see in yourself. They are people in positions or on levels that you strive to be in. They advocate for you when you're not in the room. They are endorsing, referring, and making introductions for you. They actively take steps to get you to the next level.[39]

As a species, we are neurobiologically hardwired to be in connection with others. So we need to counter the Martyr when it tries to convince us that we are alone, our needs don't matter, and we must be self-reliant. We will go further by investing in building and nurturing the three A relationships in our lives. It's not being weak or whatever else our head trash might try to tell us. It's being *effective*.

In the spring of 2025, I was fortunate to attend the WomELLE Summit and Female Voice Awards Gala and be awarded the 2024 Business Coach of the Year award. One of the incredible speakers was Chantelle Love. She said something that stood out to me and expresses the importance of not going it alone and instead investing in building and nurturing your three A relationships: "Surround yourself with people who see your success as *inspiration*, not intimidation."

It made me think about how I've leveraged the three A's to help me. I'm blessed to have a great group of allies and belong to meaningful groups where I've met both allies and advocates. As a business, we've also invested in advisors who help us take our company to the next level. And I'm regularly leveraging advisors on a personal level to help me get out of my own way. It makes a huge difference. I encourage you to do a quick inventory of the networks you have in your life and where you need to make some shifts so you feel strong and supported in all three A relationships. Remember, you are not meant to go it alone!

For more resources related to the Martyr, including downloadable exercises to start the upgrade process, scan this QR code.

CHAPTER 12

The Three Cousin Faulty Programs

Today YOU are YOU! That's truer than true! There's not one alive that's YOU-er than YOU.

—Dr. Seuss, *Happy Birthday to You!*

As you've already seen, while some people may find they are predominantly hijacked by only one faulty program, it is very common to be running more than one faulty program at the same time. In addition to the seven core faulty programs, three additional ones with their unique characteristics emerged from the data. We refer to these as faulty cousin programs because they are not as prevalent and never stand alone. They consistently show up in tandem with one or more of the core faulty programs and make their unique marks in how they keep us trapped in the Stuckness Zone. Following is a summary of the three cousin programs and which core faulty programs they tend to hitch a ride with.

Our Brains' Three Faulty Cousin Programs		
Cousin Program	**Description**	**Related Faulty Program**
The Dropout	Has a deep fear of either sounding stupid or being perceived as incompetent. Will typically either silence themselves to avoid that risk or overcompensate to try to prove their competence and intelligence.	The Mime The Control Freak The Overachiever
The Fraud	Perceives they don't belong or don't deserve their current roles and are afraid of being found out (impostor syndrome) and having it taken away. Will either hide parts of themselves they feel won't be accepted or try to prove their worthiness via achievements.	The Counterfeit The Overachiever
The Protector	Fears someone else's struggle. Holds themselves responsible for someone else's experiences or outcomes. Can show up as trying to save them and shoulder their burdens, holding back to emotionally protect them, or taking on burdens that aren't really theirs to own.	The Martyr The Mime The Control Freak The Overachiever

The reason the Faulty Program Discovery doesn't include the cousin programs is because they are secondary. But make no mistake: They are powerful in keeping us stuck and hindering progress in areas of adaptive change. Therefore, it's important to recognize if any of the cousin programs apply to you. Pay particular attention if you're running the Overachiever; it is the only faulty program that shows up in tandem with every cousin program as a powerful coping mechanism for the yuck factor present in each of them.

Additionally, you may notice that missing from this overview are the Perfectionist and the People-Pleaser. It certainly doesn't mean that you can't be running one of the cousin programs if you're also running one of these core faulty programs. But there wasn't a consistent enough pattern in our dataset to specifically note this. For example, we found leaders who are running the Protector and the People-Pleaser. However, on closer examination, the Protector is more likely related to those also running the Mime or Martyr than being a product of the People-Pleasing tendencies of avoiding rejection. With that as context, let's unpack each in a little more detail, starting with the Dropout.

The Dropout

The Dropout		
Fears	**Behaviors**	**Related Faulty Programs**
Sounding stupid	Avoids speaking up. Hijacks conversations to try to prove expertise or avoid being questioned. Takes on more work to prove their worthiness.	The Mime The Control Freak The Overachiever

The Dropout program is rooted in the deep fear of either sounding stupid or being perceived as incompetent, and in our study, it showed up in 16 percent of leaders. It can show up in thoughts like:

- *I don't want to say anything that makes me sound stupid.*
- *I don't want people to think I don't know what I'm doing or that I am not competent.*
- *My value comes from being the smart one; if I don't have that, what's left?*
- *People are counting on me to have the right answers.*
- *I can't let people think I don't know what I'm talking about.*

When the Dropout is riding shotgun with the Mime, we tend to silence ourselves and hold back so we don't risk saying something that might be inaccurate or have people question our expertise. In this case, we avoid difficult conversations and situations just like the Mime. But instead of the primary motivator being to maintain harmony, it's wanting to not risk having discord because people think we don't know what we're doing or talking about. The Dropout can tell us that we'll expose ourselves and lose credibility or respect, so it's safer to stay quiet.

Carl is a leader of a small division within a large manufacturing company. He has been in his role for several decades and is in the legacy years of his career. Despite this, he always struggled with difficult conversations and effectively providing growth feedback to others. Instead, he would either procrastinate or jump in and take care of things himself rather than have a conversation with someone. Carl's primary faulty program was the Mime. He viewed that his value and role were to play the peacekeeper and maintain harmony. At the same time, the Dropout was fighting to take over the driver's seat. Carl assumed that if he ever risked looking stupid, he would be embarrassed, he would be seen as weak, and he wouldn't be able to recover from it. Once we uncovered that, he started to understand why he had always struggled with having difficult conversations.

On further examination, it became clearer to Carl that his ten-year-old self was more in control than his sixty-year-old self. When he was ten years old, his father got mad at him for something he did and called Carl "stupid." This left its mark on him. He hated to let his dad down and get yelled at. He realized that this fear was front and center in the present as he cringed at the thought of upsetting people, hence why he avoided conversations where that was a risk.

In school, Carl was only an average student. He was okay with not being the smartest person in the room. However, he realized that he would hold back his opinions so he wouldn't reveal himself to others and risk looking stupid. Carl's Dropout-Mime combination kept him flying under the radar and frustrated with his team. He quietly became increasingly apathetic. The key to kicking his Mime program to the back seat lay in upgrading the Dropout because they were deeply intertwined, and his fear of sounding stupid was extremely dominant.

When the Dropout is riding shotgun with the Control Freak, it looks much different than when it shows up in conjunction with the Mime. In this case, we move into overcompensation mode to try to outrun our worries of not being smart or competent enough. This frequently shows up as hijacking conversations or taking over projects and tasks to avoid the risk of having people think we don't know what we're doing. It makes sense because if we can be the conductor and control situations, our brains convince us that we can engineer certainty into situations and convince other people that we have the right answers and they should trust our expertise.

Miriam is a midcareer surgeon who was brought in to help grow her specialty's practice in a new geographic area. She jumped at the opportunity and was excited to be part of something new and develop a thriving practice. However, the uncertainty and inevitable clunkiness of the new venture quickly bumped up against her Control Freak programming. Miriam prided herself on her competence, being the top of her class in school, and being looked to as the one with the "right" answers. In this new role and environment, she quickly found herself becoming increasingly frustrated and judgmental of nearly everyone and every process. Miriam would take over meetings, redo the call scheduling, and constantly vent about everyone who wasn't doing things in what she considered to be the right way. Her Dropout's need to prove her competence in this new and uncertain environment activated her Control Freak tendencies. Not only was she quickly frustrated and disengaged to the point of looking for other opportunities, but Miriam was pissing off most of the people who worked with her.

On closer examination, Miriam realized that most of her behaviors were stemming from her ten- and thirteen-year-old selves, not her thirty-something self. Several instances of being teased as she was growing up led her to assume she was and still is inadequate. Anytime she acted out or let others get the best of her, she either got in trouble or had an otherwise unpleasant experience. She determined that if she could control situations and do what's right (her definition), unpleasantness could be avoided. Additionally, she had some classes in middle school where much of her grade was based on actively speaking up and participating in class. Consequently, Miriam learned that showing how much you know was key to getting a good grade. Enter the Dropout, which found her needing to prove her adequacy in order to gain approval in the present day. But her career and the success of the new practice were almost completely sabotaged by her Dropout and Control Freak faulty programming hijacking her. Thankfully, she did the work to upgrade them. But it wasn't easy. And she had a lot of cleanup work to do in order to repair relationships with others.

When the Dropout is riding shotgun with the Overachiever, one of two conditions is typically present. The first is that we have a distorted view that our value is conditional on how smart we are. In this case, we go overboard trying to constantly show how smart we are and to prove our knowledge and expertise. If someone were to question our competence, it would mean our value is coming into question and at risk. Unfortunately, it typically comes across to others as being arrogant or critical. The second condition where the Dropout is present occurs when we have a fear of sounding stupid. In this case, we keep trying to accomplish or achieve more in the hope that we will eventually feel smart and/or competent. However, we are usually unsuccessful in outrunning that fear and end up stressed and burned out instead.

Damon had a little of both conditions, and they were getting in his way. Damon is an executive leader in an organization within the financial industry that has multiple locations in the United States and is expanding globally. He practically grew up in the business, starting as an intern and working his way up over the past twenty years in various positions. Perhaps because of this, part of him still felt like a newbie intern trying to prove himself. Damon wanted to show up with greater calm and confidence by being more authentic, assuming good intent, being more open and interactive with people, and practicing more curiosity, especially when people have different perspectives than he does. But he was quietly working against himself, running the Fraud, Counterfeit (the Fraud always goes hand in hand with the Counterfeit), Overachiever, Perfectionist, and Dropout faulty programs. He assumed that his value came from working hard and being smart, that he had to have the right answer to be considered smart, and that any failure would validate that he wasn't good enough and didn't belong. Damon realized that his forty-something self was not showing up on most days.

Growing up, Damon's dad was strict about chores and working hard; work always had to come first. He would get yelled at if he slipped and didn't do his chores or didn't do them up to his dad's standards. This fed into his head trash of not being able to do anything right and helped to form the Overachiever and Perfectionist faulty programs as a way of coping and trying to be enough for his dad.

As a kid, Damon also had some extra weight on him and was only so-so in sports. So he poured himself into getting good grades and doing well in school. He was teased about his weight, which fed his Counterfeit and Fraud programs of not belonging and not being enough. It further fueled his need to double down on proving himself. The problem is that Damon was walking into rooms hijacked and trying to prove how much he knows (fueled by his Dropout and Overachiever programs), emulate the CEO rather than being true to himself, take on more and more responsibilities to try to prove how hard he works, and outrun his ten-year-old insecurities. As he was identified as the successor to the CEO, these tendencies only grew and intensified.

Damon's upgrade process was multifaceted. He interviewed people to find out what they value about him and what it is like when he's trying to prove how smart he is. He got clear about who he authentically is (versus trying to copy someone else) and practiced leaning into vulnerability and showing up more courageously. He was eventually able to delegate more and laugh at himself when he was less than perfect. His journey is ongoing, as it is for most people. But now when he recognizes his faulty programming trying to hijack him, he leans on his tools to reground himself and get back to who he knows he authentically is. Damon trusts in his expertise and abilities while remaining open to what others can contribute.

Name It and Own It: Upgrading the Dropout

The steps to upgrading any of the cousin programs are similar to the process you need to undertake for your core faulty programs. The first is to name and own where it came from and how it shows up in the present day. Then you can start the upgrade journey in tandem with your other faulty programs.

Own It: The Dropout Expression and Origin Exercise	
Recognize how you express the Dropout in terms of what it sounds like and how you behave.	
Which core faulty program(s) is (are) in the driver's seat for you when the Dropout shows up?	

What inner head trash does the Dropout have you say to yourself?	
How do you behave when the Dropout is hijacking you?	
Next, identify the Dropout's origin. (This is a key part of the process to help you see that your brain is usually reacting from past experiences and flawed programming rather than actually responding to the present situation.)	
Identify three to five experiences from the first ten to fifteen years of your life that may have led you to conclude that either you're not smart or competent enough or that being smart is your primary value so you need to protect it or assert it wherever you can.	

Once you name and own where your Dropout program came from, how it shows up in the present day, and how it relates to your other core faulty programs, you can officially challenge it and start the upgrade process. Following the upgrade steps of your core faulty programs will typically get you pretty far in upgrading the Dropout as well. Start with interviewing people who know you well to find out what they experience when you either withhold your contributions (Mime tendencies) or try to prove how smart you are (Control Freak or Overachiever tendencies). The feedback will likely sting but hopefully help you see that it's not effective. Then try a strategy for upgrading your main faulty programs, and you will find the Dropout letting go as well.

The Fraud

The Fraud		
Fears	**Behaviors**	**Related Faulty Programs**
Being "found out" as an impostor	Hides authentic selves. Tries to make themselves indispensable. Constantly tries to prove their worthiness.	The Counterfeit The Overachiever

The Fraud program is like the Counterfeit on steroids. It is also rooted in a deep fear of vulnerability and letting our authentic selves or any weaknesses show. But the Fraud takes it to another level as it is exacerbated by adding a fear of being exposed, or "found out," as being an impostor and then having everything taken away. Our study found that this program shows up in 13 percent of leaders. It can show up in thoughts such as:

- *I don't really belong here. I don't know what I'm doing.*
- *They're going to realize they made a mistake giving me this job or opportunity.*
- *I'm a fraud; I'm an impostor.*
- *I'm not good enough. I will never be good enough.*
- *I'm not as talented, qualified, experienced, or good as they think.*
- *It's only a matter of time before they figure out I don't belong here.*

I was initially surprised that the percentage of leaders running the Fraud wasn't higher. After all, impostor syndrome is widely discussed and seems to be practically everywhere. But on closer examination, it made sense. We found that when the Fraud is present, it appears with the Counterfeit in 100 percent of leaders. They always go hand in hand. While the fear of vulnerability and letting our authentic selves be seen is real for both, a smaller percentage of people take it to the level of the Fraud. But when we do, its head trash will tell us that we don't belong or deserve our current roles or positions. We will constantly be in a state of self-protection, waiting for the other shoe to drop when we are exposed as impostor and losing respect, our reputations, and ultimately our jobs and livelihoods.

Although it's not as common, there's a double whammy for some leaders with the Overachiever joining the Counterfeit in the driver's seat while the Fraud tags along in the passenger seat, throwing out unwelcome directions and detours. When this happens, we convince ourselves that if we stay busy and productive and keep taking on more, we will eventually earn our keep and won't feel like an impostor. But no matter how much we achieve, that fear is still present.

Travis is a highly respected leader in a prominent program within a large university but was feeling stifled. He wanted to take steps more intentionally and confidently to put himself out there and find his next career move, where he felt his gifts would shine and he'd be more fulfilled. But his underlying head trash of not being enough was debilitating. Much of Travis's faulty programming stemmed from the fallout of strict religious teachings when he was growing up. When he was ten years old, he was so excited about getting a good grade on a test that he studied hard for. But he was nervous about it, so his mom prayed for him. Travis happily proclaimed that his hard work paid off only to be scolded by his grandmother, who told him that it wasn't due to his work but due to God and that it was sinful to take credit for God's work.

Around this age, Travis also started to realize he was attracted to boys. But it freaked him out because his religion taught that being gay was a major sin. He tried to do everything to pretend he met what the requirements for what his religion considered "normal," from dating some girls to trying to fumble his way through sports. All along, Travis was running a powerful narrative that he can't be accepted for "this" (that is, being gay) and needs to either fix it or be something other than who he is. He literally thought he would be morally judged and punished by God.

By the time I started working with Travis, he had spent multiple decades hating himself and wishing he weren't gay. He was lonely but had never had a relationship. He had told only a couple of people in his life that he was gay. He told me, "Look, I already have the deck stacked against me as a Black man. I don't need to give them another reason to think I don't belong and something else to hold against me." My heart ached as I listened to Travis fight who he is. He kept thinking that if he achieved more, he would somehow "make up" for his supposedly sinful nature of being gay. But it never worked. He continued to feel like a stranger in his own skin.

Although he already had multiple degrees, Travis felt like he needed more to be fully respected and further his career to prove he was enough. Every time a potential promotion emerged or he found a larger position at another university or organization, he inadvertently sabotaged himself by not following up or even applying in the first place. Even when we did a 360 assessment for him, Travis only picked people to evaluate him who he thought would be hard on him, which would further validate his "not enough" head trash. He kept feeling like he was behind and had missed his chance. But instead of taking steps to find his next role, he would get heads down in trying to be the best at things and take on more to prove himself. This left him no capacity or energy to focus on creating a future where his sparkle could shine.

Travis's upgrade journey mimicked the process for upgrading both the Counterfeit and Overachiever programs. He started with a self-gratitude practice and exercises to increase his self-compassion. Next, Travis interviewed people who know him well to find out what they value about him and the costs of him getting sucked into a mode of trying to prove himself via being productive and his accomplishments. Then he started testing the waters a bit with being a little more vulnerable and showing up more authentically. Eventually, he told a couple of his close friends he was gay. When they didn't think anything of it, Travis's confidence grew. He eventually told one or two trusted colleagues at work and even went out on a few dates. He started questioning if he needed to get a new position or if that was part of him trying to outrun his own demons. Eventually he did start actively pursuing new leadership roles, but he was doing it from a place of confidence and clarity rather than to punish himself or as a desperate effort not to be exposed for his perceived flaws.

Name It and Own It: Upgrading the Fraud

The steps to upgrade the Fraud mirror those to upgrade the Counterfeit. But because of the deep fear of being exposed, another step needs to be taken to dampen the fear-based head trash that tells you you're an impostor.

Own It: The Fraud Expression and Origin Exercise	
Recognize how you express the Fraud in terms of what it sounds like and how you behave.	
What are the biggest areas in which you fear you'll be exposed as an impostor?	
What inner head trash does the Fraud have you say to yourself?	
How do you behave when the Fraud is hijacking you?	
Next, identify the Fraud's origin. (This is a key part of the process to help you see that your brain is usually reacting from past experiences and flawed programming rather than actually responding to the present situation.)	
Identify three to five experiences from the first ten to fifteen years of your life that may have led you to conclude that you aren't enough, you can't show vulnerability, or there's something wrong with your authentic self.	

Once you own where your Fraud program came from, how it shows up in the present day, and how it relates to your other core faulty programs, you can start to challenge it via the upgrade process. Similar to what Travis did, consider starting with exercises to increase your self-compassion, like a self-gratitude practice. At the end of each day, reflect on the following questions:

- What went well for me today?
- What qualities about myself am I grateful for?
- What squiggles, detours, or setbacks am I appreciative of that brought me valuable learning?
- What did I learn about myself?

As you increasingly start to embrace who you authentically are, the next step is to practice leaning into vulnerability more and bringing more of your authentic self forward. When your "I'm an impostor" or "They'll find me out" head trash tries to take over, remind yourself that you are here for a reason. And if you respect the person who hired you or gave you an opportunity, consider that you're actually undermining and devaluing them by not absorbing the belief they have in you. Temporarily borrow their belief in you and see what starts to shift.

The Protector

The Protector		
Fears	**Behaviors**	**Related Faulty Programs**
Other people struggling	Holds back potentially difficult information or feedback. Shoulders others' burdens. Jumps in to fix or save a project when others struggle.	The Martyr The Mime The Control Freak The Overachiever

The final cousin program surprised me as it emerged from our data. Although not as common (only showing up in 10 percent of leaders), the Protector is powerful in keeping us trapped in the Stuckness Zone, elevating our stress, and frequently contributing to burnout. It is rooted in a deep fear of letting other people suffer through struggle. It can show up in thoughts like:

- *I can handle more stress than they can, so better I suffer than they do.*
- *They can't handle this feedback, news, or workload.*
- *I don't want to add anything more to their plates.*
- *I don't want to be the cause of their negative emotions, bad experiences, or struggles.*
- *It's my job to save and protect people from struggle.*
- *I hate seeing people struggle.*

Essentially, when the Protector program is present, we hold ourselves responsible for someone else's experiences or outcomes, including their emotions. When it shares space with the Martyr, we will try to save others from their own struggles and to somehow shoulder other people's burdens for them. This goes beyond simply deprioritizing our needs or feeling like we must do things ourselves. The Protector takes it to another level where we feel like our capacities for stress and struggle are greater than those of others. We feel compelled to take on tasks or perceived burdens of others because we don't think they can handle them, and it makes us feel valued by saving them from struggling.

When the Protector emerges with the Mime, we will tend to hold back difficult feedback or information in an attempt to emotionally protect others. We saw this in chapter 10 with both Rhonda's and Brett's needs to avoid conflict and stabilize situations. Their tendencies were sometimes taken to another level when the Protector was also present. They would hold themselves responsible for protecting people from the perceived emotional stress of conflict, assuming others had the same aversion as they did.

A smaller percentage of leaders running the Protector overcompensate and lean on their Control Freak and Overachiever tendencies, taking on burdens that aren't really theirs to own. For example, when the Control Freak is present, we may shy away from delegating or presenting growth and learning opportunities, or we may try to control conversations to protect people from what we perceive could be risks for greater stress. When the Overachiever is in control, we may think that by us taking on more responsibility, we are proving our value by not only being productive but by not subjecting others to extra work.

Elizabeth leads a region for a midsize, well-established distribution company. She wanted to take her growth-feedback conversations to the next level to truly foster accountability. Specifically, she wanted to be clearer, make more timely difficult decisions, and focus on calling others to greatness rather than saving them. However, as is the case when it comes to adaptive challenges, Elizabeth was quietly working against herself. She was running a powerful combination of the Perfectionist, Overachiever, Mime, and Martyr programs. As we started to look closer at the origin of her faulty programming, we also uncovered the Protector hiding out but profoundly keeping her trapped in the Stuckness Zone.

Elizabeth recalled numerous instances of her parents having pretty significant arguments when she was a young child. Sometimes, she hid in a closet with her older sister and waited for them to stop. Other times, her mom would leave, and Elizabeth would worry if she was ever coming back. This started to form some Mime tendencies and a sense that she would be abandoned. Fast-forward to around age ten. By this point, her siblings were medically fragile with many hospitalizations and required most of her parents' attention. In addition, her father's bipolar disorder worsened, and he was in and out of mental institutions. So Elizabeth was largely left to fend for herself, thus forming her Martyr tendencies of self-reliance.

Around this same time, she got all A's on her report card and was so proud. But her spirits were quickly deflated when she received no response from her parents. That was when her Overachiever and Perfectionist tendencies started to take root. Elizabeth convinced herself that being good wasn't enough. She needed to work extra hard and be perfect in order to be noticed. This eventually formed her head trash beliefs that her value was intimately tied to being perfect and that she had to work extra hard to prove her worth and value. Elizabeth realized that she tolerated being treated poorly in many areas of her life. She thought that others would see how great she is if she simply tried harder.

Elizabeth's Protector program also started to emerge around age ten. Her mom had some behavioral health challenges to the point that Elizabeth felt compelled to cover for her, to protect her. By the time she was a teenager, Elizabeth's parents divorced. Her dad moved many states away for a new job and had an affair before the family could join him. She felt betrayed and wanted to protect her mom from the pain, so Elizabeth didn't see or talk to her dad for another fifteen years.

Elizabeth had a huge aha moment when she realized that she felt abandonment was inevitable but that it was also her duty to save and rescue people. She convinced herself that if she didn't rescue people, they would feel abandoned, and she'd be doing to them what was done to her. Consequently, she went way overboard in trying to help and save employees who were underperforming. She gave them excessive chances before having accountability conversations. When Elizabeth had difficult growth-feedback conversations, she would finesse the message so much to avoid hurting their feelings that she wasn't always clear. Other times, she would do people's jobs for them rather than having them do what they were being paid to do—another way to protect and save them.

As is the case with so many other leaders, instead of her thirty-something self being in the driver's seat, Elizabeth's ten-year-old self was firmly at the wheel and getting in the way of her growth while elevating her frustration and stress. Her upgrade journey was multifaceted. It started with interviewing people to learn what they value about her, uncovering what others experience when she's messed up or failed, and gathering the yuck feedback about what people experience when she's trying to prove her worth and value by taking on more or when she's going overboard to save people. The feedback she received gave her some confidence and the momentum she needed to start to challenge her faulty programs by delegating more, holding back instead of jumping in to take over and save people, and being more clear and direct in feedback conversations—including taking corrective action with HR for habitually underperforming employees. Once Elizabeth stopped trying to save everyone and instead focused on being clear and calling them to greatness, she saw what her teams were capable of doing. Some stepped up greatly, while others were either demoted or let go. Her fulfillment increased, her region's performance got even better, and she was recently promoted.

Name It and Own It: Upgrading the Protector

The steps to upgrade the Protector follow a similar path as those taken to upgrade your other core faulty programs. Of course, that starts with naming and owning where it came from and how it shows up in the present day.

Own It: The Protector Expression and Origin Exercise	
Recognize how you express the Protector in terms of what it sounds like and how you behave.	
Which core faulty program(s) is (are) in the driver's seat for you when the Protector shows up?	
What inner head trash does the Protector have you say to yourself?	
How do you behave when the Protector is hijacking you?	
Next, identify the Protector's origin. (This is a key part of the process to help you see your brain is usually reacting from past experiences and flawed programming rather than actually responding to the present situation.)	
Identify three to five experiences from the first ten to fifteen years of your life that may have led you to conclude that it's your responsibility to save other people from struggles or that you are somehow responsible for their experiences and results.	

Once you own where your Protector program came from, how it shows up in the present, and how it relates to your other core faulty programs, you can start to challenge it via the upgrade process. My suggestion is to go right to the yuck factor. Interview people who know you well to find out what they experience when you withhold information and feedback (Mime tendencies), take over and do everything yourself (Martyr tendencies), take control and try to ensure things go the "right" (your definition of "right") way (Control Freak tendencies), or keep taking on more and saving people rather than asking them to step up or embrace accountability (Overachiever tendencies). The feedback will likely sting but hopefully help you to see that your methods have not been effective. Then develop a strategy for upgrading your main faulty programs, and you will find the Protector letting go as well.

Regardless of which core faulty programs are in the driver's seat, the key to kicking the Protector to the back seat is to regularly ask yourself, "Who is ultimately responsible for this outcome?" If it's the other person, then remember it's not helpful to save someone else from the struggle. Support them; teach them to fish. Don't just give them a fish sandwich.

I realize there is a lot to unpack in this section. Welcome again to being human! We are messy and complex. But once you name which combination of faulty programs tends to hijack you, own how they get in your way of effectively leaning into adaptive change, and at least start the process to challenge and upgrade them, you're ready to start future-proofing leadership within your organization and yourself. The last section of this book will help you do that.

PART 3

FUTURE-PROOFING LEADERSHIP AT ALL LEVELS

CHAPTER 13

Future-Proofing Your Organization's Leaders

Without learning new ways—changing attitudes, values and behaviors—people cannot make the adaptive leap necessary to thrive in the new environment.

—Ronald Heifetz and Marty Linsky, *Leadership on the Line*

Here we are. In part 1, we explored why change is so hard, why the majority of leadership development efforts aren't meeting our current and future needs, the challenges of being human in a VUCA world and how that lands us in the Stuckness Zone, and the critical importance of leveling up human-centered leadership skills to be future-ready. In part 2, we unpacked our findings from analyzing five years of leadership data by exploring the most common adaptive change goals leaders have where they find themselves in the Stuckness Zone and the faulty programs that are quietly working against us, preventing us from making progress on goals and moving well through change even when we're highly motivated to do so.

There's another critical reason why we must do the work now to future-proof leadership. A larger organizational crisis is looming with the leadership pipeline. The 2025 DDI Global Leadership Forecast reports that 71 percent of leaders are reporting significant stress, and 40 percent have considered abandoning leadership roles entirely as a result. They conclude that "the leadership pipeline is not just under severe strain; it's potentially facing a structural breakdown" and that we should have a great sense of urgency to address the stress and support leaders to perform effectively.[40] Even more troubling than current leaders wanting to jump ship is the "conscious un-bossing" of Gen Z. A Belgian study on Gen Z professionals found that 42 percent of Gen Zers don't want to become a manager, with 61 percent thinking the role is too stressful for the rewards that come with it.[41] It's worse in the United Kingdom, where 52 percent of Gen Zers don't want to become a manager, and 69 percent think the role is too stressful.[42]

If current leaders want out and potential future leaders don't want the role, it will be highly problematic. Having effective leaders now and in the future requires that we change how we develop and support them. What we've been doing is not working and has brought us to a critical tipping point. The good news is that it's time to tie everything together to provide a road map you can use to future-proof leadership at both the organizational and individual levels.

From surveying fifteen thousand leaders globally in 2025, Korn Ferry concluded that leadership success today and in the future requires adaptability, collaboration, and authenticity. They also report that the 2025 World's Most Admired Companies say that learning agility and curiosity are their top priorities when hiring for leadership roles.[43] Think about that for a moment. We need leaders to be able to move through adaptive change, play well in the sandbox with other humans, be curious rather than doubling down on judgments (which requires courage), and show up authentically rather than in self-protective mode. But we can't get there by stressing them out or without shifting our approaches.

If we're going to future-proof leadership on all levels, it's important to remember that leadership is not about a title or role. In this VUCA environment, we need to equip *everyone* to show up as a leader to move through the Stuckness Zone, effectively navigate change and disruption, and level up human-centric leadership skills. Remember that most people have not been taught these skills, yet they are the skills needed in this increasingly fast-paced world. Furthermore, we need all employees to develop skills to keep up with where the organization and world are heading. We can't just reserve it for a select group of formal people leaders. At the same time, those who have formal leadership responsibilities need another level of care because of the influence they have over culture and the employee experience. With that said, let's look more pragmatically at what this is actually like in practice.

Critical Leadership Practices for Creating More Human, Future-Ready Workplaces

In our leader interviews, we asked, "If you could challenge leaders everywhere to practice this one behavior that would create more human workplaces and equip everyone to show up as a leader, what would that be?" Some patterns emerged from the data with three key opportunities for leaders.

1. *Build genuine, caring relationships* (38 percent): The most common recommendation leaders have for creating more human, future-ready workplaces is to lead with the heart and focus on building authentic, caring, and supportive relationships. This includes taking the time to invest in relationships, check in on people authentically, and tend to people before jumping to tasks.
2. *Be authentic and vulnerable* (25 percent): A close second is being authentic and embracing vulnerability. Leaders describe this as being real when you're struggling, owning missteps, leaning into discomfort, and humanizing yourself.
3. *Embrace calm* (25 percent): Many leaders describe how critical it is to be self-aware and to lead self-first, which starts with pausing to quiet reactivity. Some describe this as having an active practice for mindfulness and self-awareness. Others describe this as remaining curious and giving themselves and others more grace.

4. *Other leadership practices:* Three additional behaviors were noted by leaders that were not as prevalent but still can make a difference in creating human, future-ready workplaces:

    - *Listen to understand* (10 percent): Many leaders noted the importance of fully listening to others and seeking to understand. We found that listening to understand is an essential part of building caring relationships and being authentic and vulnerable, and it requires the self-awareness that comes with embracing calm as a key leadership superpower.
    - *Lean into difficult conversations* (7 percent): Several leaders stated how important it is to be clear with expectations and communication, have difficult conversations sooner, and be transparent.
    - *Lead in alignment with a clear and compelling purpose* (6 percent): Other leaders noted how critical it is to start with why by identifying and then leading in alignment with a purpose that is both clear and compelling for others.

Their responses continue to support the research and findings that human-centric skills are essential for future-ready leadership, perhaps now more than ever. Once upon a time, these would've been referred to as "soft skills" but are now thankfully being recognized for what they are: *essential* or *power skills.* Yet we can't develop these critical human-centric skills by using outdated, mismatched approaches to development. As our research revealed, and as we unpacked in part 2 of the book, a key aspect of leveling up leadership for the future demands transformational, adaptive development to upgrade our faulty programming. Then we must thoughtfully integrate skills-based development and systems to support human-centric leadership.

What is fascinating to me is that the top three practices that leaders see as important for fostering more human, future-ready workplaces and upskilling leadership across organizations are also some of the most common areas where leaders are struggling and want to improve. For example, one-quarter of the leaders we interviewed believe that being authentic and vulnerable is critical to being future-ready. Yet the most common faulty program holding leaders back is the Counterfeit, leading them to avoid vulnerability and not show up authentically. Additionally, one-quarter of the leaders we interviewed also believe that embracing calm is critical to be future-ready, yet this is challenging for nearly half of leaders with the Control Freak, Overachiever, or Perfectionist faulty programs. In other words, these outdated, self-protective programs impede our ability to be future-ready. We need to take a multifaceted approach to caring for the messiness of being human.

A Three-Pronged Approach to Future-Proofing Leadership

Future-proofing leadership within your organization requires creating an ecosystem that both develops future-ready leaders and consistently supports and reinforces them in leveraging their human-centric skills, leading themselves and others through change, and being effective stewards of the organization's purpose, values, and culture. The most effective way to do that is by taking a three-pronged approach that includes:

1. Individual development
2. Team-based courage-building
3. Systems for sustained impact

I'll dive deeper into what goes into each of these aspects momentarily. But before we get to the details, a great place to start enabling more effective human-centric leadership is by conducting a short audit of your current approach to developing leaders of all levels. See where you have opportunities to better enable your leaders (formal or informal) to be future-ready and thrive in a VUCA world. The following table is an example of how you might categorize your audit and clarify where you may find the greatest benefit in focusing your efforts.

Outdated Leadership Development Strategy	Future-Ready Leadership Development Strategy
Trains selected leaders or "high potentials."	Equips everyone to show up as leaders.
Focuses on behaviors and skills.	Focuses on shifting mindsets.
Strengthens technical leadership.	Strengthens adaptive leadership.
Holds people accountable.	Develops accountable people and teams.
Only focuses on individual development.	Combines individual and team development.
Holds development separate or disconnected from systems.	Development includes system changes to reinforce and support sustainability.
Does not include cohesive strategy or sequencing for how people move through developmental offerings.	Requires that upskilling comes after inner work. Cohesive strategy and clear sequencing for how people move through developmental offerings are developed.
Operates with one-and-done workshops and learning experiences.	Uses multisession, application-based experiences to upgrade faulty programming and build courageous leadership skills.
Largely ignores purpose.	Fosters clarity of purpose.

The point of doing a quick audit is to understand your strengths and see where and why you might be struggling more than you'd like. It's not uncommon to find that a few tweaks to your leadership development strategy and approach can make a huge difference. If you want to go deeper into understanding where your organization is specifically struggling and where to best focus your efforts to be future-ready, take our Future-Ready Leader Assessment (the QR code is at the end of this chapter). You will receive your own Future-Ready Leader Scorecard with recommendations for guiding your next steps in each of the three areas that are key to your organization's leadership effectiveness. Now, let's dig into each area in more detail.

Supporting Individual Development

Bill Adams from the Leadership Circle says that "the process of developing extraordinary leadership is the same process as becoming an extraordinary person." Notice he refers to it as a "process." This is key when we think about how we need to approach development. In our desire for quick fixes, we tend to overuse one-and-done training to be efficient, like offering an annual one-day workshop or leadership summit. Then we later wonder why little was retained or put into practice in a sustainable way. Don't get me wrong. Full-day workshops and leadership summits can be important parts of developing clarity of message, foster connection, and introduce concepts and tools. But they are just one part of the journey, and more is required to be effective in the long term.

Think about the journey of babies learning to walk. They don't go from birth to running overnight. First, they must learn how to hold their heads up. Then they go through various developmental milestones like sitting up, pulling themselves up, walking assisted, and eventually walking independently. As they get closer to actual walking, they fall down countless times. Each time they gain valuable feedback on what did and didn't work. Then they try again, putting this new information into practice. They don't give up and think, *Screw this; it's too hard. I'll just stay crawling for the rest of my life.* They learn a little, put it into practice, see what did and didn't work, adjust their efforts, and try again over many months.

That is how development works. We would laugh at the thought of sending a baby to a one- or two-day off-site intensive to learn to walk. But we do this all the time when it comes to adult development. In the name of efficiency or not really valuing the difference between training (that is, information-based technical skill building) and development (transformational adaptive change), we attempt to cram in as much information as we can in a short period of time. One-and-done rarely works, especially when what is needed is adaptive development. We need to be thinking about creating journeys in which people incrementally shift their mindsets and build skills over time. This means being mindful of how much new information or how many new tools we're asking them to absorb in any given session and then providing clear action steps for applying and practicing between sessions.

As you look at your development strategy, remember that being a future-ready leader requires us to lead with human skills of authenticity, empathy, and adaptivity so we can foster greater connection and collaboration and a sense of mattering (being both significant to others and significantly contributing in service of the organization's purpose). This means that development needs to start with inner-game aspects of leadership and then move to honing the outer-game skills. Following is a summary of the key components for each aspect of future-ready leadership to include in your strategy for individual leadership development and what they look like in practice.

Inner Game (Self-Leadership) Focus: self-awareness, emotional regulation, mindset work	**Outer Game** (Relational and Tactical Leadership) Focus: interpersonal skill set, influence, adaptability
Recognize and upgrade faulty programs. We know and can name what triggers us—gets in our way—and leads to self-protection. We have established clear reset practices to use when our faulty programs hijack us.	***Actively practice empathy and connection.*** We consistently connect with others in meaningful ways to show we care and foster mattering. We promote learning agility and curiosity at all levels.
Practice self-compassion and emotional literacy. We give ourselves grace and can minimize and regulate our head trash. We lean into curiosity with our emotions and can effectively regulate them.	***Give and receive feedback skillfully.*** We actively listen to understand and openly seek and receive feedback at all levels. We skillfully leverage feedback to both recognize and foster growth in others (call others to greatness versus saving them from struggle or fixing them).
Respond versus react when triggered. We actively practice pausing, lean into curiosity, and leverage calm as a leadership superpower.	***Navigate conflict constructively.*** We leverage conflict as a call to creativity to find a win-win and improve relationships and processes; we defuse drama to focus on solutions.
Align behavior with personal values. We actively practice and ground ourselves in our values in order to lean into courage rather than self-protection.	***Foster alignment and clarity.*** We actively seek and provide clarity of direction for all strategies, initiatives, and decisions. We empower others and work to clarify priorities and remove any barriers to innovation.
Leverage a strong ability to reset. We leverage tools and practices to reset and get back up when we experience setbacks so we don't stay stuck.	***Serve as a culture steward.*** We actively live the company purpose and values and leverage them consistently in leading others. We ask strategic questions to hold purpose and value alignment at the same level of importance as results.

I unpack each of these in more detail in the next chapter as they relate to individual development. In the meantime, when you think about what this looks like at the organizational level, first go back to what you're currently doing and ask yourself three important questions:

1. Do our leadership development offerings care for the most common adaptive change goals people have or where leaders get in their own way (yet want to improve)?
2. Do our leadership development offerings care for the inner aspects that are critical for growth and moving through the Stuckness Zone?
3. Are we strengthening our overall leadership bench or only reserving development opportunities for current formal leaders?

Let's start with how you're supporting the adaptive development of your leaders. For example, it's easy to see time management goals and jump to providing productivity classes and tips. Or perhaps you might offer programs and tips for how people can better delegate or have growth-feedback conversations. Those certainly can be helpful. But people with faulty programs at play will be unable to effectively leverage those tools until they do the transformational work to reframe and upgrade their mindsets. Remember that in order for people to change their behaviors, they must first identify the false beliefs they have.

We already know from our data analysis that communication-related improvement goals are the most common, with 74 percent of leaders wanting to grow in this area. But consider who might especially struggle when it comes to communication and how you're supporting people to grow in this area. For example:

- One hundred percent of people running the Mime program are trying to get better at some aspect of communication.
- Ninety-three percent of people running the People-Pleaser program are trying to get better at some aspect of communication.
- Eighty-six percent of people running the Counterfeit program are trying to get better at some aspect of communication.

Another way to think about this is that if you have leaders who are struggling with or wanting to level up their communication skills, there's a high probability they are running one or more programs leading them to silence themselves, people-please, or avoid vulnerability. So even without having each individual leader identify their faulty programming, this data provides some helpful direction as to what inner aspects you need to include as part of your development efforts for leaders to be more effective at having growth-feedback conversations, fostering accountability, or speaking up with greater confidence. Or if we consider that nearly half of leaders want to shift and improve their mindsets—meaning they likely struggle with emotional regulation, tend to judge themselves and others harshly rather than lead with empathy, or don't listen effectively—there's a good chance they probably need to upgrade their faulty programming that is leading them to try to control things or prove their value by overachieving before they're going to be a more emotionally intelligent, growth-mindset-oriented leader.

Next, it's important to examine who gets access to development and why. Do only formal leaders get access to development? It's not uncommon for this to be the case with organizations citing budgetary constraints or needing to focus on tactical skills with nonleadership employees. Investment in humans is critical but often slighted in favor of investing in technology or operations and deemed as somehow nonessential until there is a crisis of engagement, retention, or worse. Of course, there is an elevated need to level up current formal leaders due to the level of influence and impact of their roles on people, culture, and business results. But they will struggle more than they need to as they try to lead others through change who are also trapped in the Stuckness Zone. Investing in developing people at all levels to better navigate the change and disruption of a VUCA world is a win for everyone. And it might help people shift from "conscious un-bossing" to seeing the value of moving into formal leadership roles.

One way to support everyone to show up as a more courageous future-ready leader is using the insights and resources in part 2 of this book to help them name and own their faulty programs and start to challenge them via the upgrade process to move through the Stuckness Zone. I say "start" intentionally. Your leaders, formal and informal, can get pretty far leveraging the exercises I've provided, and it will make a significant positive difference. That's why I wanted to include them so I'm not opening a can of worms and then leaving people stuck. However, keep in mind that because we're wired for self-protection, at some point your leaders will likely need some external support (for example, high-quality, adaptive-development-focused coaching) to fully get out of the Stuckness Zone. The other thing that can be helpful is to be deliberate about having a parallel process in place where leaders are doing their individual development work in conjunction with team-based courage-building work, which is the second aspect of future-proofing leadership at the organizational level.

Supporting Team-Based Courage-Building

In reality, transformation happens within relationships; it's not a solo journey. This is why including peer-based development is an important part for both individual and organizational effectiveness. However, to develop and enable people to thrive amid change and disruption, it's essential to nurture a fearless environment where psychological safety is high. Psychological safety is defined as "the belief that the work environment is safe for interpersonal risk taking . . . It is present when colleagues trust and respect each other and feel able—even obligated—to be candid."[44] If you think about it, most people will find it nearly impossible to lean into vulnerability to do inner work if they don't feel safe doing so.

Perhaps an even more compelling reason to develop and foster courage-building at the team level is that it's critical to performance. Google conducted Project Aristotle, a five-year research study of 180 teams. They aimed to uncover the secret of high-performing teams. What they learned is that the secret was less about who was on the team and more about *how the team worked together*. They identified five key attributes of their highest-performing teams:[45]

- Psychological safety
- Dependability
- Structure and clarity
- Meaning
- Impact

Above all, they determined that psychological safety is the most critical factor in team success. It serves as an enabler for the other four attributes when it is high and a gatekeeper when it is low. Additionally, their findings on meaning and impact reflect the importance of mattering that was discussed in chapter 3. So creating and nurturing a fearless environment for teams creates a safe container for people to level up their human-centric leadership skills while also fostering high performance.

There's another benefit as well. When teams lean on common tools and language to boost their individual and collective effectiveness and show up more courageously, they are able to reset quicker and support one another when their faulty programs and head trash inevitably try to hijack them. Following is a summary of the two key dimensions that are essential to team-based courage-building and leveling up how teams work together so they can have high performances and effectiveness, along with what they look like in practice.

Team Culture and Psychological Safety Focus: shared language, vulnerability, trust, mattering	**Leveraging Team Strengths and Diversity** Focus: collective intelligence, shared vision and group norms, clarity, and alignment
Use common language and tools to reset and realign. We actively use shared language and tools to quickly align, reset when challenges arise, and lean into important and difficult discussions and decisions.	***Understand each other's working styles and strengths.*** We actively leverage shared tools to understand how each of us prefers to work and communicate. We intentionally honor varying styles and create space for everyone to meaningfully contribute.
Model vulnerability, trust, and accountability. We lean into vulnerability, practice staying curious, and actively practice high-trust behaviors even when it's hard. We embrace accountability on both the individual and team levels.	***Cocreate shared group norms.*** We establish clear behavioral guideposts aligned with our purposes and values and group norms for how we interact. We actively use both to ground us, guide us, and reset when needed.
Cultivate inclusivity and mattering. We actively practice seeing one another and listening to understand. We check in as human beings first, affirm one another's contributions, and challenge one another to grow.	***Foster alignment and clarity.*** We actively leverage our company purposes and values to guide our priorities. We practice truth with care and speak up with candor and clarity, even when it's uncomfortable.

You may wonder what is entailed in enabling these courage-building aspects within your teams. While it can look different for each team and organization, there are common core elements in design and practice that we have found to be most effective. First, we always do this work via multiple sessions (anywhere from four to ten sessions, depending on the focus and group's goals) spaced out at two- to four-week intervals. Between each session, leaders are given tangible application exercises to put into practice. Each program is designed so that the sessions build on each other, starting with key self-awareness exercises and inner-game work and then moving to outer-game work. We also build in postprogram sustainability with 30-, 60-, 90-, and 120-day postprogram email reinforcements and a leader checklist on how to keep the concepts alive on a daily basis with the team. Additionally, it is common for us to do a check-in session approximately four to six months later to see what is and isn't working and help the team reset when needed. For leadership teams, it's not uncommon to build a follow-up cadence of regrouping as part of their quarterly off-site meetings to nurture ongoing support.

That is the general structure of team-based courage-building work. Here are some critical considerations necessary for a successful experience along the way and nurturing transformational development on a team level.

- *Always start with container-building:* This is critical for creating a space of psychological safety and creating shared norms and commitments on how the team will approach their work together. Do not skip this part! Something that Brené Brown said during day one of our 2019 Dare to Lead facilitator certification stuck with me and explains why this can't be overlooked. She said, "No good container means that no good work can happen—period." You will need to spend at least thirty minutes of your first session for this. People need to provide their input on things like:

    - What a successful experience looks like.
    - What they need for themselves to be able to show up and fully engage in the work.

    - Naming what will get in their way of being able to show up and fully engage in the work.
    - What support they need (and specifically what it looks like) from each other and/or their leader to lean into the work.
    - Naming the group gatekeeping behaviors to be aware of. These are the collective behaviors teams tend to default to when they're trying to control or avoid the vulnerability in the room.

  Once you've set the container, it's important to summarize it and briefly revisit it at subsequent sessions to reground everyone in their shared commitments.

- *Start each session checking in as humans and setting intentions:* Engaging in courage-building work requires intentionality. Most teams are coming to a session still immersed in their previous meeting or conversation and are in a task or doing mode. I always like to start with some sort of check-in. My favorites are doing a two-word check-in on how you're feeling today or letting people know whether you're above or below the line. Some people also use a weather forecast metaphor for checking in. This practice is important to level-set and get a temperature check of where people are as this will impact the session. By the way, this is a great practice to use at any team meeting to see people as humans before jumping to tasks.

  Once everyone checks in, we leverage one of the Dare to Lead tools of permission slips. Everyone takes two minutes to capture on a sticky note or piece of paper what they want to give themselves permission to do, feel, or let go of during the session so that they can lean in and get the most out of the time. Each person shares one of their permissions to help set the container for that session. It's basically a way of intention setting before revisiting the shared commitments.

- *Create space for self-awareness and self-reflection:* We tend to have such a bias for action that we discount how critical self-awareness and self-reflection are, even in a group setting. In each session, regardless of the topic at hand, we invite people to self-reflect first and then move into discussion. For people who are internal processors, this is essential for them to absorb and meaningfully contribute. It also creates a space for people to be more intentional and insightful as they move to discussion.

- *Focus on one or two concepts, tools, or skills at a time:* Our brains can only hold so much. After tending to the container and shared agreements for the group, I like to allow time to process learning and experiences from putting the previous session into practice before introducing anything new. Then it's key to be mindful of how much new content you introduce in each session. That depends on the complexity of the concept, tool, or skill. Set people up for success so they can practice and integrate it between sessions. If it's too much, they'll be on cognitive overload and likely won't do anything.

- *Lean into facilitation over training:* Too often we confuse development with training and use a training approach when what is needed more is facilitation, especially when we want to level up human-centric leadership skills that are messy. Training has its place. It is focused on an expert trainer imparting specific knowledge to participants when there are specific objectives to be met. Facilitation, on the other hand, is a more collaborative approach. It is focused on creating an enabling environment where people can process, discover, and think as they generate new knowledge within the group. It is critical when asking people to engage in adaptive development work in which mindsets need to shift.

- *Include a meaningful closing for each session:* Make sure there is space at the end of each session for people to synthesize their experiences.

This space serves as a catalyst for how they will put the concepts and tools into practice outside of the session. We have a handful of ways we use to close sessions or entire programs. We choose our closing based on the best fit for the group. One simple approach that many find doable and helpful is to have people reflect after each session using *what*, *so what*, and *now what* as prompts.

- *"What did I learn today?"* Have them briefly capture their insights.
- *"So what?"* Have them capture how what they learned applies to them, their work, or their team.
- *"Now what?"* Have them capture what actions they will take based on the session.

These may seem like no-brainers as you read them. If so, awesome. It means that you're approaching team-based courage-building work in a way that sets everyone up for success. On the other hand, if you're reading these guidelines and have no idea what the team learning experience is like at your organization, use the prompts as a way to inquire and find out if you need to adjust your approach. If you don't have the resources to facilitate this work internally, use them as a guide as you vet potential external facilitation partners. As with any industry and skill, the quality of facilitators varies greatly.

I know there's a lot in team-based courage-building work, but it's very important and a key to transforming culture and future-proofing leadership. Let's take a short inventory of where we are presently. We covered the components that are essential to team-based courage-building. Then I discussed key considerations to ensure that teams have a successful experience working together. Now it's time to get a bit more granular and unpack what some of the content, tools, and skills are that can be embedded into team-based work.

I'm a firm believer that one size does not fit all when it comes to the messiness of developing humans. That's why we intentionally include many tools and programs in our leadership development tool kit. It allows us to customize experiences that meet teams where they are and most effectively guide them as they progress to where they want to be. My intent in giving you the following information is to help you as you audit and adjust your efforts and perhaps enlighten you about resources you haven't considered that may be helpful. There are also likely other tools and programs I haven't listed or that will emerge after this book is published. I'm specifically including the ones we've consistently used with our clients that have been meaningful and transformative. Some are proprietary to us at Salveo Partners. Others are tools and programs we've chosen to certify our consultants in so we can be stewards of other people's work and benefit our clients. So you could look for your own certified facilitators, trainers, and consultants who also leverage these various tools and programs based on what will meet your needs (or even train people in-house).

From a programmatic perspective, we leverage four key programs with our clients. I've included abbreviations after each as a key for when you get to the summary table with all the tools and programs.

- *Dare to Lead™ (DTL):* This is an empirically based courage-building program based on the research of Brené Brown. It focuses on a collection of four skill sets that are teachable, measurable, and observable. I was fortunate to be part of a select group of facilitators personally trained and certified by Brené in 2019 to facilitate the Dare to Lead™ curriculum. Since that time, over 150,000 people across every continent have completed the courage-building program, and it is used in many high-profile organizations to level up their cultures and leaders. It's now offered through BetterUp and the Center for Daring Leadership. I am honored to continue to be a steward of this work along with many other incredible certified facilitators.

- *Showing Up and Lifting Up (SU/LU):* These are empirically based programs from Jen Marr and Showing Up that equip people on the peer-to-peer and leadership levels to foster a sense of mattering, and they tangibly equip people with the skills of human care and connection. We find it incredibly powerful with every group and a key aspect of helping to heal while so many are struggling and hurting.

The facilitator community for this work is absolutely amazing and ranges from in-house organizational trainers, nonprofit and faith communities, college campuses to support native digitals directly, and even professional sports teams. They host several certification cohorts each year. We are honored to also be stewards of this work.

- *Developing a Leadership Mindset (DALM):* This is our proprietary program designed for intact teams at all levels. Its purpose is to increase psychological safety and improve team effectiveness. It's typically six sessions long and builds from self-awareness to leveling up listening and feedback, mastering conflict, and creating a shared culture and guiding principles road map for each team that helps to remind them that they need to show up and provides clarity for onboarding new team members. I have personally trained a network of licensed facilitators who are equipped to bring this work to organizations.

- *Building a Cohesive Leadership Team (BACLT):* This is our other proprietary program designed for leadership teams. It is designed to either go before or in parallel with DALM. There is a lot of overlapping content by design so that leaders have many of the same tools and language to support and align with their teams. BACLT takes it a step further and focuses on key aspects of organizational health and how leaders are being stewards of their organizations' culture, purpose, and values.

If you want to learn more about our programs, DALM and BACLT are highlighted in greater detail on our website and in *Rehumanizing the Workplace.* In the book, we present case studies of how they have been used to transform workplace culture one team at a time. Besides these core programs, we offer our Courageous Leadership Program (CLP) to the public. This is a condensed version of what we normally offer within organizations to add value and start to explore the various tools and concepts that you might want to dig into more deeply. CLP is a live, two-day, Zoom-based workshop. *Wait, what? I thought you said that's counterproductive because our brains can only hold so much at one time.* I know that thought likely just popped into your head as you read "two-day." But hear me out on this one. We receive countless requests from individuals who want to invest in their own development but may or may not have organizational support. And we have busy leaders who are curious but want to see the work in action before they decide if it's right for their organizations. It's easier to commit to two mostly full days at once than spread it out over time for this reason. We are bridging the gap to help people get started.

To help you get started with your plans for supporting courage-building at the team level, following are key skills, tools, programs, or modules we have found to be most effective for each of the components of team-based courage-building work.

Team Culture and Psychological Safety Focus: shared language, vulnerability, trust, mattering	**Leveraging Team Strengths and Diversity** Focus: collective intelligence, shared vision and group norms, clarity, and alignment
Use common language and tools to reset and realign. • Simple, common frameworks and language so we can pause and catch ourselves when our head trash tries to hijack us. • Shared language from programs like DTL, DALM, or BACLT.	***Understand each other's working styles and strengths.*** • Team WHY.os and Working Genius sessions to understand what motivates and fulfills each person. • Other assessments to understand communication preferences and personality tendencies can include Hogan, Judgment Index, Collective Leadership Circle Profile, Strengths Finder, Predictive Index, Insights Discovery, and Enneagram.
Model vulnerability, trust, and accountability. • Vulnerability-based tools from DTL, DALM, and BACLT. • BRAVING trust model from Brené Brown. • Franklin Covey's trust behaviors. • Moving from drama to accountability. • Checking out our stories to move from reactivity to intentionality and impact.	***Cocreate shared group norms.*** • PSI—Psychological Safety Inventory—to understand current state and cocreate the path forward. • Five Dysfunctions of a Team assessment to understand current state and cocreate the path forward. • Actively use the container-building work to guide team interactions.

Team Culture and Psychological Safety Focus: shared language, vulnerability, trust, mattering	Leveraging Team Strengths and Diversity Focus: collective intelligence, shared vision and group norms, clarity, and alignment
Cultivate inclusivity and mattering. • Level up listening. • Shift from an inward to an outward mind-set. • Leverage meaningful recognition. • SU/LU workshops. • Peer learning circles.	***Foster alignment and clarity.*** • Frameworks to strengthen alignment and clarity with delegation and change. • Ground ourselves in our personal and company values. • Giving and receiving feedback well.

One of our clients comes to mind as a great example of the value of implementing a parallel process in which individual development accompanies team-based courage-building. I'm choosing to share their story because it's not a fairy-tale version of the ideal. They didn't listen to our recommendations at first but reluctantly ended up doing the work they initially fought. Before we got into any of the development work, we clarified and strengthened some of their leadership systems (which I'll detail more in the next section). We helped them to refine their organizational purpose and core values and then established clear guiding principles of leadership and leadership competencies for each level of the organization.

Next, we inched our way into leader development work by first setting the stage with a keynote and follow-up values clarification workshop at their annual leadership summit. During this time, we introduced the concepts of VUCA, the Stuckness Zone, and the need to develop courageous leaders and cultures. This was to provide some initial common language and foundation as the developmental work would unfold over the upcoming months and years. What is funny about this is that a couple of members of the executive team (including the CEO) told me they thought that "this vulnerability stuff is bullshit" and they didn't want us using Brené's term of "armoring up" to describe our self-protective instincts.

There is also a generational divide on this particular executive team. The Gen X and older leaders were the ones fighting the work initially. The millennial leaders embraced it. So the CEO encouraged starting with the millennial leaders, thinking the older leaders (including himself) didn't need it. While that went over about as well as a lead balloon, the millennial executives went first and embraced the opportunity to do their individual and semigroup work. Each of them completed a suite of assessments and then coaching to help them identify and upgrade their faulty programming. We also facilitated small-group work with just the millennial leaders. We introduced some of the exercises from the Dare to Lead and Building a Cohesive Leadership Team programs to help provide them core and common language and tools to get out of their own way and strengthen their team cohesiveness (at least among this subset of the executive team). Unfortunately (and not surprisingly), this started to create a greater divide within the executive team. As the younger leaders started to step into their greatness, the others felt uncomfortable. After many months of this, the other executives finally decided they would also benefit from working on themselves and began their individual developmental journeys. Better late than never, right?

With all the executive team members finally engaged in doing their individual development work to move beyond their ten-year-old selves, they found their executive team meetings becoming more effective. This is primarily because several of the executives were challenging the validity of their faulty programs by showing up differently in those meetings. Additionally, they created a shortcut for each other by announcing when they had "Rosie homework," which became code for them to know each was getting out of their comfort zone and to give one another extra grace. Thankfully, they all viewed it as important and prioritized it. They became more blatant about stating and owning when their thinking wasn't in a good spot by saying when they were "below the line" (one of the core exercises we always use with teams).

A game-changing practice they started using was checking out their stories. They all started regularly saying, "The story I'm telling myself is . . ." and found themselves better able to lean into curiosity than into judgment and frustration.

On more than one occasion, they all shared how valuable it is to have a shared language to cut through the fog and quickly find alignment and understanding. I laughed when the CEO told me during one of our individual coaching sessions, “You’re all around us,” as he referred to them using a new shared language. I inserted a self-deprecating joke, saying something like, “Yeah, I’m that annoying parasite that won’t go away.” But he very clearly corrected me and said, “More like a fine wine that we can’t get enough of.” This is from one of the people who initially said this was bullshit. It made my day to hear that shift in him.

Eventually we reached the point where they all shared their adaptive change goals and faulty programs with each other. This humanized them with each other and fostered even greater understanding of each other. It also helped fill in the gaps from earlier work we did leveraging both the WHY.os Discovery tool and the Six Types of Working Genius assessment to specifically focus on how the executive team worked together and where they had gaps. (I’ll talk more about these in the next chapter.) We also had each executive share signs that their colleagues would know they’re getting hijacked and what they’d like from them if they notice it before they can reset and course correct. It was powerful and started to build real team health, not the false harmony they had experienced for many years. If they only did their individual development work or only tried to do team-based courage-building, it wouldn’t have been as effective. However, combining both accelerated their effectiveness and set the stage for their growth strategy.

As they continued to assess and strengthen their leadership bench across the organization, the executive leaders were better able to take their experiences and support other levels of leaders who were next up to do their individual work. As we facilitated our talent review process with more of their leaders, some concerning patterns emerged. The talent review process is where we use the guiding principles of leadership and leadership practices determined by level to start a leader’s evaluation process. Their leaders complete a survey on how effectively they embody both and key examples of strengths and growth opportunities. Then we convene a small group to build upon that leader’s feedback. During this short, small-group meeting, we ask about the next best role for that person within the organization and what he or she needs to be ready. We also ask about retention risk.

When leaders are being evaluated, they complete a suite of assessments and have debriefs with us so they can better understand themselves. Then we create a final profile for each leader outlining key strengths, opportunities, and recommendations for nurturing their development (including a development plan). This is a key process for individualizing development and using meaningful data to guide succession planning.

What we saw consistently in the Leadership Circle Profile 360 feedback and small-group conversations were comments worrying about the leader's stress and bandwidth and how much more the organization would ask of them. At the same time, the talent team was seeing a lack of interest in people wanting to become formal leaders. We shared our concerns and told them that without changing the mindset around work and leadership, all the efforts they had put into their culture would be in vain. Additionally, it seemed they were getting pulled out of alignment with one of their guiding principles of leadership, which centered on the importance of fostering well-being. They were already starting to see the threat to their leadership pipeline. This further illustrated the need for a collective mindset shift across leadership and to be deliberate about realigning with their guiding principles of leadership.

This client is future-proofing their leaders by shifting the leadership culture bit by bit, a far cry from when they initially dismissed the value of leaning into the messy, human-centric work. We have also trained some of their learning and development team as DALM facilitators so they can nurture team-based work for informal leaders. Now they are building a common language throughout their organization that quickly lowers the threat responses and gets people on the same page. Additionally, they are building the other wraparound systems that are critical for having sustained impact, which is the final aspect of the three-pronged approach.

Systems for Sustained Impact

Individual development and team-based courage-building are only part of the equation. When it comes to any meaningful change, our chances for success significantly increase when there are systems in place to support and reinforce any changes. Furthermore, you can't put a changed person in an unchanged environment and expect things to be different. They're interconnected. Many organizations miss the mark by not being thoughtful and deliberate about leveraging systems that are critical for ongoing sustainability.

To start, make sure your organization has established clear guiding principles of leadership. These are nonnegotiables for all leaders, regardless of level, and they set the tone for your leadership culture. Think of them as leadership mindset practices that are essential to support a consistent experience of the culture you want to create and maintain and for truly living your purpose and values daily. Most organizations have between three and five guiding principles of leadership that include nonnegotiables for leading oneself and teams and being a steward of the organization's culture. Following are a few examples from some of our clients.

- Continuously invests in personal well-being and ongoing development (self).
- Demonstrates a high degree of emotional intelligence (self).
- Shows genuine willingness and commitment to give and receive feedback and engage in ongoing development (self).
- Creates and fosters a respectful environment with the willingness to experiment, fail, and learn with a sense of belonging (others/team).
- Fosters an environment that prioritizes people's well-being so they can show up authentically (others/team).
- Fosters a physically and psychologically safe environment (others/team).
- Models actively living the company's purpose and values and behaves consistently with holding others accountable to living them at the same level as performance and results (organization).
- Leads by example by holding self and others accountable to consistently living the company's desired culture and experience (organization).
- Models the company's desired culture and experience through knowing, growing, and engaging talent and business (organization).

Much like your organization's values, the guiding principles of leadership become an active tool that guides behaviors and helps to reset when people's default instincts try to take over. Of course, it requires having deliberate practices in place to support leaders in actively embodying them and using them as a filter for how they lead. Once you have established your guiding principles of leadership, it's important to clarify (and likely update) the leadership practices you see as essential at each level (including informal leaders) for people to be aligned with your organization's purpose, values, and vision and that effectively contribute to your goals. These serve as the foundation for your leadership culture, guiding how leaders show up on a daily basis and how you evaluate their leadership effectiveness. Every development effort should connect back to your guiding principles of leadership and established leadership practices. And these should be reinforced in your performance and recognition systems as well as leveraged to guide thoughtful succession planning.

When it comes to systems to support sustained impact, we like to think of the systems in two main areas: (1) leadership practices and succession and (2) meeting and communication hygiene. Essentially, you're establishing deliberate practices and ways of operating that consistently reinforce the leadership and overall culture you want to create and nurture for your organization. These systems are critical to support leaders when their ten-year-old selves inevitably try to resurface and leaders fall back on the familiar, comfortable ways of doing things. To help you get started with your plans for creating and leveraging systems that support sustained impact, here are examples of what each aspect of the systems looks like in practice.

Leadership Practices and Succession Focus: formal and informal systems that reinforce growth	Meeting and Communication Hygiene Focus: operationalizing purpose and values
Use guiding principles of leadership and specific leadership practices to guide development. • Embed your leadership nonnegotiables and specific leadership practices you've identified into your annual performance appraisal process. • Anchor all development on your guiding principles of leadership and leadership practices. Be specific on how any program, tool, or project will help them more effectively embody the skills and traits you desire in your leaders.	***Ensure purpose-driven and human-centered meetings.*** • Create standards of practice in which leaders check in on how people are doing both at and outside of work. Check in as humans before moving to tasks and agendas. • Keep the purpose and values at the forefront by asking people to share recent stories in which people were both in and out of alignment with the desired culture, purpose, and values and the resulting impact. • Embrace clear meeting hygiene aligning with the work at hand (versus "meeting stew"), ensuring meetings have a clear purpose and action items that foster a sense of mattering.
Leverage visual reminders of key leadership tools for leaders to reference and reset. • Create a leadership playbook that includes reminders of your guiding principles of leadership and key common tools and language you want leaders to leverage. • Create a visual dashboard of specific leadership tools and when to use them so leaders can quickly refer to them.	***Align recognition and feedback with company purpose and values.*** • Explicitly link all information to how people's actions are aligned with and support living your purpose and values. • Create standards of practice so growth feedback is also framed in terms of how improving in a specific area will foster more alignment with the company's values and/or support people in better aligning with the company's purpose.
Embrace thoughtful succession planning and mentoring. • Leverage a talent review process to formally evaluate leaders so you're using meaningful data to inform succession planning as well as evaluating your overall leadership bench strength. • Implement thoughtful mentoring to support ongoing growth for leaders that is linked to their development plan. Check in with the development plan quarterly and adjust so it's a meaningful, evolving guide.	***Maintain alignment with purpose and values in one-on-one and team meetings.*** • Create standards of practice for how leaders conduct one-on-one meetings so that they are fostering a sense of mattering, ensuring that ongoing two-way feedback is the norm (both recognition and growth), and they frame development and task-specific conversations in terms of the importance to organizational priorities, furthering the purpose, and aligning with the core values. • Create standards of practice for how leaders meet with their teams to maximize effectiveness and support the work at hand. Additionally, ensure leaders engage their teams in culture-focused discussions.

When it comes to systems, something that I keep coming back to is a gem I got from one of my podcast guests, Matt Tait (CEO and cofounder of Decimal, a high-growth bookkeeping company). He said that he views his role as that of chief reminding officer.[46] What he means is that it is critical as leaders (of all levels, not just the actual CEO) that we regularly remind people of our purpose, values, where we're headed, and how their work matters. We can't assume that it's something we only need to do once or that people inherently know. Remember, in our VUCA world, people are distracted, stressed, and likely in the Stuckness Zone, so leveraging systems that support sustained impact surrounds leaders with the reminders and tools they need to stay grounded in human-centric leadership practices and effectively serve as stewards for their organization's culture. And then it's important to measure the impact of your efforts so you know what is serving you well and where you may need to make adjustments.

Measuring the Impact of Your Efforts

I would be remiss if I didn't talk about the importance of measuring your future-proofing leadership efforts. One of the reasons I believe too many organizations undervalue or underresource investing in developing and nurturing future-ready leaders is that they either don't know how to or aren't effectively measuring the impact of their efforts. Or if they do, the evaluation usually stops at the level of assessing participant satisfaction with a program and doesn't assess meaningful change or how the development connects to the organization's priorities. A starting point is to determine what key performance indicators (KPIs) you want to track. Next, decide how you can link leadership effectiveness to those KPIs in a meaningful way.

A 2025 Workday report examined the connection between leadership skills and business impact. The report specifically highlights the business value of human-centric leadership skills in an AI world. Survey respondents state that adaptability, emotional intelligence, and resilience are critical for navigating business disruptions. They also report that human connection, teamwork, and healthy conflict resolution are key during an AI revolution.

Finally, the findings support how critical it is for leaders to leverage the company's purpose and values to support ethical reasoning and decision-making.[47] Some of these human-centric skills can initially appear harder to measure, but they are just as—if not more—critical than other KPIs. So think about how you can measure the human impact of your leaders and how you're equipping them to be future-ready.

Many of our clients leverage our proprietary Thriving Workplace Culture Survey (TWCS) as one aspect of their KPIs to help measure aspects of human-centric leadership. They are able to see how they are doing in terms of both strength and alignment in five key areas of culture: organizational identity (purpose and values alignment); leadership; climate, growth, and development; and work–life integration. One of our clients repeats their TWCS every eighteen months. We've seen scores improve in the areas of focus, and it helps identify any new issues or locations that may need more attention. They heavily rely on their results to track progress of their culture and leadership efforts because they significantly invest in both. As a generous employee-owned company, they view this as critical. Their other KPIs, besides culture survey scores, include safety, ESOP evaluation, and overall financial performance. We started partnering with them in 2018, and they intuitively felt a difference, plus the subsequent surveys indicated an overall positive trend. But it wasn't until 2024 that they finally connected all the dots. The CEO realized that they had been financially flat from 2010 to 2018, but since 2018, they had consistent financial growth (including two record years, even during COVID-19) and increased their stock valuation. They realized that the investment they make in their culture and leadership was paying off and view it as key to their success. Safety is huge for them as well, and they realized that the years they don't do as well from a safety perspective are those when there are challenges with some of the leadership. The link is clear for them.

Instead of specifically measuring culture, another of our clients heavily measures employee engagement using a third-party vendor conducting quarterly pulse surveys. They had all their leaders complete a well-known behavioral and skill-based leadership program. Shortly after implementing this program, they also started providing our inside-out approach to development. Leaders who wanted to do the work to upgrade their faulty program engaged in ten ITC coaching sessions over a six- to eight-month period. Leaders completing ITC coaching did so in parallel with team-based courage-building work in one of two ways. Some were also completing one of our workshop series with other leaders, allowing them to build a structure of support while strengthening team health. Others completed one of our team-based workshop series with their direct reports to help foster greater team effectiveness. All our group development options include postprogram reinforcement and tools to foster sustainability.

This client wanted to see what impact their development efforts were having on some KPIs, specifically employee engagement and turnover. To their surprise, despite spending a significant amount of money on this well-known program, they found that the behavior and skill-based training didn't have any clear impact on engagement or turnover. However, the leaders who completed the inside-out approach to development by upgrading their faulty programs, doing team-based courage-building work, and leveraging the sustainable systems had significantly higher engagement scores and significantly lower turnover rates. Had they not decided to measure the impact in terms of their KPIs, they could have kept investing more money in the wrong area.

When you effectively invest in and nurture each of the three key aspects of future-proofing leadership within your organization, everyone wins. Also remember that it's a journey and more like a marathon than a sprint. The key is to know where to start so the process will be most impactful and build momentum and then create a plan from there. If you want a deeper and more specific understanding of where your organization is and where to best focus your efforts to be future-ready, scan the QR code to complete our Future-Ready Leader Assessment. You will receive a detailed scorecard outlining your strengths and opportunities and tailored recommendations to guide your next steps.

KEY POINTS

- Being a future-ready leader requires us to lead with human skills of authenticity, empathy, and adaptivity so we can foster greater connection and collaboration and a sense of mattering (feeling significant to others and significantly contributing in service of the organization's purpose).
- Leverage a three-pronged approach to future-proofing leadership within your organization that includes individual development, team-based courage-building, and systems for sustained impact.
- One-and-done rarely works when what is needed is adaptive development. Think less about annual one- or two-day leadership workshops and more about a leadership series approach with shorter sessions over time focused on meaningful application between sessions.
- Leverage team-based courage-building in a parallel process with individual development. This helps to foster common language and tools leaders can use to support one another, align, and more quickly reset when their faulty programs try to take over.
- Think of systems that foster sustained impact as providing structure, support, and deliberate practices to help mitigate the messiness of being human. Equip your leaders to not only leverage human-centric skills but to be ongoing stewards of your purposes, values, and culture, and serve as "chief reminding officers" to nurture a sense of mattering for your people.
- Don't forget the importance of measuring the impact of your efforts in a meaningful way. Identify your essential KPIs and determine how you will evaluate and link your efforts so you know if you're on the right track or need to make adjustments.

CHAPTER 14

Future-Proofing Leadership in Yourself

The truth is that our finest moments are most likely to occur when we are feeling deeply uncomfortable . . . For it is only in such moments, propelled by our discomfort, that we are likely to step out of our ruts and start searching for different ways or truer answers.

—M. Scott Peck, *The Road Less Traveled*

One of the reasons I felt compelled to write this book and share the findings from our research is that I consistently see a great deal of shame and self-judgment by leaders who think they should somehow have it all together or be immune from the messiness of being human. So if you've found yourself struggling in many of the same areas as the leaders in our data, please stop the head trash. Instead, congratulate yourself for being human and know that you're not alone. This is a shared human experience.

Future-proofing ourselves as leaders is an ongoing journey. It doesn't matter how long someone has been on this earth, how many degrees and certifications someone has, whether or not they have formal leadership roles, or how long they've been in that role. *No one* is above development. The second we stop working on ourselves or think we've somehow "arrived" and no longer need additional development is the second we stop being effective. I always tell our clients that it is a huge red flag and deal-breaker when they have leaders who think development applies to other people but not themselves, because in a VUCA world, our faulty programs will be activated. The most effective, courageous, future-ready leaders are not immune to being human. They are well aware of their inner operating system. They know what activates it and have the tools and deliberate practices to lean on to reset when that happens. Additionally, because life isn't static, we need to continue learning about ourselves and adding new tools and practices. Selfishly, one reason I love supporting individual leaders, teams, and entire organizations in being future-ready is that it keeps these tools in the forefront for me, making it easier for me to leverage when my humanity gets the best of me.

In the previous chapter, I provided a high-level summary of the key components to individual development. It's now time to dig into each aspect in more detail and provide you with some of the core tools and considerations we use with our clients. My hope is that you can leverage these to level up your effectiveness and lean on these to reset along the way because you will need it; we all do. The late leadership guru Peter Drucker said, "You cannot manage other people unless you manage yourself first." Most leadership training and education is backward; it starts with strategy, finance, operations, and people management. According to Drucker, this approach is like building a house starting with the roof; it starts at the end and misses the beginning.[48]

We need to start tending to our messy inner game before we strengthen and hone our outer-game skills. Below is the high-level summary of the inner- and outer-game aspects to include in your developmental journey. The rest of this chapter goes deeper into each component.

Inner Game (Self-Leadership) Focus: self-awareness, emotional regulation, mindset work	**Outer Game** (Relational and Tactical Leadership) Focus: interpersonal skill set, influence, adaptability
Recognize and upgrade faulty programs. We know and can name what triggers us or gets in our way and leads to self-protection. We have clear practices to use to reset when our faulty programs hijack us.	***Actively practice empathy and connection.*** We consistently connect with others in a meaningful way to show care and foster mattering. We promote learning agility and curiosity at all levels.

Practice self-compassion and emotional literacy. We give ourselves grace and can minimize and regulate our head trash. We lean into curiosity with our emotions and can effectively regulate them.	***Give and receive feedback skillfully.*** We actively and openly seek and receive feedback at all levels. We skillfully leverage feedback to both recognize and foster growth in others (call others to greatness versus saving them from struggle or fixing them).
Respond versus react when triggered. We actively practice pausing and lean into curiosity and leverage calm as a leadership superpower.	***Navigate conflict constructively.*** We leverage conflict as a call to creativity to find a win-win and improve relationships and processes. We defuse drama to focus on solutions.
Align behavior with personal values. We actively practice and ground ourselves in our values to lean into courage rather than self-protection.	***Foster alignment and clarity.*** We actively seek and provide clarity of direction for all strategies, initiatives, and decisions, and we empower others. We work to clarify priorities and remove any barriers to innovation.
Leverage a strong ability to reset. We leverage tools and practices to reset and get back up when we experience setbacks so we don't stay stuck in them.	***Serve as a culture steward.*** We actively live the company purposes and values and leverage them consistently in leading others. We use strategic questions to hold purpose and value alignment at the same level of importance as results.

Recognize and Upgrade Your Faulty Programming

The key starting point to developing yourself as a future-ready leader is identifying and naming which faulty programs make up your IOS. Because this programming powerfully shapes our default thinking and behaviors, it's essential to own how much of our daily experiences are due to the ten-year-old version of ourselves taking over the driver's seat in our lives. If you skipped over taking the Faulty Program Discovery, I encourage you to go back to the end of chapter 4 and complete it. Also, keep in mind that the discovery provides your most likely top three faulty programs. But it's possible to be running more than just three. We did this intentionally to avoid cognitive overload. Additionally, pay close attention to the three cousin programs detailed in chapter 12. If any of these resonate with you, it will be important to include them in your upgrade plan.

Once you name which faulty programs you are running, you can then start the upgrade process by owning them (understanding more about their origins and how they show up for you in the present day). Don't skip over that part; it is key to how you design your upgrade journey. Then challenge them by using the exercises provided for each faulty program in part 2 of the book and the additional resource page provided for each program. It's also helpful to remember that upgrading your faulty programming requires getting out of your comfort zone. The metaphor I always use with our clients that helps them level-set their expectations is that of a swimming pool. You want to think about easing into the zero-slope shallow end of the pool and gradually going deeper, not jump into deep water before you've had a swimming lesson and panic. In other words, start slowly with a reasonable amount of discomfort, and gradually go further as your confidence and tolerance for discomfort grow.

Upgrading and moving beyond these faulty programs requires courage and intentional, vulnerability-based work. Remind yourself over and over that this is a journey, a marathon and not a sprint. My experience is that it takes most people somewhere between six and eight months of intentional work to complete the initial upgrade and make significant progress toward their adaptive change goals; some may take longer. But I've rarely seen people complete their upgrade in fewer than six months. Yes, the initial upgrade process will take a while and be messy. But once you've done that hard work, it will be easier to reset and do mini-upgrades in the future. So use the exercises and resources included with each faulty program to guide you through your upgrade process. You will get pretty far just using those. And if you get stuck, know that is normal and it's not because there is something wrong with you. Remember that we are wired for self-protection, so most people at some point need some external support (for example, coaching or peer group development) to fully complete their upgrades.

As I've shared in previous chapters, my default wiring is shaped by five of the faulty programs: Counterfeit, Overachiever, Martyr, Perfectionist, and People-Pleaser. I'm constantly working on myself and use many of the tools I've outlined here to reset because they work. I regularly receive my own coaching and have specifically gone through the ITC coaching process multiple times. Each time, new limiting assumptions emerge that connect back to one or more of my core faulty programs. I've mostly retired the Counterfeit and Perfectionist programs. I've gotten much better at regulating the Martyr and People-Pleaser programs, but I still occasionally need to use the tools to ground myself when they try to creep back in and take control. My ongoing kryptonite is the Overachiever and probably always will be—with an important caveat. I no longer believe my value depends on my accomplishments or how productive I am. That part is long gone. But the wiring of taking on too much runs deep and is a constant work in progress. So I regularly talk about it with my team, fess up when I've mismanaged my calendar and capacity, and have created a support network around me. It's the only way for me to keep that one in the back seat because it's a determined little sucker for me!

My point of sharing this is to illustrate that we are all works in progress; this is a lifelong journey. Just because I research, teach, facilitate, and coach using these concepts doesn't mean I'm immune to the messiness of being human. Run far, far away from anyone who pretends to be. And even when you think you've mostly retired one or more of your faulty programs, new variables and VUCA-ness will emerge and invite you to revisit both your inner and outer game of leadership. With that being said, let me give you a gift my first ITC coach, Barbara Sanderson, gave to me, and it has stuck with me and helped thousands of our clients.

> Remember to embrace the AFOG:
>
> **A**nother **F*****ing **O**pportunity for **G**rowth

I kid you not. Back in the day, our COO had rubber bracelets made for the leadership team with "AFOG" printed on them to serve as a reminder. We'd take a deep breath, put our hands up to the side like we're about to say a yogic chant, and say, "Embrace the AFOG" whenever we were faced with discomfort. This is also a great tool to lean on as you practice self-compassion and emotional literacy.

Practice Self-Compassion and Emotional Literacy

If part of the common human experience is to be hijacked by our faulty programs and corresponding head trash, and we're all running around to some extent, trying to hide our flaws and inadequacies, then wouldn't it be easier if we stopped fighting ourselves and just did the work to accept ourselves? There is tremendous value in building a practice of self-compassion. In fact, thousands of research studies show that our lives radically change for the better when we learn how to practice self-compassion. People who are more self-compassionate tend to be:[49]

- Happier, more hopeful, and more optimistic.
- More satisfied with their lives and grateful for what they have.
- Less anxious, depressed, stressed, and fearful.
- Less likely to contemplate suicide or abuse drugs and alcohol.
- Wiser and more emotionally intelligent and able to regulate their negative emotions more effectively.
- More positive about their body image and less likely to develop eating disorders.
- More likely to engage in helpful behaviors like exercise, eating well, and seeing a doctor regularly.
- Physically healthier; they sleep better, get fewer colds, and have stronger immune systems.
- More motivated, conscientious, and able to take more responsibility for themselves.
- More resilient when faced with life challenges.
- In possession of more grit and determination to reach their goals.
- In possession of closer and more functional relationships.
- More forgiving, empathetic, and able to take others' perspectives.

Who wouldn't want to experience all these benefits? And if a key part of leadership is maximizing our positive impacts on others, it's evident that self-compassion is a critical part of that equation. Let's look at it a little more closely.

When a friend or colleague is struggling, think about how you typically respond. My guess is it's usually with some sort of empathy or compassion and asking what they need. But what happens when *you* struggle? We don't typically treat ourselves with the same degree of compassion. Instead, we are more likely to judge ourselves, jump to problem-solving, or simply freak out. Look at how you treat your closest friends in times of struggle—your tone of voice, the words you use, your gestures, and your posture. Then look at the difference in how you treat yourself. We need to learn to talk to ourselves like we would talk to someone we love.

Kristen Neff's research in this space has been groundbreaking. It's not just about being kinder to ourselves; kindness is not enough. She describes three aspects of self-compassion:[49]

1. *Mindfulness.* This is the foundation of self-compassion and is our ability to turn toward discomfort and acknowledge its presence. It is important because the default mode of our brain creates our sense of self, projects that self into the past or future, and scans for problems. So rather than being present with what is, we get lost in worry and regret. We have to be present to know that we're struggling; the intentional focus of mindfulness deactivates the default mode so we can be present with our pain as we're feeling it instead of getting caught up in stories.
2. *Common humanity.* This is what differentiates self-compassion from self-pity. The word *compassion* means "to suffer with." So connectedness is inherent to compassion. When we turn compassion inward, we acknowledge that all humans are imperfect. Unfortunately, more often than not, we fall into a trap of thinking and assuming things should always go well and that there is something wrong when they don't. Then we end up beating ourselves up and feeling alone and isolated. But when we remember that pain is part of a shared human experience, we can escape the hole of self-pity. How we treat ourselves affects our interactions with others.

3. *Kindness.* This is the motivational core of self-compassion and is the desire to alleviate suffering. We experience it with our impulse to help. Turned inward, it's having a warm, friendly, and supportive attitude toward ourselves as we wade in the messy middle of life. Too often we do the opposite; we beat ourselves up when we struggle or realize we've made a mistake. But we can't be perfect, and our lives will inevitably involve struggle. When we can respond with benevolence and good will to our pain, we can generate feelings of love and care that make a positive difference.

When we practice self-compassion, we have a stable sense of self-worth, which leads us to treat others better as well. And while we're talking about embracing our imperfect selves, one myth that I think is important to squelch here is that self-compassion equates to complacency. We can accept who we are at this moment and believe we are enough as is *and* be working to become a better version of ourselves. Both can be true at the same time. In fact, if we are stuck in a pit of self-loathing, any changes we try to make become more fear-based and aren't likely to last. In an interview with Tim Ferris, Brené Brown put it well when she said, "I don't think you can truly change for the better—in a lasting, meaningful way—unless it is driven by self-acceptance."[50]

If we want to become stronger, better versions of ourselves, we need to do it from a place of self-compassion and self-acceptance. I have to constantly work on this because I can be pretty ruthless when it comes to beating up on myself, and I know I'm not alone. A great practice to include as part of nurturing self-compassion is identifying and replacing your head trash (see the examples for each faulty program in part 2 of the book). The next aspect is acknowledging that one thing that activates our faulty programs and head trash is our emotional reactivity.

As human beings, we are emotional creatures, even though we may like to think otherwise. Brené Brown put it well in her book *Atlas of the Heart* when she wrote, "We like to think we are rational beings who occasionally have an emotion and flick it away and carry on being rational. But rather, we are emotional, feeling beings who, on rare occasions, think."[50] The problem is that most of us can only identify three main emotions: happy, mad, and sad. Not having nuanced language to describe our emotions impedes our ability to move through it. That's why leveraging tools like a Feelings Wheel or the How We Feel app can be powerful. How We Feel is a free app from Mark Bracket's groundbreaking work with Yale's Center for Emotional Intelligence. It helps expand your emotional literacy, giving you more accurate language to name the emotions you're experiencing.

Having a robust emotional vocabulary is also important when we move into the outer game of leadership and can support us in being more effective with feedback and conflict. Additionally, expanding our emotional literacy and emotional intelligence is a key aspect of being able to move from reactivity to responding with intentionality. We have to recognize that we're triggered and having an emotional response before we can name and regulate it.

Respond Versus React When Triggered

Regardless of which faulty programs are present, understanding and recognizing what triggers or activates them enables us to act with greater intention and calm rather than reactivity. We like to anchor this work on the concept of the Frame,[51] the lens through which we view the world that influences the choices we make and actions we take.

The Frame

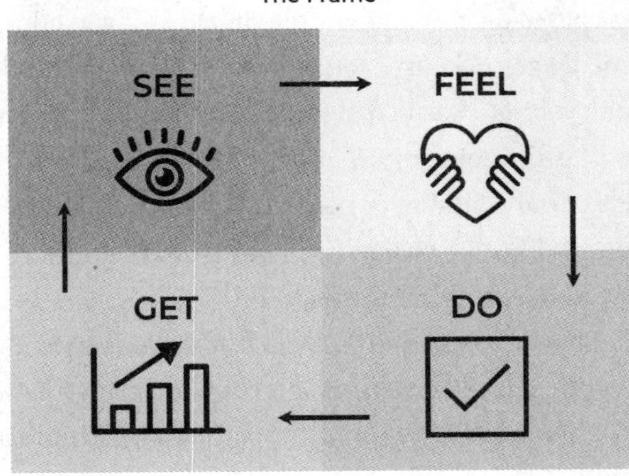

How we choose to *see* a person, ourselves, or a situation (that is, our inner narrative) influences how we feel about it and ultimately what we *do*. What we *do* gets us a result that we usually use to reinforce how we *see* it. Here's the example we always use: Let's say you're going for a walk. You look over in some nearby woods and *see* an angry-looking tiger. How are you probably going to feel? If you're like most people to whom we ask this question, you probably instinctively said, "Scared." And if you're scared, what are you likely going to do? Again, if you're like most people we asked, you probably instinctively said, "Run." That will get you a pretty predictable, physiological fight-or-flight response that will reinforce your *see* of averting a near-death experience. And now you'll probably have a nice dramatic story to tell at social gatherings for months, or even years, to come.

Now let's say you're going for a walk. You look over at the same nearby woods, but you don't see a tiger. This time you see a cardboard cutout of Tony the Tiger, the Frosted Flakes mascot. How are you likely going to feel? If you're like most people to whom we ask this question, you probably didn't have a quick answer. Perhaps you said, "Amused" or "Confused" or "Hungry" or "Grrrrreat!" And with those guiding your *do*, you probably didn't say you'd run. Perhaps you'd keep walking. Or perhaps you'd go up and take a selfie with it. Regardless, you're not going to have that same fight-or-flight response. You'll likely have a much less dramatic and significant result that you may never mention to anyone.

The point of these examples is that, in either case, your actions make complete sense based on how you saw the situation. If you honestly thought your life was in danger, of course you're going to protect yourself and run. If you didn't think your life was in danger, it would be a little odd to run. If we perceive a threat, we're going to self-protect. Our behaviors are the outward manifestations of our thinking or how we *see* things. If we want to behave differently and have lasting change, we need to do the work to rewrite our inner narrative and how we *see* things.

One of the best ways to do that is to build our pause muscle. Kevin Cashman describes the "pause principle" as something that is universal and inherent in humans. He says it "is the conscious, intentional process of stepping back, within ourselves and outside of ourselves, to lead forward with greater authenticity, purpose and contribution."[52] In our VUCA world, this becomes even more important. Cashman suggests that we need to step back to find clarity in order to step forward to be able to deal with complexity. It seems counterintuitive, but pausing helps us to regain our balance and feel grounded and centered. Machines may be able to keep going and going. However, humans need to rest and regenerate. We need to shift from doing more to *reflecting* more; pausing powers performance.

As we strengthen our ability to pause, we are able to move to a place of owning and caring for ourselves when our faulty programming and head trash try to take over. Another core exercise we use to help strengthen the *see* part of the Frame is based on *The 15 Commitments of Conscious Leadership*[53] and what we refer to as "the choice line." How we *see* things is fundamentally different depending on whether we are "above the line" or "below the line." When we are above the line, we tend to be more open, curious, collaborative, empathetic, resilient, and energetic. As a result, we are more committed to learning. But when we're below the line, we tend to be judgmental, defensive, closed off, guarded, pessimistic, and sometimes apathetic. As a result, we tend to be committed to being right. When we're committed to being right, we cannot show up authentically or leverage human-centric leadership skills.

One of the simplest but most impactful exercises we've leveraged for decades on the individual and collective level is walking through self-reflection questions to help people identify how they show up and know whether they are above the line or below the line. Use the following questions to walk yourself through this exercise.

- How do you know when you're above the line? (Identify your mindset, emotions, and behaviors.)
- How do you know when you're below the line? (Identify your mindset, emotions, and behaviors.)
- What are some common triggers that tend to bring you below the line? (List circumstances, situations, environments, or people.)

- When you recognize you're below the line or know you have a high probability of encountering a trigger, what are some things that can act like a trampoline to provide an immediate reset in the moment and spring you back above the line? (For example, do you find yourself going for a short walk, listening to a favorite or motivational song, watching a funny video clip, reading an inspirational quote, looking at pictures of loved ones, getting out in nature, or simply taking a few deep breaths and repeating personal mantras?)
- How do you view others (that is, what are the assumptions or stories you create) when you're above the line, and how does that shift when you're below the line?

You will see that the differences in your experiences and impact largely depend on your mindset. I'll share with you what I always share with our clients. Going below the line is not a bad thing; it's a *human* thing. Too often we convince ourselves that we're supposed to always have it together in order to effectively lead others; we must always be above the line. But that's not realistic. A key difference between people who are able to show up as courageous, future-ready leaders in their lives and those who leave a swirl of collateral damage around them is that they are keenly aware of where they are in relation to the choice line and tend to it when they're below the line. It's really that simple.

On days when I'm below the line, I feel like everything is in slow motion. I reread text messages, emails, and Slack messages multiple times before I send them. I find myself exercising my pause muscle constantly. And perhaps most helpful is that I call in reinforcements from my team. This exercise is also a key part of team-based courage-building development. From a team perspective, it starts to give people a common language. We encourage people to check in at the start of their day, meetings, or huddles with a quick pulse of where everyone is in relation to the choice line. Some teams even use quick hand signals—thumbs up for above the line, thumbs down for below the line, or a flat hand for hovering at the line.

Most important, it's critical to communicate when we're below the line because, let's admit it, there will be days when there isn't a trampoline in the universe large enough to bring us back above the line. Here's why it's so critical to recognize, own, and communicate when we're on the struggle bus. You see, if I'm below the line but don't say anything, my team will experience my faulty-program-hijacked self that is more task-focused, intense, and less communicative than normal. Most certainly, their brains will fill in the space with assumptions, worries, and a bunch of other nonsense that could've been avoided if I simply spoke up and shared where I'm at. By me sharing that I'm below the line, they don't have to make up a story.

Now, sharing when we're stuck below the line does not give us a free pass to be a jerk to others. It does, however, let others know this may be a day to give us more space or not go to us with something requiring our best thinking. It also gives team members a nonthreatening way to check in with each other and be more intentional about owning their inner narratives.

There are many other tools we can leverage to help us quiet our reactive instincts, allowing us to pause and proceed with greater intentionality and impact. But hopefully, this gives you a tangible place to start. Like anything, the more you practice, the easier it will become. And even so, you will screw up. The key is recognizing it, owning it, and then circling back to clean up our messes when our ten-year-old selves hijack us.

Despite using the choice line exercise and language for over twenty years, I'm still a flawed human being. Many months ago, I was having one of those days when everything that could go wrong from a technological standpoint did. I was so far below the line that I couldn't see straight and was not fit for human consumption. I was in the middle of trying to problem-solve when my son, Peyton, opened my office door without knocking or checking (which he's supposed to do when I'm working) and came in talking about wanting some game on his phone. I'm not a yeller, but in a pretty short and frustrated tone, I said something like, "Good God, Peyton, not now! I'm in technology hell and can't deal with this right now."

As he put his head down and left my office, I went into a good ten-minute shame spiral. *I should know better. I'm a crappy mom. How am I going to clean this up? But what the hell was he thinking?* Because I know how our brains work, especially during our key developmental years, I knew it would leave a mark. Eventually, I took a few deep breaths and walked out into our loft area to clean up my mess. I apologized to Peyton and let him know that I wasn't frustrated with him and was just having a really frustrating day. He thanked me and said he was sorry my day was crappy, and we hugged.

A vice president at a client's business shared how impactful having this language and tool has been for her. Mary was having a frustrating day. Luckily, she had built a routine of reflecting either on her way home or when she gets home. Specifically, she reflects on what went well and what she wanted to do differently. She didn't like how she interacted with one of the directors on her team. Mary didn't feel that she was overly rude but knew she wasn't as present and collaborative as she would normally like to be. So the next day, she found that director and said, "I just want to apologize because I realize

I was really below the line yesterday and didn't show up as the best version of myself." Her director seemed a little surprised. She told Mary it wasn't that bad but appreciated her circling back with her.

Too often when we don't show up well, we move on and hope it will be forgotten. But it leaves a mark and can become the proverbial elephant in the room. Courageous leaders recognize their missteps, own them, and make them right. More often than not, it increases trust and enhances their effectiveness. And owning our humanness gives other people permission to do the same. Remember that most people want realness and authenticity over polish and perfection any day of the week. When we learn to pause, lean into curiosity, and leverage calm as our leadership superpower, everyone benefits. A key way to help us to stay calm and courageous is to ground ourselves in our values.

Align Your Behavior with Your Personal Values

Courageous, future-ready leaders actively practice and ground themselves in their values to mitigate self-protective instincts. I like to refer to this as clarifying and leveraging our lighthouse. Think about what a lighthouse does. It cuts through the fog and provides clarity and direction to guide ships even in the most tumultuous of waters. For us, our lighthouse consists of knowing our purpose or our "WHY" operating system and actively leveraging our values to guide our behaviors. When we know what we believe, what makes us tick, and our core values that give us the strength to navigate our VUCA world, and when we show up as the best versions of ourselves, it's a game changer.

In his best-selling book *Start with Why*, Simon Sinek asserts the importance of clarifying and anchoring our work and life on a higher purpose. He states that great leaders are able to inspire people to act by providing a sense of purpose or belonging; they create a following of people who act for the good of the whole because they *want* to, not because they've been manipulated using fear, peer pressure, or incentives. Great leaders start with WHY.[54]

Simon uses the Golden Circle to provide a framework for inspiring action. It starts from the inside out with WHY we do what we do.

- WHY is our purpose, cause, or belief about our contributions to impact and serve others.
- HOW includes our core values and is the process we use or actions we take to bring our WHY to life. It is only through the discipline of HOW and being true to our core values to guide every decision we make that we can realize and live our WHY. The HOW enables the WHY. They go hand in hand.
- WHAT is simply what we do and what people can count on us to deliver.

Dr. Gary Sanchez is the founder of the WHY Institute and a pioneer in this space. Many years ago, he hired Simon Sinek as his coach because he wanted to find his WHY. Over many months, Gary interviewed people in his life to try to understand his contributions and impact. Then Gary started replicating this process with others to help them find their WHY. At some point, he thought, *There has got to be a better way to help people find their WHY!* This is when the WHY Institute was born. Gary created the world's first WHY discovery tool. Over time, it expanded to also help identify people's HOW and WHAT—or our full WHY operating system, the WHY.os. The WHY.os Discovery tool is a key first step in self-awareness and something we have found impactful to leverage on our team and with our clients. In a few short minutes, it gives clear language for us to use about what makes us tick and how to talk to one another. You can certainly do the work to clarify your own Golden Circle the old-fashioned way, but I'm a fan of shortcuts.

I liken the WHY.os to the beacon of light coming from the lighthouse that guides the way and tells us where to go. But it needs a solid base. The base of the lighthouse is your core values in active practice. There's a great list of core values in the book *Dare to Lead* as well as on brenebrown.com that you can use to help you identify your top two core values. As you look at the value words, it's important to remember that your core values are not who you wish you were or aspire to be. They are who you authentically are, specifically when you're at your best, and something you lean on to give you the courage and strength to move through challenges.

Then comes the essential part so you can actually practice your values. Identify the behavioral guideposts for each core value; these are the behaviors that tell you if you're in alignment or out of alignment with that value. I like to create a summary grid that I keep hanging by my computer and as a picture on my phone so I can quickly reference it to ground myself when I need to lean on my courage.

When you clarify your lighthouse, it becomes easier to set boundaries, advocate for yourself, and know how you need to show up so you can be in integrity and feel proud of yourself. Our purpose and values are an active force to ground us, making it a little easier to lean into the inherent discomfort the VUCA world brings and to help keep our ten-year-old selves in the back seat.

Another key aspect of being able to align your behavior with your values is being clear and intentional about who you are at your best. Since the core of showing up as a leader is becoming the best version of yourself, one of the exercises I like to leverage is called "Ingredients to Be My Best." We ask people to think about who they are when they're at their best and what the surrounding conditions around them are that allow them to show up as their best selves. We literally give them a paper with several of the following statements and ask them to fill in the blanks:

I'm at my best when ______________________.

For example, Roger was doing this exercise and started filling in the blanks of when he's at his best. His answers included: when I've had a good night's sleep; when I start my day with quiet time with the newspaper and a cup of coffee; when I've had time to be fully present with my kids; when I can get out in nature; when I have downtime at the end of the day.

Then we ask people to think about the recipe that allows the "I'm at my best when" statements to be realized. What ingredients make up that experience and increase the likelihood that experience will happen? As Roger thought about his list, he noted the following ingredients:

- Going to bed by 10:00 p.m.

- Setting up the coffee maker the night before and setting my alarm for 5:00 a.m.
- Not taking work home.
- Putting my phone away when I'm with my family.
- Watching the weather forecast the night before.
- Planning a walking break into my day by scheduling it as a recurring meeting.
- Blocking my calendar at the end of the day.

It may seem like an obvious no-brainer, but making the list was eye-opening to Roger. He realized he could take many simple actions that would support him in showing up as the best version of himself. Yet he was mostly leaving it to chance or ignoring their importance. We frequently hear this. We'll ask people, "For how many of you is this the first time ever—or in a long time—that you've actually thought about what you need to be your best self?" Most people's hands will go up. How can we even begin to work toward bringing more of our best selves out into the world if we don't even know what that looks like or what we need for that to happen? And from a team standpoint, we encourage people to share some of their lists so they can support each other in tending to those ingredients. They know that when everyone has the ability to show up as their best selves, the team and the organization benefit.

In recent years, I have found that revisiting this exercise regularly is helpful. Many of our clients now have a practice of revisiting it quarterly. If you're navigating a significant change, you may want to revisit it to see if there are new things you need or adjustments you need to make. For example, high-intensity workouts are my jam and a key to feeling my best and navigating stress. And as difficult chapters emerge in my life, I have to rethink what that can feasibly look like. The workouts may have to be shorter and less frequent than my ideal, or I may need more of something else in my life for that period. Revisiting what I need to be my best helps me to move from self-judgment to self-acceptance and self-compassion. I remind myself that this is a chapter in my life and try to be mindful of what I need to move through that chapter as best as I can. I encourage you to do the same. Knowing who we are when we're at our best and anchoring ourselves on our lighthouse provides a strong foundation to help us reset when we fall.

Leverage a Strong Ability to Reset

One of the things that I always come back to from my Dare to Lead facilitator training is something Brené Brown says in one of the videos we provide to participants to tee up the Rising Strong process, "If you're signing up to be a daring leader, you're signing up to fall." We can't lean into vulnerability and expect that we're not going to have a few bruises. The key is to have the right tools and practices so that we can get back up when we experience setbacks.

As human beings, we make sense of our experiences by creating narratives and stories. And in the absence of data, our brains fill the spaces with stories that are usually not true. So the more we can acknowledge and own that we're telling ourselves a story, versus running with it as fact, we open the ability to fact-check our stories and be more curious about their accuracy. One of the best ways to reset and not be hijacked by our crappy stories is to start using the language, "The story I'm telling myself is . . ." and then see how you could check to see if that story is true. Remember, just because we have a thought doesn't mean it is true. We need to stop believing everything we think and start building our muscles to pause and reflect before we act.

The more we develop the habit to state that we're telling ourselves stories and then fact-check those stories, the less drama we experience and create and the quicker we can bounce back when we stumble. Another practice that can be helpful I learned from my friend Kristen Hadeed. She talks about the value of creating a resilience résumé. It's just like it sounds. Create a repository of the times you've faced a challenge and gotten through it. Include what you learned about yourself in the process. We can refer to it when we face challenges to remind ourselves of just how strong we are and to remind us how we got through things in the past. When we're struggling, we too often forget that we're not alone; others struggle too. But when all we see on actual résumés or social media profiles is the filtered final product, we forget all the messiness that transpired along the way.

Let's get real. There will always be noise, competing demands, and distractions pulling you away from what truly matters. But leadership isn't about reacting to the loudest thing. It's about pausing, tuning in, and choosing to respond from your inner compass, not the chaos. Strengthening your inner game is about giving yourself permission to breathe, listen inward, and act from clarity, not reactivity. The more grounded you are in your own values and purpose, the more powerfully you'll show up for others. In other words, when the world gets loud, listen inward. *Your clarity is louder than the chaos.* As you do, you'll be better equipped to hone your Outer-Game, human-centric skills. And it starts with fostering connection with others.

Actively Practice Empathy and Connection

As we learned in chapter 3, our world is hurting, especially for native digitals. We need to speak to our shared humanity so we can consistently connect with others in a meaningful way to show care and foster a sense of mattering. It also means we need to promote learning agility and curiosity at all levels to help mitigate when our faulty programming wants to hijack us. The problem is that we can take the inner work too far and become so engrossed in our own world and problems that we fail to look up and see others around us. Just take a look the next time you're in a line at a store, boarding a plane, or even in an elevator. The second people have free time, their faces are in their phones and devices. We've lost the ability to see other people. We must get over ourselves and take practical steps to help other people feel that they matter. Remember that nearly half the leaders in our data (49 percent) have difficulties with adaptive change when it comes to their mindsets, including practicing empathy and curiosity and listening fully.

In addition to leveraging the tools and exercises I outlined that can help us to be curious and fact-check our stories so we can lead with greater empathy and less judgment, I love all of the exercises from Jen Marr's *Showing Up* programs. These are the peer-to-peer programs teaching the tangible skills of human care and support. In her books *Showing Up* (the peer-based work) and *Lifting Up* (builds on that with a leadership focus), she outlines many practical things you can do. One of my favorites is something called the 3x3x3 Challenge:

- Three minutes per day
- Three people
- Three months

Essentially what you do is list the people in your life—including your family, work team, close circle of support—who might need support. Take three minutes out of your day to reach out to three of those people, and do this consistently for three months. This can be as simple as sending a text letting them know you're thinking about them or offering them support. It can also include more involved ways of connecting and everything in between. Even when we think we don't have time, what we find is that showing up for others in simple but tangible ways also boosts our sense of well-being and mattering.

One of the things that was eye-opening for me as I started this challenge was how I was neglecting my circle of support, those people who show up for me when things are tough. I noticed a difference in myself just a couple of weeks into more intentionally and actively finding ways to reach out to people. It's simple and impactful!

In one of my *Show Up as a Leader* podcast episodes, Miriam Meima shared a powerful story about being in a long, hectic Starbucks line. When she got up to the counter, although she was tired and frustrated, she intentionally took a moment to actually see the barista and authentically ask how she was doing. That small action brought tears to the barista's eyes as she conveyed that in a rush of three hundred people, no one bothered to look her in the eyes or see her. Her admission profoundly impacted Miriam. That simple action of seeing another person impacted both of them.[55] We all have the opportunity to be a bright spot in someone else's day and connect in an authentic and meaningful way. After all, feeling lonely isn't about being alone.

Rather, it's feeling that no one cares. One of the ways that we can invest in others and promote a sense of mattering is by effectively leveraging feedback.

Give and Receive Feedback Skillfully

One of the best gifts we can give another human being is the gift of our full presence. Unfortunately, we rarely do that in our distraction-filled world. Changing that is so important because the core of giving and receiving feedback well is being fully present so we can effectively listen to understand. Most people don't listen from a place of curiosity with the intent of fully understanding another person's experience. We listen with the intent to reply. Listening well is a skill. When done well, it is an incredible strength; it's more like a superpower! But it can't be done if we aren't self-aware and are showing up guarded in self-protective mode.

Remember that 74 percent of leaders in our dataset are actively trying to get better at communication. Almost a third specifically want to get better at feedback conversations. As we've seen, the reason this is so challenging is due to how our faulty programs inherently work against us. This is why whenever a client approaches us wanting to do a feedback workshop, we first make sure that we've at least equipped them with core self-awareness tools. Next, we equip them with tools to listen well. Then we move into feedback. You can't jump to feedback on a foundation of judgment, self-protection, and half-ass listening. It doesn't work.

Once your inner game is better positioned to support honing your feedback skills, start by leveling up your listening skills. When we can give someone the gift of being fully present, hold a safe space for them to share, allow them to be heard, and focus our energy on simply understanding them, it's transformative. Not only does it quickly build trust and connection, but it actually fosters greater clarity and increases the likelihood that we're working with what actually matters. As a result, we become smarter with our contributions to conversations.

In their book *Get to What Matters*, Wendy Lynch and Clydette de Groot discuss some key tools for transforming conversations at work so we address what matters most to people. One of their tools we leverage in our work with groups is the power of setting intentions for the other person and for ourselves.[56] We have pairs practice listening with setting intentions to feel the difference between two different conversations. In both conversations, the person talking is asked to offer ideas and suggestions for an improvement at the organization. The first conversation reflects more typical listening to reply and how we listen when we're operating in self-protection mode. The second question reflects authentic listening when we're operating from a place of self-awareness.

Conversation One

- *Intention for the other person:* Dismiss them because they don't know the situation or have the expertise like you do.
- *Intention for yourself:* Assert your rightness and how smart you are.

Conversation Two

- *Intention for the other person:* Help them feel valued and heard.
- *Intention for yourself:* Pause, let go of needing to be right, and be curious.

When we debrief conversation one, the people bringing forward the ideas describe being frustrated, wanting to shut down, feeling like they were going in circles, and feeling that the conversation was useless. When we debrief conversation two, people describe feeling heard, energized, connected, and collaborative. This is why it is so important to pay attention to our inner narrative, know when we're triggered to self-protect, and be able to pause. It makes a profound difference when we can set aside our own stuff, choose to show up for other people, and give them the gift of our presence. Imagine if before every important conversation, you were to make a conscious decision to be fully present, hold back and be curious, learn as much as you can, and find some common ground.

Andrew was a member of one of the teams we were working with. He never realized how poorly he listened to people and how much that cost him. Andrew saw himself as a doer and was always pushing himself to have an immediate answer. He thought he was disappointing people if he didn't quickly reply with his thoughts or fix things. As we worked through the self-reflection and listening exercises, he felt a pit in his stomach. He started realizing how little he really knew about his coworkers, his wife, and even his kids. His interactions had become more about transactions than connections.

Although he wasn't sure he could change after all these years, Andrew decided to humor us and try putting some of our suggested concepts into practice. He started paying attention to how often his inner narrative was focused on being "right" and practiced setting an intention for himself to pause, be curious, and make the conversation about the other person. He also practiced pausing for five seconds before jumping in to offer his thoughts. And when he did contribute to the conversation, Andrew asked more questions to try to understand the other person's experience.

It didn't take long before Andrew became emotional with not only sadness and regret but also love and excitement. He said, "I can't believe how much time I've wasted! How frustrating it must be for people to be around me. Here I thought I was being helpful, and instead I've been railroading people. I feel like a jackass; my own kids have probably been thinking I don't really care. At the same time, I feel like I'm getting to know them again. We're having better conversations and more quality time. My wife even thanked me the other day for listening and not trying to be 'the fixer' all the time. Maybe there's something to this stuff after all."

Being self-aware, pausing, setting clear intentions, and holding back are all critical aspects of authentic listening. If we are going to shift from listening to reply to listening to understand, we need to be able to ask open and honest questions that help foster greater clarity and understanding. Open and honest questions are designed to elicit broader thinking in others, encourage answers that we could not predict the answer to, and help us better understand what it's like to be the other person in any given situation. Here are some sample questions that can be helpful:

- “What was that like for you?”
- “What is the impact that had on you?”
- “What are you wanting for yourself in all of this?”
- “What did that prevent you from doing? And what’s important about that?”
- “Given what you experienced, what feels really important to you right now?”
- “Given what transpired, what are you wanting more of for yourself? Less of?”
- “What will tell you you’re headed in the right direction?”
- “How will you know what’s the right decision or next step?”

When we ask open and honest questions, it not only helps us and the other person gain more clarity about what really matters, but it also sends a clear message to others that they are valued as people. Start leveraging these tools to begin leveling up your listening game. They will also come in handy when it comes to feedback.

Receiving and giving feedback are critical skills. Yet too often we focus primarily on giving feedback and ignore strengthening our ability to receive it well. Given everything you’ve been learning about yourself thus far and about our faulty programming, it’s not surprising that many people find their head trash taking over when on the receiving end of feedback. In fact, Douglas Stone and Sheila Heen describe our challenges with receiving feedback in their incredible book *Thanks for the Feedback*. They talk about how our mindsets and triggers get in our way:

> Our triggered reactions are not obstacles because they are unreasonable. Our triggers are obstacles because they keep us from *engaging skillfully* in the conversation.[57]

This is where emotional literacy becomes important in addition to knowing our faulty programs and triggers. We must be able to recognize when we’re emotionally hijacked and becoming defensive so that we can leverage our courageous leader tools to pause, be curious, and better receive feedback. And when it comes to leading others who are challenged in receiving feedback, it's not uncommon to get stuck. Too often I see leaders give up rather than address the issue.

There have been several times in my leadership journey when I've had team members consistently become defensive and deflect growth feedback. That behavior sparked its own growth-feedback conversation. I've had to move beyond my previous People-Pleasing tendencies and instead clarify expectations on the other's ability to receive feedback well and work through their development plans for how they will level up that skill because it's a deal-breaker at all levels.

When it comes to providing feedback, it is very common for it to activate one or more faulty programs. In addition to doing the work to upgrade any that are getting in your way, it can be helpful to remember that fostering growth in others requires us to focus more on calling others to greatness rather than saving them from struggle (which shows up frequently with the People-Pleaser, Mime, Martyr, or Protector programs) or trying to fix them (which shows up frequently with the Overachiever and Control Freak programs). As we work to move past them and poke holes in their validity, it can be helpful to leverage tried and true feedback tools.

One of my favorites is *Radical Candor,* by Kim Scott. She describes a simple yet powerful formula needed for building trust and having open and direct communication that helps achieve results: the intersection of caring personally and challenging directly.[58]

- *Care personally:* Being curious and seeing others as human beings. In other words, we need to be able to see people as unique individuals with needs, objectives, and challenges and truly care about their well-being and success. It's caring enough about people to let go of our own vanity and worries about what they'll think of us because it isn't about us.
- *Challenge directly:* Providing personal and specific feedback and recognition. This is not a license to be harsh or insulting, and it is

not an invitation to nitpick. Challenging directly recognizes that we all have blind spots. It involves telling people when their work isn't good enough—and when it is, when they're not going to get the job they wanted, and when the project they've been working on isn't getting the results desired and will be redirected to another person. It's delivering the hard feedback and making the difficult decisions that are necessary for the organization to live its purpose and achieve desired results.

One humorous example of caring personally and challenging directly that comes to mind is a Snickers commercial. In the commercial, two guys who have been friends since third grade are at a party talking to two gals. Brad (being played by Joe Pesci until the final scene) is acting like his common hotheaded gangster character and starts yelling at the gals. His friend pulls him aside and gives him a Snickers bar.

- Friend: "Brad, eat a Snickers."
- Brad: "Why?"
- Friend: "Because you get a little angry when you're hungry."
- Brad starts to eat the Snickers bar; the camera goes back to his friend.
- Friend: "Better?"
- Brad: "Better."

Besides being a funny commercial, it shows Kim Scott's *Radical Candor*. Brad's friend cares enough about him to pull him aside, give him feedback, and help him get back to his best self. As simple as it sounds, most people fall short of being able to operate from a space of caring personally and challenging directly. Most of the time, it's due to our head trash keeping us in self-protective mode because we bump up against our faulty programming and adaptive challenges.

To further enhance the effectiveness of Radical Candor conversations, we have also been using the FBI Feedback Formula for giving feedback that we got from our friends at Chapman and Co. Leadership Institute, and it has been transformative. This formula is a way to be relevant and meaningful by being as clear and specific as possible to help the recipient understand the impact of their behavior. It stands for Feelings, Behavior, Impact:

- F: This part of the message includes your feelings about the other person's behavior. The more you can focus on how you feel (versus how you perceive the other person feels), the more impactful the feedback is.
- B: This is where you are specific about what the person did—their behavior. The recipient of the feedback needs to know what they did that led to you feeling a certain way. The more specific you can be, the better.
- I: Most of us have blind spots and may not be fully aware of the impact we have on others or the organization. Including this in the feedback helps to connect the dots for people so they see the results of their behavior, including the impact it has on you, others, customers, their team, or the broader organization.

These components can be in any order, but all need to be included for the message to be clear and meaningful. For example, let's say one of your colleagues has been showing up in hyper self-protective mode, hasn't been very collaborative, and dropped the ball on something important. You could say, "I really care about you and have noticed something's been off with you lately. I'm worried about you as you've been short, distant, and uncollaborative with the team. And now with you missing this critical deadline, I feel disappointed and frustrated. The impact on me is that it hinders my ability to trust and rely on you. And the impact on the team is that we've all had to jump in and work extra to make up for this. I want us all to be successful. Can you give me some insight into what is going on with you?"

With this approach, we're not shaming anyone. We're showing we care and being specific about the behaviors, our concerns, and the impact of what happened. It helps to create a safe space where others can hopefully let go of defensiveness and self-protection, be authentically human, and admit and learn from their mistakes. If we want people to grow and develop, we need to help provide clarity of expectations and then be willing to care personally and challenge directly to help them see their path for success.

The FBI Feedback Formula can also be used to structure recognition feedback in a meaningful way. Instead of a generic "thank you" or "I appreciate you," which can be nice but fall flat, focus on being clear and specific and help foster a sense of mattering so people understand the significance of their contributions.

I would be remiss in discussing clear, transparent feedback without addressing one of the most noncourageous approaches to feedback. One of the old-school feedback models we need to be aware of and stay far away from is the so-called crap sandwich. We've all probably received one of these:

Half-ass compliment + critical feedback + disingenuous praise

Here's an example: "Becky, I really appreciate how hard you work and think you're doing great on most things. *But* I need you to be more detailed on XYZ. Other than that, you're doing great."

I hear people all the time say they were taught to start with something good before giving critical feedback. Who in the world thought this approach was a good idea? When we do this, we've just negated everything before the "but." The compliment is now seen as disingenuous. And the same goes for any half-hearted praise after the criticism. The criticism also fails to be direct and clear by being "watered down" on either side. Additionally, the chances are that anytime in the future when we want to genuinely recognize people, they will be skeptical and wait for the other shoe to drop.

Let recognition and praise stand on their own. And use Radical Candor and the FBI Feedback Formula to have effective growth-feedback conversations. Drop the "but," and don't combine them. Please, please, please, no more crap sandwiches! Once you're more skilled in listening to understand as well as giving and receiving feedback, you will be better positioned to navigate conflict more effectively as a tool for strengthening, rather than straining, relationships and processes.

Navigate Conflict Constructively

Whenever two or more people are present, at some point there's bound to be conflict. Most people tend to view conflict as something that is negative. However, when approached effectively, it's a useful tool that can strengthen relationships and processes. When we work with groups on effectively leveraging conflict, we always go back to the Frame. It always starts with how we see things, not how we feel. This is important because if we're telling ourselves stories that are negative and self-limiting, we're going to experience more negative feelings.

Another important consideration is that we usually end up in conflict because we are seeing things from a win-lose orientation. With that, we tend to get into conflict about *strategies* for meeting our needs rather than discussing our actual needs. We become attached to our stories and then get married to a specific strategy as if it's the only strategy that will work for meeting our needs. Yet there are likely many strategies that can work to meet our needs. Instead, we want to shift from a win-lose to a win-win orientation where both parties can have their needs met. From this perspective, conflict becomes nothing more than a call to creativity to find a sustainable solution recognizing everyone's needs. But to do this, we must start with identifying and naming our needs.

When we feel anger or other negative feelings, it's usually a sign we have an unmet need. So it's important to first identify what need was *not* met and resulted in the negative feelings. When you gain more clarity about what needs are important, you can start to look for a variety of strategies that will help meet them. Typically, conflict conversations consist of a repetitive cycle of:

- You: "I feel ____."
- Other person: "Well, I feel ____."

Here, each person keeps working harder to justify being right about their feelings.

Eventually, with training and experience, conflict conversations can shift to something more like "I feel ____, and I realized I have core needs of ____. What do you need, and how can we work to find a win-win so we both have our needs met?"

I always ask people to consider this:

> Is being *right* more important than the quality of this relationship or having a successful outcome?
>
> Would you rather be *right* or *wildly successful*?

One of the exercises we invite people to complete is called "My Top Three Button-Pushers." List the top three things at work that push your buttons. Then, for each button-pusher, challenge your assumptions, reframe, and then rewrite your narrative by reflecting on the following:

- My button-pusher is: _____
- My assumptions going into this situation are: _____
- The story I'm telling myself about this is: _____
- What I'm noticing about myself in this situation is: _____
- How else I could try seeing this situation is: _____

Most people realize just how married to their stories they are and how much they're assuming without knowing. I encourage you to practice using the language, "The story I'm telling myself right now in this situation is . . ." This helps you start to own that your reaction is based on the story you're holding as true. I also challenge you to call yourself and others to greatness and move beyond excuses, blame, and drama by asking:

- What is the next action you or I could take that would add value?
- What can you or I do to help?

Conflict is never fun, but it can be a productive conduit to elevate our effectiveness and improve outcomes. Instead of shying away from it or entering into it ready for battle, we need to leverage our courageous leadership tools to stay grounded and in a place of openness and curiosity. We are then better able to foster alignment and clarity with what is next.

Foster Alignment and Clarity

In this VUCA-extreme world, I frequently see challenges with implementing change and effectively executing strategy because we haven't accounted for the messiness of being human and haven't been deliberate in fostering clarity and alignment. Part of being a future-ready leader requires instilling a sense of clarity and purpose. And remember that purpose also has a protective factor when it comes to stress. One of the most effective tools I have found comes from the original Dare to Lead program curriculum called the five C's. The premise is that you need to include all five C's when aligning on decisions, deliverables, and delegating.

- *Color:* Paint the picture of what you're trying to do, how it aligns with the organization's purpose and goals, and the priority level, intentionally aligning on what "done" looks like.
- *Context:* Provide additional information about what else is happening in other departments, the industry, and so on that might impact your project or decision. Recognize the impact your project or decision could have on other stakeholders.
- *Connective tissue:* In this age of cognitive overload, people need to understand how what they're being asked to do connects to something else (that is, other organizational projects and initiatives) or lays the foundation for something forthcoming.
- *Cost:* There are certainly hard financial costs, but most people need to know how much time, energy, bandwidth, and focus are required of them.
- *Consequence:* What is at stake if this project or decision is abandoned, if it's postponed, or if we don't get it right? This is not an invitation to be threatening or blaming but rather to align on importance and impact by understanding what is at stake.

I have at least five conversations each week with leaders who are struggling with alignment, people not meeting expectations, or pushback on change and other initiatives. When I ask them if they leveraged the five C's in their communication, they inevitably did not. When they go back and fill in the gaps, things go much smoother. Of course, there will be bumps in the road along the way, but we give people less of an opportunity to fill in the gaps with head trash when we're clear and take the time to ensure we're aligned before jumping to action or assumptions.

Not only can we use the five C's to help us lead others, work, and projects, but we can also use them to foster clarity and alignment with our peers. We can even use them to lead upward to seek the clarity we need to be successful in our work. For example, imagine you are interviewing for a new job (or having a stay interview or one-to-one conversation with your leader) and leveraging the five C's. It might look like something like this.

- *Color:* What does success in this role look like?
- *Context:* What other functions are impacted by this role and the work of this role?
- *Connective tissue:* What current or future problems does my role exist to solve?
- *Cost:* What might my work cost others in time, tradition, bandwidth, and so on?
- *Consequence:* What are the consequences of not doing this? Doing this slowly? Differently?

Few people have this type of conversation and have full clarity over their roles and work. Imagine how energizing it would be if everyone had these conversations and was clear and aligned on their roles and the work. If you want to start putting the five C's into practice, here are three areas to consider.

1. *Revisit your meeting invites.* For the next thirty days or so, look at every meeting invitation you've initiated. Add in notes to the invite and include the five C's so people are clear on the intent, purpose,

and importance level of the meeting; what you're looking for from them as participants; any context that will be helpful for them to be prepared to meaningfully contribute; how this discussion and content connect to other organizational initiatives; what it will cost them in terms of energy or time to prep before and follow up afterward; and anything important regarding consequences.

Then look at any meetings you've been invited to. Email the meeting organizer and ask for clarity around the five C's. See what happens when you start to be more intentional about creating clarity so people know how to best contribute.

2. *Revisit communications.* Pay attention to communications regarding programs, processes, policies, and initiatives. When you communicate or launch something, make sure to include key information related to the five C's so people have a greater line of sight into what is being asked of them and why. Also, as you're thinking about work and decisions, ask who needs to be kept up to speed and be aware of what is transpiring and who else might need to be consulted and weigh in on things. So often we're missing key voices or are not staying connected to people who are impacted by the work at hand or who can impact the work, and we end up with unnecessary struggle. Start being deliberate about how and whom you communicate with, and see what happens.

3. *Revisit delegation.* We've all probably experienced a "Just get it done" moment where we were either delegating a task to someone else or on the receiving end of that delegation. In hindsight, there was likely confusion, and even frustration, due to some key aspects not being present or not having full alignment. Be deliberate when it comes to including the five C's when you are delegating work and see how it helps foster greater alignment, provides opportunities for a learning or teaching moment, and supports a better outcome.

The other tool that I have found incredibly helpful in fostering clarity is making it simple for yourself and your team to prioritize where they spend their time. Too often I hear leaders complain that they have hundreds of priorities or that everything ends up in the urgent and important area. Remember that in this VUCA environment, many people are on cognitive overload. So simplifying things to speak to our ten-year-old brains can be helpful. On our team, we like to use the bucket of balls approach to help align on priorities. Basically, imagine that all of your to-dos represent a ball in a bucket. Are you trying to hold the entire bucket of balls equally, or do you see clear delineation between the balls in the bucket?

- *Glass balls:* These are essential because if dropped, they will shatter and likely have irreversible consequences. Think of these as mission critical.
- *Wood balls:* These are important. If dropped, they'll have some damage, but it's not debilitating. Think of these as important but perhaps not essential.
- *Rubber balls:* These have a lot of bounce. If dropped, they're easily recoverable. Think of these as nice to have but not essential.

For us, glass balls are always client deliverables along with well-being and self-care. This includes caring for self but also for family. Everything else we negotiate from week to week as to whether it's a wood or rubber ball. Sometimes a previous week's wood ball gets promoted to glass; sometimes it's demoted to a rubber ball. This helps our team to not be overwhelmed as they add the ball priority label to their to-dos and calendars for the week to help them stay focused. As simple as this sounds, it really is a quick way to align and help work feel more manageable.

Once you've aligned on priorities, it's important to regularly ask if anything is getting in the way of people's abilities to tend to the priorities and how you can best support them in removing any obstacles. This is not about saving them but supporting them and clearing a path for them to meaningfully contribute to the organization and feel connected to its purpose and values. It's a key part of leading that helps you serve as a steward for the organization's culture.

Serve as a Culture Steward

The final aspect of being a future-ready leader is actively living the company purpose and values and leveraging them consistently in how you lead others. In a world of never-ending to-dos, it can be easy for this to go out the window and not receive the attention it deserves. However, culture is like a garden and must be regularly tended, or it can quickly get away from you. It's also important to consider that culture is not the job of HR, the CEO, the executive team, or any one person or team. Culture is *everyone's* responsibility. Every single one of us has the opportunity to show up as a culture contributor or a culture contaminator, so there's even more reason to intentionally develop everyone to be able to show up as courageous, future-ready leaders.

But if you're a formal leader of a team, you play the greatest role in your team's experience of the culture, so it's critical that you are intentional about it. This means holding purpose and value alignment at the same level of importance as results. Too often I see leaders ignore misaligned behaviors because the person is technically skilled or because they simply don't want to deal with it. But enabling people to continue to show up out of alignment with your stated company values will erode culture quicker than you think and frustrate your highest-performing and most committed team members.

Our friends at the Chapman & Co. Leadership Institute have a great process to guide organizational improvements and foster alignment with purpose (that is, WHY).

Everything starts with the company's purpose or WHY. Essentially, our WHY is who we are on our best days. But we're only human and will get in our own way. So this process is about identifying the gaps and root causes of what keeps people from being able to live and further the organization's purpose and show up as leaders. It becomes the foundation for any and all improvement efforts.

Ask people, "What's getting in the way of you living our WHY today?" or "What's getting in the way of you showing up as a leader and being fully effective today?" After they reply, ask them, "And what impact does that have on you?" This second question is important because it weeds out "recreational complaining" and helps decipher legitimate frustrations and gaps versus someone who is showing up triggered and committed to being right and blaming others. These questions can be asked at a formal meeting, a quick huddle, or a one-on-one. As you listen to understand, listen for themes regarding the barriers and gaps. Then categorize the gaps (that is, improvement opportunities and suggestions) into one of three categories.

1. Start with WHY

2. Engage the Organization

LISTEN to Identify Themes & Understand Gaps (not to problem-solve)

"How does that impact you?"

3. Bring your WHY to Life

Quick Fixes	Short-Term Projects	Long-Term Solutions
Easy, low-hanging-fruit items that can be fixed with minimal cost or effort yet can make a huge impact in building trust and showing people they are heard. Examples: • Updating an outdated policy. • Fixing something that's broken. • Providing adequate supplies.	Changes that take a little more effort but can likely be accomplished in a fairly short time. Examples: • Creating more opportunities for people to get to know their colleagues better. • Improving timeliness and relevance of communication.	Solutions that will take deliberate thought, planning, and resources to support. Examples: • Developing and communicating clear career paths. • Changing organizational structure to improve collaboration and reduce silos.

The final step of this process is to bring your WHY to life by addressing the gaps. In order to do this, it's important to determine if the gap is due to behaviors or systems. Most of the time, a faulty system is at play (for example, clunky processes requiring workarounds, outdated procedures, or operational hiccups). A faulty system will circumvent good intentions any day of the week. This is an opportunity to engage others in discussions to cocreate the path moving forward. We have found this process to be extremely helpful. People often think that this step is reserved for executive leaders or people whose roles are in business development. However, in a VUCA world demanding that everyone show up as leaders, we need to enable everyone to be able to identify and address gaps and leverage the wisdom of those closest to the work.

We do a lot of culture visioning work with our clients. When people are engaged in the process to create a shared vision of what a thriving workplace looks like and what it will take to make that vision a reality, they show up as leaders fueled by energy and passion. The Chapman & Co. Leadership Institute process helps guide people to make productive, solution-oriented contributions.

With one of our clients, we facilitated several culture visioning sessions. During each session, people were invited to provide their input on what "thriving" looks like to them when they are consistently living their WHY and people are able to show up authentically, have fulfilling work, learn and grow, become the best versions of themselves, and then go home with energy left to show up fully in their personal lives (part 1 of the alignment process). Then we asked people what they collectively need to start, stop, and continue doing in order for that shared vision to be a reality (part 2 of the alignment process). We summarized the collective feedback and then leveraged their culture ambassadors for step 3 of the process. We asked them to categorize each start and stop suggestion as a behavior or system improvement and whether it was a short-, medium-, or long-term change. Finally, because we can only do so much at one time, we asked them to determine their priorities for the upcoming year by selecting one long-term change, two or three medium-term changes, and three or four short-term quick fixes. The culture ambassadors then communicated the improvement plan and the process for how they landed on their priorities to their colleagues and engaged them to continue to be part of the process to implement the improvements. By including everyone in the process, there was greater energy to share responsibility for the next steps to grow and improve the organization.

I know there's a lot that goes into future-proofing yourself as a leader. Whether or not you're in a formal leadership role, leaning on these components will serve you and others well. Simply take it one step at a time and go in the order in which each component is listed, moving from the inner to the outer game. And remember, you will need to revisit these tools more than once to reset and recalibrate.

KEY POINTS

- Being a future-ready leader requires us to be willing to be uncomfortable and engage in an ongoing journey. No one is above or beyond development. We need to equip *everyone* to show up as courageous, future-ready leaders, starting with self-leadership.
- Future-proofing ourselves as leaders requires starting with the messy inner game and then progressing to honing outer-game skills.
- Once you've leveraged the insights and tools from part 2 of this book to identify and start the upgrade process so your faulty programs are no longer in the driver's seat (or at least not as much), you're in a great spot to start leveling up your self-leadership. Leverage the tools for strengthening your inner game so your mindset works with you rather than against you, and you can leverage calm as a leadership superpower.
- With your inner game in a good spot, start honing your outer game. Like anything, this will take repetition and practice. You have an incredible opportunity to be the leader you were meant to be and that others deserve and support the organization's culture. Take it one step at a time.

Conclusion

By being yourself, you put something wonderful into the world that was not there before.

—attributed to Edwin Elliot

I would love to tell you that I have some sort of "easy" button or magic potion that shortcuts the process to future-proofing leadership. But when we're dealing with messy and complicated human beings, quick fixes simply don't cut it. I believe that's why we've struggled more than necessary. Rather than acknowledging and addressing the discomfort that comes with our shared humanness, we keep trying to work around it. What limits our leadership is not our knowledge but what we believe to be true about ourselves.

We must remember that it is *human* to be triggered to self-protect, and our VUCA world doesn't make it any easier. Our world is not going to become any less disruptive. This means that the Stuckness Zone will continue to grow unless we identify and upgrade our faulty programming and level up our abilities to effectively navigate through adaptive change. We also need to stop reaching for technical fixes to address complex adaptive challenges. Remember that when information is primarily what is needed, we're dealing with a technical challenge or change. But when information isn't enough and what we really need is transformation, requiring a shift in both minds and hearts, we're dealing with an adaptive challenge or change. Most of the challenges and changes we face today are largely adaptive in nature. And more often than not, what is contributing to the cringey adaptive nature of the change is our faulty programming and its corresponding head trash.

I firmly believe that most people are not intentionally trying to be difficult. They've just been hijacked by their ten-year-old selves and fallen into the trap of impression management, coping in all kinds of unproductive ways. I'm grateful for the past—and ongoing—work I've done to identify and upgrade my faulty programming as it allows me to do the work I love and has brought us to a spot of releasing our research into the world to help others. There's something incredibly magical about watching people move beyond impression management to get out of their own way and step into their greatness. Being able to play a part in that journey is something I don't take lightly. I spent decades stuck in impression management, dimming my sparkle while trying to be accepted and holding myself back, thinking I couldn't make a difference. It's exhausting!

How many of us withhold our contributions, overcompensate, self-silence, or pretend to be something we're not out of fear of those darn critics? All the motivation in the world can't help us in any sustainable way until we heal the sources of our head trash by upgrading our faulty programming. It made me think about a conversation I saw in 2023 that P!NK had with Kelly Clarkson while on the latter's talk show. First, anyone who knows me knows that I'm obsessed with P!NK for many reasons. I think she's a great example of strength and authenticity, she doesn't take herself too seriously, and she's a champion of the underdogs. Even if you're not a P!NK fan, here's the thing she said that has stuck with me since this show aired:

> One of the things that my dad taught me is that my voice matters, and I can make a difference, and I will . . . One person can change a lot. And I think if we all had a chance to experience each other more, things would be a lot different.[59]

It is a core human need to feel like we're heard and seen and that we matter. We are wired for human connection. But we need to be intentional to nurture that in this digital age. That pertains even more for native digitals. Human-centric leadership is the future and is critical to organizational performance and effectiveness. This means we need to create safe spaces for people to show up authentically, stretch themselves out of their comfort zones, be supported in upgrading their faulty programming, be able to meaningfully contribute to the organization's purpose and goals, and feel that they are valued and matter to other people. We need to ground ourselves and others in clarity of purpose and values to help serve as lighthouses to cut through the fog, guide us, and ground us. This is what ultimately moves us through the Stuckness Zone.

We aren't going to fix the leadership pipeline issue, the growing rates of stress and burnout, and the growing generational divide by continuing to do the same things we always have. As Peter Drucker is widely credited as saying, "The greatest danger in times of turbulence is not the turbulence; it is to act with yesterday's logic." In other words, the risk we face from a leadership standpoint isn't about the VUCA nature of our world; it's about staying the same and not evolving beyond our ten-year-old selves. What we need to do is normalize the discomfort of adaptive change and be thoughtful about how we future-proof leadership on both the individual and organizational levels.

The other thing we must realize and remind ourselves of is that we make sense of our experiences by creating stories, and in the absence of data, our brains fill in the space with stories. Part of the messiness of being human is that most of the stories we create and use to fill in the gaps stem from our faulty programming and are part of our psychological immune system doing its job to protect us and keep us safe. This keeps us from embracing the discomfort of VUCA and keeps us trapped in the Stuckness Zone. Remember that the first step in moving beyond our faulty program is to name it. We need to name our head trash when it surfaces—it loses some of its power when we call it what it actually is. Then we can own how it's showing up in our lives and its impact and finally be deliberate in challenging it by asking ourselves:

Is this story actually true today, and is it serving me well?

or

Is it preventing me from growing and having the impact I desire?

We must remind ourselves that just because we have a thought doesn't mean it's true. I know I just said this, but being human is messy. Thankfully, we now have greater understanding, direction, and tools to help us move forward and thrive in a disruptive world. When our faulty programming hijacks us, we're not showing up as adults; we're showing up as the ten-year-old versions of ourselves. So think about what your ten-year-old self needs to hear right now. Your ten-year-old self might need to hear what mine still does:

- You don't have to be perfect!
- You are enough!
- You matter!

Then think about what your colleague's ten-year-old self needs to hear. Let's start caring for and treating each other in ways that help us to heal, thrive, and connect so that we can move beyond our childhood insecurities and faulty programming and let our courageous, connected, kick-ass adult versions usher us into a new and brighter future. Let's create a new normal in our workplaces where we acknowledge our shared humanity rather than pretend it doesn't exist or judge one another for it. We can work to become better versions of ourselves *and* be enough just as we are.

I hope you find the tools in part 2 of the book insightful and helpful in guiding your upgrade journey. And I hope you leverage the guidance and tools in part 3 of the book to level up how you are fostering future-ready leadership at all levels. The world needs more courageous future-ready leaders. It needs you! For now, I'll leave you with one of my favorite quotes by Debbie Ford:

> The greatest act of courage is to be and to own all of who you are—without apology, without excuses, without masks to cover the truth of who you are.[60]

Or as I like to say, *never* let anyone dull your sparkle!

Acknowledgments

To my amazing husband, Dave, and my incredible son, Peyton. You are both my heart and inspire me to keep growing myself and sparkling. Thank you for your support and for being my biggest cheerleaders. I love you!

To my team at Salveo Partners, y'all simply rock! I'm blessed to have you all, by the work we get to do, and by the difference we're making in the world. Thank you for embracing our messy human journey and challenging me to grow.

To Lisa Rosemeyer specifically, this wouldn't have happened without you picking up the slack and digging into the data analysis to get it across the finish line. You are amazing and the wind beneath my wings.

And to all the incredible clients I've been privileged to support—past and present—who have contributed to this work: I'm deeply grateful. You all inspire me, and I learn and grow from you every day.

Notes

Introduction

1 Dana Mao, Hans-Werner Kaas, Kurt Strovink, and Ramesh Srinivasan, *The Journey of Leadership: How CEOs Learn to Lead from the Inside Out* (Portfolio, 2024).

2 Bernard Burnes, "Introduction: Why Does Change Fail, and What Can We Do About It?," *Journal of Change Management* (2011): https://www.tandfonline.com/doi/abs/10.1080/14697017.2011.630507.

3 Gartner, "Top 5 HR Trends and Priorities That Matter Most in 2025," https://www.gartner.com/en/human-resources/trends/top-priorities-for-hr-leaders.

4 Josh Bersin, "Companies Have Been Neglecting Their Leadership, *And It Shows*," November 6, 2023, https://joshbersin.com/2023/11/companies-have-been-neglecting-their-leadership-and-it-shows/.

5 Showing Up Insights Report, "Why Care Can't Wait: The New Working Reality," https://www.flipsnack.com/C89CF85569B/inspiring-comfort-insights-report/full-view.html.

Chapter 1

6 American Psychological Association, "Stress in America," March 2022, https://www.apa.org/news/press/releases/stress/2-22/march-2022-survival-mode.

7 Gartner, "Top 5 Priorities for HR Leaders 2022," http://www.gartner.com/en/documents/4009421.

8 Ronald Heifetz and Donald Laurie, "The Work of Leadership," *Harvard Business Review*, December 2001, 131–141.

9 Ronald Heifetz and Marty Linsky, *Leadership on the Line* (Harvard Business Review Press, 2017).

10 Ronald Heifetz, *Leadership Without Easy Answers* (Harvard University Press, 1998).

11 Brené Brown, *Dare to Lead* (Random House, 2018).

12 Viktor Frankl, *Man's Search for Meaning* (Beacon, 1959).

Chapter 2

13 David Rock, "SCARF: A Brain-Based Model for Collaborating with and Influencing Others," *NeuroLeadership Journal* (2008): http://web.archive.org/web/20100705024057/http://www.your-brain-at-work.com:80/files/NLJ_SCARFUS.pdf.

14 Bruce H. Lipton, *The Bridge of Belief: Unleashing the Power of Consciousness, Matter & Miracles* (Hay House, 2008).

15 Bruce H. Lipton, "Dr. Bruce Lipton Explains How to Reprogram Your Unconscious Mind," May 29, 2019, YouTube, https://www.youtube.com/watch?v=xsA91lxuF00&ab_channel=FightMediocrity.

16 Robert Kegan and Lisa Laskow Lahey, *Immunity to Change* (Harvard Press, 2009).

17 Jacqueline Brassey, Aaron De Smet, and Michiel Kruyt, *Deliberate Calm: How to Learn and Lead in a Volatile World* (HarperBusiness, 2022).

18 Robert J. Anderson and William A. Adams, *Mastering Leadership* (Wiley, 2016).

Chapter 3

19 Zach Mercurio, *The Power of Mattering: How Leaders Can Create a Culture of Significance* (Harvard Business Review, 2025).

20 DDI, "Global Leadership Forecast 2025: Insights and Trends," 2025, https://www.ddiworld.com/research/global-leadership-forecast-2025.

21 McKinsey & Company, "Take a Human-Centric Approach to Avoid AI's Leadership Traps," February 10, 2025, https://www.mckinsey.com/capabilities/people-and-organizational-performance/our-insights/the-organization-blog/take-a-human-centric-approach-to-avoid-ais-leadership-traps.

22 Workday, "Elevating Human Potential: The AI Skills Revolution," 2025, https://forms.workday.com/en-us/reports/elevating-human-potential/form.html?locale=enus&aud=wd&stage=any&size=all&pblr=wd&assettype=rep&productfocus=alp&utm_medium=pres&utm_source=pres&step=step1_default.

23 Jason Murray, "Native Analog or Digital: Are You Ready for a New Type of Employee?," *Forbes*, March 14, 2024, https://www.forbes.com/councils/forbesbusinesscouncil/2024/03/14/native-analog-or-digital-are-you-ready-for-a-new-type-of-employee/.

24 Jonathan Haidt, *The Anxious Generation* (Penguin, 2024).

25 Sumathi Annamalai, Aditi Vasunandan, and Aveshi Mehta, "Social Isolation and Loneliness Among Generation Z Employees: Can Emotional Intelligence Help Mitigate?," *Cogent Business & Management*, December 2024, https://www.researchgate.net/publication/387143389_Social_isolation_and_loneliness_among_Generation_Z_employees_can_emotional_intelligence_help_mitigate.

26 UKG, "Perspectives from the Frontline Workforce: A UKG Global Study," October 2024, https://www.ukg.com/resources/industry-brief/perspectives-frontline-workforce-ukg-global-study.

27 Deepa Shivaram, "Pediatricians Say the Mental Health Crisis Among Kids Has Become a National Emergency," *NPR*, October 20, 2021, https://www.npr.org/2021/10/20/1047624943/pediatricians-call-mental-health-crisis-among-kids-a-national-emergency.

28 SHRM, "The State of Employee Mental Health in 2024," 2024, https://www.shrm.org/content/dam/en/shrm/topics-tools/employee-relations/shrm-mental-health-info-1.jpeg.

29 Gallup, "State of the Global Workplace," 2024, https://www.gallup.com/workplace/349484/state-of-the-global-workplace.aspx.

30 US Surgeon General, "Our Epidemic of Loneliness and Isolation," 2023, https://www.hhs.gov/surgeongeneral/reports-and-publications/connection/index.html.

31 John C. Maxwell, *High Road Leadership: Bringing People Together in a World That Divides* (Maxwell Leadership, 2024).

32 Constance Noonan Hadley and Sarah L. Wright, "We're Still Lonely at Work," *Harvard Business Review*, November–December 2024, https://hbr.org/2024/11/were-still-lonely-at-work.

33 Workforce Institute at UKG, "Mental Health at Work: Managers and Money," 2023, https://www.ukg.com/resources/white-paper/mental-health-work-managers-and-money.

34 McLean & Company, "HR Trends Report 2023," 2023, https://hr.mcleanco.com/research/ss/hr-trends-report-2023.

35 Dana Maor, Hans-Werner Kaas, Kurt Strovink, and Ramesh Srinivasan, *The Journey of Leadership: How CEOs Learn to Lead from the Inside Out* (Portfolio, 2024).

Chapter 4

36 Robert Holden, *Be Happy!: Release the Power of Happiness in You* (Hay House, 2010).

Chapter 7

37 Brené Brown, *The Gifts of Imperfection* (Random House, 2010).

Chapter 10

38 Google re:Work, "Understand Team Effectiveness," https://rework.withgoogle.com/en/guides/understanding-team-effectiveness#introduction.

Chapter 11

39 Mark McFatridge, "Leading Out Loud: Permission to be Real," *Show Up as a Leader* podcast, https://drrosieward.com/leading-out-loud-permission-to-be-real-with-mark-mcfatridge/.

Chapter 13

40 DDI, "Global Leadership Forecast 2025: Insights and Trends," 2025, https://www.ddi-world.com/research/global-leadership-forecast-2025.

41 Robert Walters, "42% of Gen Z Professionals Don't Want to Be Middle Managers," December 23, 2024, https://www.robertwalters.be/insights/hiring-advice/blog/Gen-Z-does-not-want-to-be-middle-managers.html.

42 Robert Walters, "Conscious Un-Bossing: 53% of Gen-Z Professionals Don't Want to Be Middle Managers," September 23, 2024, https://www.robertwalters.co.uk/insights/news/blog/conscious-unbossing.html.

43 Korn Ferry, "Workforce 2025 Global Insights Report," April 2025, https://www.kornferry.com/insights/featured-topics/leadership/top-5-leadership-trends-2025.

44 Amy C. Edmondson, *The Fearless Organization* (Wiley, 2019).

45 Google re:Work, "Understand Team Effectiveness," 2016, https://rework.withgoogle.com/en/guides/understanding-team-effectiveness#introduction.

46 Matt Tait, "Building a People First Culture," *Show Up as a Leader* podcast, https://drrosieward.com/building-a-people-first-culture-with-matt-tait/.

47 Workday, "Elevating Human Potential: The AI Skills Revolution," 2025, https://forms.workday.com/en-us/reports/elevating-human-potential/form.html?locale=enus&aud=wd&stage=any&size=all&pblr=wd&assettype=rep&productfocus=alp&utm_medium=pres&utm_source=pres&step=step1_default.

Chapter 14

48 Peter Drucker, *Managing Oneself, The Drucker Lectures: Essential Lessons on Management, Society and Economy*, ed. R. Wartzman (McGraw-Hill, 2010).

49 Kristen Neff, *Fierce Self-Compassion: How Women Can Harness Kindness to Speak Up, Claim Their Power, and Thrive* (HarperCollins, 2021).

50 Brené Brown, *Atlas of the Heart* (Random House, 2021).

51 Top 20 Training, "Check Your Frame," https://top20training.com/check-your-frame/.

52 Kevin Cashman, *The Pause Principle* (Berrett-Koehler, 2012).

53 Jim Dethmer, Diana Chapman, and Kaley Warner Klemp, *The 15 Commitments of Conscious Leadership* (Conscious Leadership Group, 2014).

54 Simon Sinek, *Start with Why* (Portfolio, 2009).

55 Miriam Meima, "Maximizing Our Impact as Leaders," *Show Up as a Leader* podcast, https://drrosieward.com/maximizing-our-impact-as-leaders-with-miriam-meima/.

56 Wendy Lynch and Clydette de Groot, *Get to What Matters* (What Matters Press, 2017).

57 Douglas Stone and Sheila Heen, *Thanks for the Feedback* (Penguin, 2015).

58 Kim Scott, *Radical Candor: Be a Kick-Ass Boss Without Losing Your Humanity* (St. Martin's, 2017).

Conclusion

59 Pink and Kelly Clarkson, "5 Songs," *The Kelly Clarkson Show*, February 26, 2023, https://www.youtube.com/watch?v=bKRxpQgFMfw&list=RDbKRxpQgFMfw&start_radio=1.

60 Debbie Ford, *Courage: Overcoming Fear and Igniting Self-Confidence* (HarperCollins, 2013).

About the Author

Dr. Rosie Ward is a sought-after leader, consultant, coach, speaker, and author known for transforming leaders, teams, and organizations to move beyond their innate self-protective wiring to maximize their impact. She serves as CEO and founder of Salveo Partners, an award-winning consulting firm focused on future-proofing organizations by strengthening culture and equipping leaders and teams to show up courageously and more effectively navigate change and disruption.

Rosie's first book, *How to Build a Thriving Culture at Work,* provides a blueprint for organizations to break past old, outdated paradigms and rehumanize their workplaces. Her second book, *Rehumanizing the Workplace,* won a Readers' Favorite award. She also hosts the award-winning podcast *Show Up as a Leader*.

Rosie has an incredible gift for synthesizing complex ideas about culture, leadership, behavior change, and what it means to be human and presenting them in a way that makes them relevant, understandable, and meaningful for people.